America's Obsession

Sports and Society Since 1945

Richard O. Davies
University of Nevada, Reno

Under the General Editorship of
Gerald D. Nash and Richard W. Etulain
University of New Mexico

THOMSON

WADSWORTH

Australia • Canada • Mexico • Singapore • Spain

United Kingdom • United States

Wadsworth/Thomson Learning
10 Davis Drive
Belmont CA 94002-3098
USA

For information about our products, contact us:
Thomson Learning Academic Resource Center
1-800-423-0563
http://www.wadsworth.com

For permission to use material from this text, contact us by
Web: http://www.thomsonrights.com
Fax: 1-800-730-2215
Phone: 1-800-730-2214

Printed in the United States of America
10 9 8 7 6 5

To my father—
Robert O. Davies
athlete, teacher, coach

Preface

Each day millions of Americans emulate a ritual followed by Earl Warren throughout his life—they turn first to the sports section of their morning newspaper before tackling the national and international news. "I always turn to the sports pages first," Warren once commented. "They record people's accomplishments; the front page, nothing but man's failures." Like millions of his fellow Americans, the former chief justice of the Supreme Court maintained a lifelong interest in sports. His was an innocent fascination that often revolved around his favorite college team, the Golden Bears of the University of California. Like this leading jurist Americans follow with considerable interest their own special high school, college, and professional teams, whose victories and defeats add an important dimension to their daily lives. Millions of Americans have also become dedicated participants, faithfully attending aerobics classes, struggling with their tennis or golf game, lifting weights at a health club, or placing a wager at the racetrack. Within the past several decades, sports have become a vital part of the lives of the American people.

The close observer of contemporary American sports can learn much about the national condition. Sports have become a microcosm of national life. Once relatively isolated from national issues, sports in recent decades have lost whatever innocence they might have once enjoyed and moved into the mainstream of national life. At times they have mirrored national trends and issues, at other times they have forced national policymakers to act. Thus the following pages only occasionally describe the exploits of star performers and the record-setting achievements of great teams. Instead, the reader has an opportunity to delve into the relationships between sports and such major issues as sex discrimination, labor-management relations, substance abuse, destructive compulsive addictions, the powers of television, racism, and the condition of urban America. The intense American-Soviet competition for gold medals at the Olympics even added an important dimension to the Cold War. Instead of providing a safe harbor from the turbulence of modern life, sports since World War II have often served as both a contributor to and a reflection of the major issues of our time.

Sports have traditionally provided Americans with a temporary haven from the tensions and problems of everyday life. One can only wish that such a benign view holds today, but it has been reported over and over again by sociologists and psychologists that sports have taken on a central role in the daily lives of millions of Americans, sometimes even exceeding politics, community service, religion, or family in importance. If kept in a healthy perspective, sports can provide a particularly effective escape valve from the daily grind—a pleasant afternoon at the ballpark, a casual round of golf with friends, a few hours before the television set on an autumn Sunday afternoon. But such is not the case for the growing numbers of Americans who have become obsessed with sports, who have elevated their interest to a level that can be destructive to themselves and their families. Public officials and case workers bemoan the actions of parents who convey to their children that winning the Little League championship, or making the cheerleading squad, or becoming a junior ice skating (or swimming, or tennis, or gymnastics) champion takes precedence over schoolwork or other social outlets. College officials have yet to find a way to prevent the booster from slipping a promising recruit a hundred-dollar bill, or to keep a coach with a "win at any cost" attitude from forging an athlete's transcript or behaving in an embarrassingly unacceptable way by berating game officials.

Many fans readily confess that their addiction to a particular team has produced more frustration and agony than pleasure. Over the years sports fans are certain to learn much more about coping with defeat and disappointment than about enjoying the thrill of victory. For some it seems, the quest for triumph is more important than ever achieving it. The long-suffering sports fans of New England have waited since 1918 for their beloved Red Sox to win a World Series, but their dedication to the Boston baseball team is unquestioned. There is no more meaningful or powerful unifying factor in the life of the several states in New England than the ebb and flow of the fortunes of the Bosox. Chicago Cub fans proudly wear T-shirts that boldly proclaim "Chicago Cubs, World Series Champions" in large print; below in tiny letters is inscribed the year "1908."

The homes of the Red Sox and Cubs, Fenway Park and Wrigley Field, are considered historical shrines in Boston and Chicago, as full of symbolic meaning for their populations as are ancient cathedrals of European cities. The millions of dollars that in recent years have been poured into the construction of arenas and stadiums to house professional teams is powerful testimony to the priorities of a community. Often those dollars could have been used instead to bolster severely declining school systems, to offer enhanced public services, or to rebuild deteriorating city streets and other physical facilities.

For millions of Americans, however, sports provide a much needed diversion from the complexities and frustrations of their daily lives, from the often disturbing events reported on the evening news.

Sports offer not only an avenue of relief from the pressures of the moment, but also instill a sense of continuity and meaning into the lives of American sports fans. They have come to recognize that the opening of spring training is the harbinger of the end of winter, that the first Saturday of May is the day for the running of the Kentucky Derby, that Memorial Day weekend means the Indianapolis 500 auto race, that the dull plunk of a toe smacking into a football signals the coming of the harvest season, and that the first blasts of wintry weather indicate the hockey and basketball seasons have arrived. Americans associate New Year's Day with college football bowl games, the turning of the leaves with the World Series, and the last Sunday in January with our newest, but perhaps most celebrated informal national holiday, Super Bowl Sunday. They look forward to their weekly tennis game with a friendly rival, savor the joy derived from a solitary run along a country road, and take personal pride in mastering the intricacies of using a nine iron. Sports in America is not just millions of people glued to their television set during the seventh game of the World Series or cheering the local team to victory. It is a young boy persistently working on his jump shot in a neighborhood park, a teenager spending hours each day perfecting her backstroke in preparation for the state swim meet, an elderly citizen faithfully listening on the radio to the games of his or her favorite major league baseball team.

This book was written between 1991 and 1993 and a careful rereading indicates that very little has transpired in the intervening decade that changes the underlying assumptions and interpretations that I initially advanced about the role of sports in American society. If anything, the obsession that I described a decade ago has only expanded with the passing of the years. ESPN has expanded from one to two full-time cable television networks and it and *The Sporting News* have launched competing radio sports networks. Sports betting, always an important but oft-overlooked aspect of the American sports world, has grown exponentially in recent years with the establishment of hundreds of off-shore internet sports books. No one really knows how much Americans wager each year on sports, but the annual figure is in the billions of dollars. The obsession for winning that drives Division I college sports programs has produced a continuum of shameful ethical transgressions and rules violations, including not only the garden variety of cash bribes to recruits, but also far-reaching academic fraud committed by university officials, and a spate of violent crimes committed by athletes. The obsession of boosters and senior university officials to produce winning football and basketball teams has severely tarnished the reputation of American higher education. The never-ending quest to be "Number One" has helped drive up coaches salaries far beyond what is paid to senior faculty, even campus presidents. By 2004 more than thirty head basketball and football coaches were paid in excess of one million dollars, and scores of others were earning in the high six figures; the highest salary thus far, undoubtedly soon to be exceeded, was the 2004 pay package of $2.7 million for Louisiana State's Nick Saban. That daunting salary was apparently the reward the school was willing to pay for the Tigers 2003 national football championship. Arguably the two most popular Americans during the last decade have been Tiger Woods and Michael Jordan. Their multi-million dollar deals with sporting goods giant Nike, along with their other commercial endorsements, far exceeded their earnings on the PGA golf circuit and in the National Basketball Association, providing ample testimony to the importance bottom-line businessmen attach to identifying their products with charismatic sports superstars.

A careful examination of the role of sports in modern American society provides a useful and valid way to explore broader themes of American life. Whether the topic is the importance attached to high school basketball in Indiana and football in Texas, the emotional intensity exhibited by parents while watching their youngsters performing in Little League or soccer games, the willingness of taxpayers to fund lavish new stadiums and arenas to attract a "major league" professional team to their city, the $6 billion CBS was eager to pay for the rights to telecast the NCAA men's basketball tournament, or the estimated $350 million Americans bet illegally on the Super Bowl, the truth is that sports in America is not only big business, but transmits important symbolic meaning in a broader cultural sense. Unlike many aspects of daily life which are filled with uncertainty and ambivalence, where political and social issues are subject to different and conflicting interpretations, the attraction of sports on a simplistic level is that competition provides clear-cut winners and losers. In their obsession for a favorite team, many Americans have unfortunately taken too literally the myth-enshrouded comment attributed (inaccurately) to famed football coach Vince Lombardi: "Winning isn't everything, it's the only thing." But as the pages that follow indicate, sports also is filled with its own moral ambiguities that are but reflections of the larger social and cultural issues at work within American society.

Sports can and does, however, provide a wholesome and positive way for millions of Americans to enrich their daily lives. That has been the case in my own life as I have struggled over the decades to lower my golf handicap and increase my tennis ranking. I have known the intense emotional joy when my favorite team has won an occasional championship or pulled off an improbable upset, but my memories of devastating losses remain much more vivid. I have dedicated this book to my father, who instilled in me at an early age an appreciation for the positive benefits one can derive from a healthy participation in athletic competition. On special summer days he took me to Reds' games at decrepit Crosley Field in Cincinnati, and on glorious autumn afternoons we were in Oxford to watch the Miami (Ohio) Redskins play in their mid-century glory days under coaches Sid Gillman, Woody Hayes, and Ara Parseghian. We traversed many a dark and sometimes snowy Ohio road to watch an important high school basketball game. Together we worked—with limited success—on my two-hand set shot and left-hand dribble during basketball season and getting into proper position to field a hot grounder at shortstop and how to lay down a perfect bunt during steamy Ohio summers. Those times will forever be among my valued memories.

Richard O. Davies
University of Nevada, Reno

March 31, 2004

Contents

Branch Rickey, General Manager of the
Brooklyn Dodgers, and Jackie Robinson, the
first African-American to play major league
baseball in the twentieth century.

HARBRACE
BOOKS
ON AMERICA

SINCE 1945

Chapter
1

The Postwar
Era Takes
Shape

It was a typical languid summer day in Brooklyn—hot, humid, a day to go to the beach. But August 15, 1945, would not be another uneventful day in Flatbush. Everyone in Brooklyn, as well as across the United States, eagerly anticipated the end of the most devastating war in the history of the world. Hitler's Germany had surrendered three months earlier, and now, with the United States having destroyed the cities of Hiroshima and Nagasaki with nuclear bombs, the end of the war in the South Pacific was obviously at hand. The morning newspapers announced the first landing of American troops on the Japanese mainland and the entrance of the American fleet into Tokyo Bay. Four years of sacrifice were about to come to an end.

Behind the doors at 215 Montague Street, the office of the Brooklyn Dodgers of the National Baseball League, however, little thought was being devoted to these momentous events. History of another sort was being made in the steamy non-air-conditioned office of the Dodgers' sixty-three-year-old chief executive, Wesley Branch Rickey. In a carefully planned secret meeting, the rumpled, cigar-smoking Rickey informed a stunned twenty-six-year-old black athlete, Jack

Roosevelt Robinson, that he was contemplating sign-ing him to a Dodger contract. Robinson had almost decided to forgo the meeting, assuming that Rickey merely wanted to recruit him to play for the Brooklyn Brown Dodgers of the Negro leagues. The former UCLA star athlete was relatively satisfied with the $400 a month salary he earned playing for the Kansas City Monarchs and saw no reason to switch teams.

What Robinson did not know was that for more than two years Rickey had pursued a secret plan to bring down the racial barrier that had denied black athletes the opportunity to play in organized base-ball. Like the rest of American society it so often mir-rored, the national pastime had maintained a rigid racial barrier since the 1890s that denied black ath-letes an opportunity to compete. Branch Rickey fully understood the hazards implicit in the actions he con-templated. He alternatively lectured and questioned the man whom his years of careful research had in-dicated was best suited to challenge baseball's un-written but rigidly enforced color line.

"I'm rounding first and I come into second. It's close. It's a very close play. We untangle our bodies. I lunge toward you." Sweating profusely, Rickey brought his fist close to Robinson's face. "Get out of my way, you black son of a bitch, you black bas-tard!" He paused, then asked, "Now what do you do?"

Transfixed by Rickey's impassioned lecture-performance, Robinson thought for a moment, then inquired, "Mr. Rickey, do you want a ballplayer who's afraid to fight back?"

Rickey quickly retorted, "I want a ballplayer with enough guts not to fight back."

Robinson quickly grasped Rickey's reasoning and reassured his future employer, "I get it. You want me to say that I've got another cheek."

Dodger scout Clyde Sukeforth, who had recom-mended Robinson to Rickey as the best of several black prospects, watched this improbable drama unfolding before him in amazed silence. For nearly three hours Rickey continued, warning Robinson about the impending racial insults, the beanballs, the flashing of sharpened spikes, and the taunts from cruel fans, adamantly insisting that Robinson be willing to accept humiliating abuse while refusing to respond verbally or physically. Rickey's investigation had convinced him that Robinson possessed the intellectual and temperamental qualities necessary for the historic mission he had planned. Only Robinson's intense competitive zeal and record as being outspoken at times on racial matters gave Rickey pause. Assured that Robinson could control his emotions despite the racial taunts of opponents and fans, the Dodger executive offered him a contract—a $3,500 signing bonus and $600 a month to play for the Dodgers' top minor league team in Montreal. Robinson eagerly signed, and one of the great dramas in modern American history began to unfold.

No mere whim prompted Rickey's audacious move. He brought to his work a perspective unique among the group of white businessmen who ruled the world of organized baseball. During his lengthy career as a baseball executive, he had demonstrated a remarkable ability for innovation and long-term planning. "Luck," he liked to say, "is the residue of design." Born in 1881 and raised on a small farm in southern Ohio, Rickey put himself through Ohio Wesleyan University playing professional baseball and football and coaching the Wesleyan baseball team. He later earned a law degree from the University of Michigan while playing professional baseball in the American League for the St. Louis Browns and the predecessors to the Yankees, the New York Highlanders. Rickey played for a few years in the major leagues, but his physical talents were at best average; he survived by bringing to the game an intellectual approach unique for its time. In 1907, suffering from a lame throwing arm, he set a dubious major league record for catchers by permitting thirteen stolen bases in one game. After surviving a potentially fatal bout with tuberculosis and in the aftermath of a disappointing attempt to establish a law practice in Boise, Idaho, he became the field manager for the Browns. In 1917 he joined the St. Louis Cardinals, serving in various capacities as field manager and director of operations.

Never a consistent winner as a field manager, Rickey moved to the front office and soon became recognized as one of baseball's most successful executives. To stimulate attendance he offered special "ladies day" ticket discounts and Sunday doubleheaders. A strong believer in the importance of fundamentals, he revolutionized the traditionally lazy days of spring training by introducing such innovations as mechanical pitching machines for batting practice, sliding pits, instruction on running techniques by college track coaches, and lengthy strategy sessions. He even required his players to attend lectures on the dangers of alcohol and tobacco. Most important, he built the first comprehensive minor league farm system and assembled a scouting system that brought to the Cardinals a steady stream of superior talent. The result was five league championships and three World Series titles during his seventeen years at the Cardinal helm, including the classic victory by the rambunctious "Gas House Gang" in seven games over the Detroit Tigers in the 1934 World Series.

In 1942 Rickey moved to the Brooklyn Dodgers and immediately began to work his magic once more. Although other teams were biding their time until the end of the war, Rickey took advantage of the hiatus and implemented his plan to make Brooklyn a championship caliber team when peace returned. He created an enormous farm system of twenty-five affiliated teams. He stocked these teams with hundreds of would-be major leaguers identified by his extensive scouting system. In 1945 Rickey purchased a closed military base in Vero Beach, Florida, and turned it into a spring training facility at which more than seven hundred players received instruction on fundamentals from the coaching staff.

Within the context of building a championship team, Rickey decided in 1943 to take advantage of the large but untapped pool of talented black players who played in the obscurity of the loosely organized Negro leagues. Rickey later insisted that his motivation was merely to win ball games and that he should not be honored for being a pioneer in racial justice. Like most baseball executives, his political inclinations had always been distinctly conservative—he was a consistently outspoken critic of Franklin Roosevelt's New

Deal. But unlike the preponderance of his peers in baseball management, throughout his life Rickey had expressed deep concern about racial discrimination in America. His commitment led him to read widely about the history of slavery and contemporary race relations; friends and associates often heard him refer to such important books as Frank Tannenbaum's *Slavery and Society* and Gunnar Myrdal's *An American Dilemma.* He frequently spoke of an episode that haunted him throughout his life. While serving as the youthful baseball coach at Ohio Wesleyan in 1903, he had taken his team to play Notre Dame. Much to his anguish, the one black player on the team was denied the right to register at a South Bend hotel with his teammates. The embarrassed player had broken into tears and began rubbing away at his skin in frustration, telling his coach, "Black skin, black skin. If I could only make it white."

Rickey's strong moral and religious convictions, a product of his strict Methodist upbringing, often led him to be ridiculed by others in baseball. He stubbornly adhered to his strong prohibitionist convictions by never drinking alcoholic beverages—surprising behavior for a baseball player at the time. He also drew mockery for his strict observance of the Sabbath: he never played in or attended a game on Sunday, apparently the result of a promise he had made to his mother when he first signed a professional contract as a young man. (He was known, however, to rent a hotel room on Sundays overlooking the playing field when his teams were playing crucial games, and he promoted Sunday doubleheaders as a means of stimulating ticket sales.) His only vice was his well-known affection for premium cigars from Havana; the phrase "Judas Priest" was the closest he came to using profanity.

As he quietly developed his plan to sign a black player to a Dodger contract, Rickey did not operate in a vacuum. Events now increasingly pointed toward the end of racial segregation, not only in baseball but in American society at large. The all-too-obvious irony of the United States fighting Nazi Germany and its racist doctrines with its own rigidly segregated military system invited criticism. In 1941 the pioneering black labor leader A. Philip Randolph had attracted national attention with his highly publicized protest against racial discrimination in hiring practices by industries accepting federal defense contracts. Brutal race riots in Harlem and Detroit during the war had further intensified attention on American racial practices, and Myrdal's disturbing revelations that vividly described the great gulf between America's democratic ideals and its segregated society placed civil rights squarely on the public agenda. In New York City a committee formed to push for the integration of the major leagues published a brochure that proclaimed, "Good enough to die for his country . . . not good enough for organized baseball." Political pressure even forced the autocratic —and determinedly racist—baseball commissioner Judge Kenesaw Landis to proclaim in 1943 that "each club is entirely free to employ Negro players," although his every action sought to thwart such an eventuality. Pressure from black spokesmen forced several teams to announce the abolition of their Jim Crow seating practices, but the pressures to maintain the racial status quo of major league baseball team rosters remained powerful. At war's end baseball's leadership showed no inclination to change its racial policy. New York Yankees President Larry MacPhail bluntly announced in 1945, "I have no hesitancy in saying that the Yankees have no intention of signing Negro players."

MacPhail's comment accurately depicted the over-whelming sentiment of the leadership of organized baseball. Even after the announcement of Robinson's signing, the chief executives of the major league teams voted 15–1 in a secret meeting to instruct the commissioner to forbid a black player to enter the major leagues. Not surprisingly, Branch Rickey cast the one dissenting vote. Such opposition notwithstanding, Rickey correctly perceived that the time had come for decisive action. Despite intense criticism from many quarters—the *New York Daily News* mockingly said Rickey had "a heart as big as a watermelon"—he refused to be deterred. Rickey subsequently extended contracts to such outstanding black players as Roy Campanella, Joe Black, Don Newcombe, Junior Gilliam, and Sam Jethroe. Ever the pioneer, Rickey gained an important competitive advantage for the Dodgers by providing a foundation of outstanding young talent. In the process he lived up to his own demanding moral code and contributed greatly to the rapidly developing civil rights movement.

The Triumph of Jackie Robinson

Rickey's careful selection process paid enormous dividends, both for the Dodgers and for American society. Jackie Robinson soon came to symbolize the struggle of all black Americans to achieve fundamental rights within a nation whose laws and customs were still discriminatory. The "separate but equal" doctrine established by the U.S. Supreme Court in 1896 remained in force; even brutal lynchings in the Deep South still occasionally made headlines. As the civil rights movement began to gather momentum in the late 1940s, Jackie Robinson's struggle to succeed on the baseball diamond came to symbolize to a nation the dawning of a new era. Jackie Robinson was indeed the right person to break baseball's color barrier. A superb athlete, Robinson had lettered in four sports at UCLA. He had attended nearly four years of college and had served his nation during the war as a member of the U.S. Army. He held several UCLA track records and had been a consensus all-American halfback as well as a top scorer for two years on the Bruin basketball team. He had even won national recognition as an amateur tennis player in black tournaments. Recognized for his high moral standards and respected for his intelligence and competitive spirit, for years Robinson had quietly seethed at the racial insults he had encountered. He fully understood that when he entered the all-white world of professional baseball, his ability to control his emotions would be severely challenged, but he understood the importance of restraining the urge to fight back.

Jackie Robinson made his professional minor league debut at Jersey City with the Montreal Royals on April 18, 1946, before a standing room crowd estimated at 24,000. Robinson, who later admitted he was extremely nervous, grounded out to shortstop in his first at bat, an inauspicious start. But in the third inning he lashed a line drive over the left field fence for a home run and later displayed the special qualities that had initially attracted Rickey: he worked the pitcher for a base on balls, stole second base, and after advancing to third on a ground ball, faked a steal home, so flustering the pitcher that he committed a balk.

As Robinson trotted across home plate even the home crowd loudly cheered his effort. But he was not yet done for the day and scored two more runs, both resulting from base hits and stolen bases. After that impressive start, he went on to enjoy a banner year, batting .349, leading the league in runs scored, ranking second in the league in stolen bases and first among all second basemen in fielding percentage. At the end of the season he led the Royals to an exciting seven-game victory in the Little World Series; following the final game happy Montreal fans carried him off the field on their shoulders. Newark manager Bruno Betzel marveled at his baseball skills and instincts: "I'd like to have nine Jackie Robinsons."

Despite Robinson's outstanding season at Montreal, Branch Rickey gave no public indication whether he would be brought up to the Dodgers in 1947, all the while carefully orchestrating Robinson's promotion to the parent team. Fearing possible ugly racial incidents in Florida, Rickey moved the Dodgers' spring training camp to Cuba and scheduled several of the team's exhibition games in Panama. He also curtly put down a potential mutiny by several southerners on the team, led by the popular, aptly named outfielder Dixie Walker. He and several other players had indicated to the press they might refuse to play or would demand trades to other teams rather than accept a black as a teammate. The possibility of a racially inspired walkout fizzled, in large part because of Rickey's behind-the-scenes management as well as the courageous leadership provided by Pee Wee Reese, himself a proud southerner. The star shortstop refused to support any organized action, and the threat of a walkout quickly dissipated.

Ultimately, Robinson himself won over the skeptics with his baseball skills and his courage. Racial prejudice notwithstanding, these were baseball men who soon recognized that Robinson could help them win games, even get to the World Series. As the combative Dodger manager Leo Durocher put it in a dramatic no-holds-barred locker room confrontation with the dissidents, "I don't care if a guy is yellow or black or if he has stripes like a fuckin' zebra. I'm the manager of this team and I say he plays." Jackie Robinson, Durocher emphasized, "is going to put money in your pocket and money in mine." When Rickey announced shortly before opening day that Robinson would be the Dodgers' first baseman, most newspapers, uncertain and confused about the implications of the impending historic event, confined their comments to the sports page. The *New York Times*, however, correctly observed in an editorial, "If Robinson was a white man, his name would have been there long before this," while the *New York Post* predicted that the great majority of fans "will be rooting for him to make a good showing."

Robinson won the overwhelming support of baseball fans and the grudging respect of other major leaguers with the quality of his spirited play. After getting off to a slow start in April, he hit his stride a month into the season. His daring base running, consistent hitting, and superior play in the field helped propel the Dodgers to the National League pennant, seven games ahead of the St. Louis Cardinals. Only a late season slump, most likely the result of the cumulative effects of the intense pressures he faced, caused Robinson's batting average to drop below .300. Playing in 151 of 154 regular season games—the most of any Dodger—he batted a hefty .297 and led the National League in stolen bases while finishing second in runs scored. Only years later did friends learn that the season took a heavy toll, causing him to suffer from high blood pressure, depression, and related nervous problems.

Durocher's prediction that Jackie Robinson would put World Series money in the players' pockets proved to be right on the mark. Although Durocher himself would shortly be suspended for the season by Commissioner A. B. "Happy" Chandler for allegedly consorting with gamblers, the Dodgers, under interim manager Burt Shotton, easily won the National League pennant, only to lose to the crosstown Yankees in a memorable seven-game World Series. Robinson's performance proved decisive in propelling the Dodgers to the league championship. Despite more unpleasant incidents than anyone cares to recall, Robinson adhered to Rickey's counsel to avoid confrontation, even when he was the target of an inordinate number of brushback pitches and brutal racial epithets from the dugouts of opposing teams and from the grandstands. When he was viciously kicked by Chicago Cubs shortstop Len Merulla after a close pickoff play at second base, Robinson instinctively started to retaliate, then, remembering Branch Rickey's insistence on nonviolence, lowered his clenched fist and turned away from his assailant. "Plenty of times I wanted to haul off when somebody insulted me for the color of my skin," he later recalled. "But I had to hold to myself. I knew I was kind of an experiment." He fully understood that "the whole thing was bigger than me." A Pittsburgh sportswriter, observing Robinson's coolness under such intense pressure, noted, "Throughout it all he has remained a gentleman and a credit to the game, as well as to his race."

Even his early nemesis, Dixie Walker, agreed that Robinson had proven the determining factor in the Dodgers' pennant, telling a reporter, "No other ballplayer on this club, with the possible exception of Bruce Edwards [the catcher], has done more to put the Dodgers up in the race than Robinson." *Sporting News* concurred and, overcoming its own prejudices—the *News* editorial policy had long opposed integration—named Robinson its rookie of the year.

Robinson's impact far transcended the won and lost standings. Attendance at Dodger home games jumped to a record 1.8 million, and when the Dodgers took to the road, spectators turned out in unprecedented numbers. Attendance by black fans increased appreciably, and black newspapers proudly highlighted Robinson's daily performances. The pride and excitement he generated among blacks was equaled only by Joe Louis's spectacular knockout victory over Max Schmeling in 1938. "How'd Jackie make out today?" became a standard daily question in black neighborhoods across the country. He also converted a generation of blacks into loyal Dodger fans, who expressed their appreciation to the team that broke the color line by abandoning earlier team allegiances. Fan letters flooded in to Ebbetts Field in enormous quantities. From rural Arkansas came a typical letter: "I own and operate a rural general store and right now the farmers are gathering for your game this afternoon . . . . There is no greater thrill than a broadcast of a Dodgers' ball game . . . . We are so proud of you." Quickly jumping on the bandwagon, numerous black organizations showered awards on the Dodger first baseman.

As the historian Jules Tygiel observes in his excellent monograph, Robinson also stimulated the interest and support of a large and rapidly expanding group of white fans. They too flocked to their local ballpark to witness baseball's new sensation, many of them jostling with black fans after the game in quest of Robinson's autograph. Brooklyn's own rooters evidenced strong support for Rickey and his experiment, enthusiastically cheering for the rookie first baseman. As Tygiel points out, they were also cheering the concept of the racial integration of baseball. He quotes a leading Brooklyn journalist who wrote in his sports column that the fans "were with him, not just Jackie, they were with the idea. He became a state of mind in a community that was already baseball oriented."

The drama of Jackie Robinson captured the attention of the American people in 1947. The symbolism provided by the integration of the national pastime was clear: race relations in the United States would never return to their prewar status. Robinson's exploits also served notice that things would never be the same in the life of American sports. Like the society it so often mirrored, America's sporting world, however reluctantly, entered a period of pervasive change.

A New Era Dawns

The knowledgeable sports fan of the 1990s would scarcely recognize the American sports scene during the years immediately following World War II. Professional sports had a modest, even provincial, quality about them. Only professional baseball and boxing attracted substantial national attention. At a time when teams still traveled by train, major league baseball was confined to the Northeast and upper Midwest. The St. Louis Cardinals and Browns were the western outposts of the two major leagues, and the Washington Senators were considered a southern team! Attendance during the prewar period for each of the sixteen major league teams seldom approached a million fans, often hovering below half a million. Salaries for professional athletes were modest, with the average major leaguer earning less than $5,000 annually, roughly approximating the income earned by college professors or small businessmen. Ruthlessly exercising their strong bargaining position—derived from special treatment by federal courts and the Congress—baseball owners kept salaries and expenses low. Ted Williams of the Boston Red Sox, one of the greatest hitters in baseball history, received vast publicity when his pay reached $100,000 in 1950.

Most fans followed their favorite team through the sports pages, where uncritical writers overlooked the many human imperfections of the athletes while writing about their accomplishments in heroic terms. (The harsh, even cruel, treatment accorded Williams by several Boston journalists was the major exception.) All of the teams now broadcast their games on the radio, although many reluctant owners feared they were giving their product away and that broadcasts reduced ticket sales. Teams either employed the broadcasters themselves or insisted on the right to approve those hired by the radio station. In 1946 only the New York Yankees sent their popular broadcaster Mel Allen on the road with the team to report the games live. Several other broadcasters, such as Cincinnati's Waite Hoyt, were forced to sit in a studio and recreate the game from a teletype report when the team played away from home. Millions of fans raptly followed their teams' fortunes on the road with the sound of a Western Union machine clicking in the background.

Professional football, in one form or another, had been around since early in the century, but the National Football League that had been formed in 1922 was barely a pale imitation of baseball in popularity or influence. Franchises frequently folded or moved from city to city, making the composition of the league uncertain from year to year. A few stalwart teams—the Washington Redskins, Green Bay Packers, New York Giants, Philadelphia Eagles, and Chicago Bears—provided a modicum of stability. As late as 1945 most players received only a few hundred dollars per game, and crowds seldom exceeded twenty thousand, even for championship games. The highest salary in 1947 was the Washington Redskins' quarterback Sammy Baugh's $17,500; the salary of one of the all-time best pass receivers, Don Hutson of the Packers, never exceeded $15,000, while the parsimonious owner/coach of the Chicago Bears, George Halas, never paid all-league quarterback Sid Luckman more than $12,500 a season. Ominously, the leadership of the league had devolved largely on a group of individuals recognized for their close associations with professional gamblers, and an unreported bribe offer to two members of the Giants backfield before the league championship game in 1946 threatened the integrity of the sport.

In that same year, investors formed the new All-American Football League to capitalize on the sport's potential, and as a harbinger of events to come, awarded franchises to the West Coast cities of Los Angeles and San Francisco. Competition between the rival leagues for players immediately stimulated salary increases, but cooler heads among management prevailed and the few financially viable teams of the new league were absorbed by the NFL in 1950. Much to management's relief, the escalation in salaries quickly ended.

Professional basketball lagged far behind football and baseball in fan appeal; divided into two competing leagues with a total of only fourteen teams, professional franchises were located in major cities like Boston, Philadelphia, Chicago, and New York, as well as such small markets as Fort Wayne, Rochester, and Syracuse. In 1950 the two rival leagues combined to form the National Basketball Association. NBA teams seldom played to full houses, and only occasionally mustered sufficient interest in their product to enjoy the luxury of commercial sponsors of radio broadcasts of games. In search of paying customers they often played "home" games in such out-of-the-way locations as Dayton, Ohio; Charleston, West Virginia; and Harrisburg, Pennsylvania. Well into the 1950s professional basketball found itself in a serious rivalry for both fans and players with semiprofessional teams sponsored by such corporations as Phillips Oil and Goodyear Tire and Rubber, whose teams competed under the aegis of the American Athletic Union. One of the nation's first 7-foot centers, all-American Bob Kurland of Oklahoma A&M, for example, opted to play for the Phillips 66ers rather than for an NBA team.

At war's end professional boxing enjoyed substantial national interest, much of it stimulated by gambling and publicity generated by major bouts between boxers embodying the pride of ethnic and racial groups. Like other professional sports, boxing's headquarters lay on the eastern seaboard. In the late 1940s the Gillette Razor Company began to sponsor the radio broadcasts of fights held in New York City's Madison Square Garden; public interest started to grow and then increased dramatically when in 1950 the fights were also televised. Boxing's close ties with organized crime and gamblers, however, provoked many government inquiries and considerable public skepticism. During the immediate postwar years the dubious sport of boxing lived, as it had for more than half a century, on the fringes of respectability.

The other most popular sport was college football, but with the exception of the two military academies and the University of Notre Dame, no team enjoyed anything approaching a national following. By the mid-1920s most teams played a schedule of eight or nine games. The press produced a "top ten" listing each week, and substantial interest focused on the selection of the nation's top team and an all-American team. Postseason games were few in number, with the Rose Bowl enjoying the most prestige. Even such relatively major bowl games as the Cotton, Orange, and Sugar struggled to survive financially. Still, autumn Saturday afternoons on the campuses of such powerhouses as Ohio State, Alabama, Texas, and Southern California generated immense excitement with sellout crowds. In 1946 the mid-November game between Notre Dame and Army attracted a capacity crowd to Yankee Stadium, as millions of fans across the nation listened to Bill Stern's dramatic description of the big game—which ended in a 0–0 tie despite the highly publicized offensive reputations of both teams.

While big-time college football attracted large crowds, thoughtful observers raised penetrating questions about the questionable methods used by coaches to recruit their players. Critics also made much of the often lax academic standards to which many colleges held their athletes. Despite a continued barrage of criticism from faculty and critics, those in control of college athletics were content with the status quo and routinely deflected efforts of well-intentioned reformers.

College basketball took a distinct backseat to football. Few fans concerned themselves about national rankings or even the National Collegiate Athletic Association (NCAA) tournament. Most basketball enthusiasts considered the National Invitational Tournament (NIT) held each March in New York City to be the more prestigious postseason event. During the immediate postwar years, major college basketball revolved primarily around promoter Ned Irish, who operated the NIT and throughout the winter months attracted large crowds every Tuesday and Saturday nights to his immensely popular Madison Square Garden doubleheaders. These sellout events usually featured such premier teams as Manhattan, Long Island University, St. John's, Seton Hall, St. Joseph's, LaSalle, City College of New York, Niagara, and Siena. Occasionally, these eastern teams would be challenged by such inland powerhouses as Kansas, Kentucky, or Bradley. Unfortunately, observers close to the New York college basketball scene recognized that the surge in the popularity of college basketball resulted in part from involvement by professional gamblers. The recent introduction of the point spread had revolutionized sports gambling, stimulating unprecedented wagering on college basketball games; no longer did a gambler merely bet on one team to win based on established odds, but rather on how a team would fare against a predetermined number of points set by odds makers to offset perceived differences between teams. Following revelations of fixed games involving Brooklyn College players in 1945, rumors about the "fixing" of games became rampant on the streets of the city in the late 1940s, a disquieting precursor of major problems to come.

Sports Reflect Major Social Changes

College athletics mirrored the racial patterns of American society. Although a few black players dotted the rosters of northern college and university teams, white players dominated the squads of all but the traditional black colleges. Such leading conferences as the Southeast and Southwest rigidly excluded blacks; consequently the black colleges in the South reaped a bountiful crop of players each year until major northern universities began systematic recruiting of southern black talent in the 1960s. Such renowned coaches as Adolph Rupp of the University of Kentucky adamantly refused to recruit black basketball players, even after the university began to admit black students in 1949. Rupp's outlook represented not only popular opinion in the bluegrass state but also the sentiment prevalent among college coaches that black players lacked the discipline, dedication, and intelligence to be successful major college competitors.

Racial stereotypes pervaded other sports as well. Professional golf and tennis were considered a special preserve for whites, extending down to local country clubs, where racial and religious restrictions applied. This exclusivity determined that the athletes who rose to national prominence in these sports would be almost exclusively white. In tennis only Althea Gibson during the 1950s and Arthur Ashe in the 1960s managed to crack the racial barrier and win national championships. Similarly, the professional golf tour remained an all-white event until the late 1960s when Lee Elder and Charles Sifford gained begrudging entrance into tournaments. It was not until 1970 that a black played in the most prestigious of all tournaments, the Masters, held at Augusta, Georgia. America's Olympic delegation in 1948 exceeded five hundred athletes, but included only a handful of nonwhites.

This cozy and confined world of American sports did not last for long, however. The war had unleashed powerful social, economic, political, and technological forces that drastically altered the structure of American society. The economic boom created by the war quickly manifested itself after 15 million military personnel returned home from the war. A rapidly expanding economy propelled millions into the relatively affluent lifestyle of the middle class. Developers throughout the land replicated the concepts first employed in the building of the spectacularly successful middle-class community of Levittown, New York. The flood of new residents to the suburbs led to the decline of the central urban cores of many leading metropolitan areas; in 1963 the Bureau of the Census announced that more Americans lived in the suburbs than in the central cities of America. A high birthrate further served to fuel the ascendancy of suburban America. Once ensconced in new split-level suburban houses, America's thriving middle class soon evidenced a new lifestyle that many social commentators were quick to criticize. Not only did the suburbs afford a white haven far from the racial, ethnic, and social diversity characteristic of the central cities, but they seemingly produced a new and disturbing conformity of thought and behavior. A typical critic, writing in a popular magazine, dismissed the new suburbs as a place where there existed "few of the opportunities for individuality found in the big city. One moves there, buys the right car, keeps his lawn like his neighbors, eats crunchy breakfast food, and votes Republican." This blanket condemnation—correctly

dismissed in 1969 as the "suburban myth" by scholar Scott Donaldson—
obviously overlooked many positive aspects of the new lifestyle on the
edges of American cities. But that a new lifestyle had emerged was
unmistakable.

The impassioned debate over the merits of suburbia notwithstanding, within a decade after V-J Day the suburban explosion had funda-
mentally altered the nature of American society. Although there were
distinct working-class, middle-class, and more exclusive suburbs, all
were manifestations of the rising affluence of America's postwar economic boom. The new consumer culture, symbolized by such icons as
the two-car garage, the television antenna atop the roof, and the suburban shopping mall, swept across the American landscape.

The availability of substantially more leisure time helped make
this new lifestyle possible. The "good life" available in suburbia required a substantial amount of discretionary income, a new force that
had a direct impact on sports. In the immediate postwar years, attendance at professional baseball and college football games increased
appreciably. Several baseball franchises established new attendance
records. The Brooklyn Dodgers drew only 482,000 in 1937, but by
1946 more than 1.7 million fans paid their way into Ebbetts Field. The
New York Yankees had claimed more than a million paying spectators
each year during the heyday of Babe Ruth and Lou Gehrig during the
late 1920s, and by the early 1950s the new version of the Bronx
Bombers drew in excess of 2 million fans annually. In 1948 more than
20 million fans attended major league baseball games, double the prewar total of 1941. Similarly, attendance at professional and college
football games, automobile races, boxing matches, horse races, and
other sporting events grew substantially.

Insightful businessmen quickly recognized that big dollars awaited
creative sports promoters. After the long years of war, Americans eagerly anticipated the resumption of full sports competition, and they
had more money to spend in their quest for entertainment. "THIS IS WHAT
WE'VE BEEN WAITING FOR," the *Cleveland Plain Dealer* headline enthusiastically proclaimed in late 1945 when the fabled Bob Feller returned
from military service to pitch for the Indians. More than sixty thousand
war-weary fans turned out late in the season to Municipal Stadium to
witness the recently discharged   pitcher crank up his famed 100-mph
fast ball.

Not content to be merely spectators, Americans eagerly plunged
into sports participation on an unprecedented scale. Public golf courses

soon encountered great pressure from a rapidly expanding golfing population; by the mid-1950s middle- and even working-class Americans had discovered the pleasures—and frustrations—of a sport that only a generation earlier had been viewed as reserved for the upper levels of society. City governments responded by building hundreds of new courses to meet the demand. Many new private clubs were also established, often with annual fees set within the reach of the middle class. Similarly, city parks and recreation departments across the country constructed tennis courts to meet growing demand. Sporting goods manufacturers encouraged the democratization of golf and tennis with national advertising campaigns. Consequently, sporting goods stores enjoyed a thriving business, providing a new generation of participants with a set of Ben Hogan autographed golf clubs or the latest model Jack Kramer wooden tennis racket. Across the nation, in communities big and small, men and women—well into middle age—flocked in extraordinary numbers to join softball leagues, often playing on newly lighted fields.

No participant sport grew as rapidly as bowling. Once a furtive stepchild of the sports world, bowling polished its image and moved into the mainstream of American life during the postwar years. The relatively few bowling establishments in operation before the war had usually been dingy, smoke-filled places, smelling of stale beer and greasy food, often competing with the local pool halls for their clientele. No longer. A new generation of operators successfully appealed to an enormous new market by emphasizing that bowling could be a family activity. The advent of automatic pinsetters greatly speeded up the game, and the construction of air conditioned, attractively appointed new facilities added to the attraction. New bowling establishments, costing in the range of $2.5 million, became the country clubs of America's blue-collar class. By the mid-1950s what had once been a sport with very limited interest now claimed in excess of 20 million regular bowlers. The AMF and Brunswick corporations, leading manufacturers of pinsetters and other bowling equipment, became two of Wall Street's most spectacular growth companies until they eventually saturated the market in the 1960s. In addition to expanding the interest of adult males by establishing leagues for bowlers of all skill levels through their place of work or worship, the companies also discovered they could keep their bowling lanes busy throughout the normally slow weekdays by forming leagues for housewives; they even provided child care for mothers. One lady summarized the appeal: "I get out of the house and meet new people. My daughter is having a good safe time in the nursery. And I get to exercise the fun way, not by listening to someone telling me to stretch and bend by the numbers."

Given the immense proportions of the postwar baby boom, it is not surprising that the new emphasis on participation included the nation's youth. Although the public schools and the YMCA and YWCA had long provided structured sports programs as a means of character development, parents now sought to supplement those opportunities with more competitive programs. Youth football had begun in 1929 with the establishment of the Pop Warner program, and Little League baseball was founded ten years later, but the size and scope of the programs remained minuscule until after the war. Within a decade after the war more than a million young boys participated annually in Little League baseball; Pop Warner football enjoyed a lesser but nonetheless impressive level of popularity. These programs for boys twelve years of age and younger placed special emphasis on adult supervision and coaching, snazzy team uniforms, the "drafting" of players, and league standings and postseason playoffs, with careful attention paid to the enforcement of rules and regulations. Seeking to impose on youth the regimentation and adherence to team rules practiced by college and professional teams, these programs emphasized organization, discipline, and the importance of the team over the individual. Protestations by program spokesmen notwithstanding, these highly structured programs also placed a heavy emphasis on the importance of winning. Both programs conducted national championships, a dubious enterprise that even high school sports programs had avoided. Eager parents also sought to provide young girls with opportunities for participation, namely cheerleader squads for Pop Warner teams and somewhat later the formation of Bobby Sox softball leagues.

The Crisis of College Athletics

From its very early days intercollegiate athletics had been defended by its many and enthusiastic advocates for providing participants with the opportunity to learn the values of competition, good sportsmanship, teamwork, and physical conditioning. It is also true that from the beginning college athletics was pervaded by a hypocrisy so great that it called into question the intelligence if not the integrity of university officials. The much publicized problems of contemporary major college athletics of the 1990s are nothing more than a continuation of practices begun a century ago. These abuses revolved around the incessant quest for winning teams, which led to academic dishonesty, renegade recruiting practices, willful exploitation of athletes, and unprincipled intervention by outside booster groups.

Intercollegiate competition originally grew out of the informal games played by various clubs and fraternities. By the 1870s formalized competition between colleges in baseball, crew, and track and field had become commonplace. During the last two decades of the nineteenth century the game of football emerged as the most popular sport, a result in part of the creative genius of Walter Camp of Yale University, whose innovations included such fundamental aspects of the game as the line of scrimmage, the first down, and the use of diagrammed offensive plays.

Dollar-conscious college administrators quickly recognized that a winning team provided an effective means of publicizing their institution and generating funds. The innate values of competition and sportsmanship quickly gave way to the overriding importance of victory. Winning teams stimulated ticket sales; it was also believed, although unproved, that successful teams produced increased giving by alumni. Some colleges and university officials also discovered that a winning football team could generate amazing loyalty among individuals who had never attended their institution, even to the point of inspiring them to contribute large sums. By the late 1920s the dedication and size of Notre Dame's "subway alumni"—ardent fans who had never attended any college—had already reached legendary proportions.

From the inception of college athletics, money became the fundamental driving force. To satisfy rapidly growing public and student interest in football, college institutions began to erect large stadiums. One of the first of such new campus landmarks was the enormous Yale Bowl, which seated sixty thousand. Following the First World War, many universities determined to pursue football on a major scale. Typical among these was Ohio State University which, after years of playing the likes of Oberlin and Ohio Wesleyan, decided to test its mettle against the nation's best teams. In 1922 the mammoth horseshoe-shaped Memorial Stadium appeared along the banks of the Olentangy River; it soon became a statewide mecca for football fans on autumn Saturday afternoons, as more than seventy thousand people gathered to cheer on the Buckeyes. The fortunes of the football team became a common point of interest among Ohio's 6 million residents. The popularity that surrounded big-time football at Ohio State during the 1920s was emulated across the country on campuses in such communities as Lincoln, South Bend, Ann Arbor, Austin, Baton Rouge, and Champaign-Urbana. Radio stations further stimulated interest with their broadcasts of important games, and moviegoers thrilled to such stars as "Red" Grange of Illinois or the famed "Four Horsemen" of Notre Dame, whose daring exploits were highlighted in the popular newsreels shown before the feature film.

The emphasis on winning, which translated into dollars generated at the ticket office, led inevitably to a scramble to attract the best athletic talent. As early as the 1890s, critics denounced the devious means used to entice nonstudent players to perform for college teams, including cash payments to "tramp" athletes who seldom bothered to enroll in classes and moved from school to school playing for many years, even for more than one team in a season. Although such practices angered faculty, their demands for reform were usually ignored. In 1905 reformers succeeded in forming the Intercollegiate Athletic Association with some sixty-two founding members. In 1910 this fledgling institution became the National Collegiate Athletic Association (NCAA), but its powers were largely restricted to the establishment of game rules. Especially pressing was the need to reduce the mayhem on the football field, which resulted in an inordinate number of deaths each year.

The NCAA was founded as a cooperative organization of member institutions; it sought to encourage adherence to academic standards and fair recruitment practices by appealing to the presidents, faculties, and coaching staffs of member institutions *to police themselves*. Although this policy—a logical adaptation from established academic accreditation procedures—succeeded at colleges that resisted the allure of big-time athletics, it failed almost universally at those institutions that sought to win national recognition. Although individual conferences and the NCAA established relatively strict regulations governing athletic eligibility, such rules were routinely ignored. By the 1930s most major athletic programs offered "scholarships" that were based solely on an individual's athletic skill, not his academic abilities or financial need. Determined boosters and overly aggressive coaches found many creative ways to reward star players. For example, when the president of Ohio State University threatened to cancel the 1936 football season, a year when the Buckeyes were considered to be a leading contender for the national championship, if Ohio governor Martin L. Davey persisted in his determination to reduce the university's budget, the public outcry proved decisive in protecting the budget before the legislature. The iconoclastic Davey, however, created a furor when he responded tartly to President George W. Rightmire's threat: "We recognize the fact that football has become the supreme purpose of higher education. We certainly have done our part, because we have most of the football squad on the state payroll." Much to the embarrassment of state and university officials, the accuracy of Davey's shocking revelation was soon verified. Defenders of this practice rationalized that players actually did the work for which they were paid, a contention many skeptics found hard to believe. But the flap Governor Davey had created soon faded away when it was learned the practice was commonplace in many states where the football fortunes of the state university had become an important priority.

Winning, not the building of character or academic integrity, became the unquestioned goal of many college football programs. College presidents often lamented their lack of control over their virtually independent athletic departments, but they willingly acquiesced to the demands of influential boosters that a coach with a losing record be fired, and refused to require that their coaches adhere to the academic and recruiting rules to which the institution had formally pledged itself. Unfortunately, the general public and, in particular, deeply involved and politically well-connected boosters, had in practice assumed de facto control of big-time college athletics.

Controlled by its member institutions, the small staff of the NCAA could not effectively combat this squalid situation. Instead, the NCAA stubbornly adhered to the naive and impractical policy that the extent of its responsibility did not go beyond encouraging each member institution to police its own academic and recruiting practices. This was like letting the fox patrol the henhouse. In 1948 the NCAA established a so-called Sanity Code, which set strict limits on the financial aid a member institution could provide an athlete; it even required that any part-time job provided an athlete had to entail actual work—a sharp change in practice for many institutions. Opponents quickly scuttled the Sanity Code. Seven prestigious institutions (including the University of Virginia, The Citadel, and Colgate University) denounced it as "sheer hypocrisy" and threatened to resign from the association rather than enforce it on their campuses, contending that their opponents would certainly circumvent the new code. A badly shaken president of the NCAA feared the worse, predicting "we will have chaos in college athletics." Perhaps not chaos, but at least a continuation of what one federal judge in 1951 condemned as a pervasive system that created an atmosphere of "commercialization and professionalization," and that condoned the practice of permitting "unqualified students to matriculate." Judge Saul Streit went on to denounce an environment that encouraged "flagrant violations of amateur rules by colleges, coaches and players, and illegal scouting, recruiting and subsidization of players." It was not until 1958, when the cry of critics could no longer be ignored, that the NCAA finally established a modest enforcement division to investigate violations of its policies governing intercollegiate athletics. The outside observer has to question the sincerity of the organization in identifying and punishing violators; in 1990 its enforcement division had finally reached the total of ten full-time investigators!

College athletics thus moved into the postwar period carrying a heavy ethical burden. The problems would only intensify in an environment that saw a rapid increase in public interest in athletics. Because intercollegiate athletics had proved itself incapable of preventing wholesale cheating by its own members, it should come as no surprise that it also proved equally unable to fend off threats to its integrity from the outside. In late 1947 officials at the U.S. Military Academy and at Notre Dame quietly announced they would not continue their football rivalry; they did not announce, however, that they did so upon learning that an estimated $20 million had been wagered on their last two games. They rightfully feared the possible influence of gamblers playing for high stakes. Unfortunately, other institutions were not as perceptive, and as a result a major gambling scandal in 1951 engulfed many major college basketball teams. By the late 1940s bookies routinely set a "line" on major games utilizing the new point spread concept; according to law enforcement officials, gamblers illegally bet an estimated $10 million a day on college basketball in the major eastern cities alone.

As public interest in Ned Irish's Madison Square Garden Saturday night basketball extravaganzas grew with the advent of television, so too did rumors that the fix was in. Gamblers recognized that it was much easier to determine the final score of a basketball game by bribing one or two key players than to control the outcome of the much more complex game of football. By early 1951 the sports editor of the *New York Journal American*, Max Kase, had become convinced that rumors about fixed games he was picking up on the street were accurate. For more than a year he had watched games in which such national powerhouses as Long Island University (LIU) and City College of New York (CCNY) won games by only a few points (i.e., below the point spread) over obviously inferior opposition; his sources in bars and bookie joints confirmed his suspicions that several of the best players in the country were on the take, making an errant pass or missing an easy shot at critical times. Buttressed with incontrovertible evidence, Kase informed District Attorney Frank Hogan of his facts, giving him a week to act before he broke the story in his newspaper. Hogan's investigation confirmed Kase's allegations, and in late January, as teams pointed toward postseason tournaments, the district attorney stunned the nation by arresting three members of the defending national champion CCNY team. Hogan also announced that he had arrested an ex-con and well-known gambler, Salvatore Tarto Sollazzo, on charges of bribery and conspiracy.

The arrest of Sollazzo and the three CCNY players proved to be just the beginning. A few weeks later Hogan arrested three LIU starters, including forward Sherman White, who had just been named player of the year by *Sporting News*. At precisely the same time White and his two teammates were being placed in custody, across town their renowned coach was in the process of strongly denying to a luncheon audience that any of his players were involved in the unfolding scandal. "You've got to believe in your kids and you've got to stick up for them," Clair Bee said. The point-shaving scandal devastated the veteran coach. He had won a national championship in 1940, and his current team was considered a strong challenger to unseat CCNY for national honors. Shortly before the disaster hit, LIU had powered to a 16–0 record, before losing four games on a tough road trip to the West Coast. In his eighteenth season as coach of the Blackbirds, Bee enjoyed a national recognition for his disciplined offense and aggressive man-to-man defenses. The author of an acclaimed set of technical books on the art of coaching, he had also tried his hand at writing fiction, with considerable success. In 1948 he published the first of a series of popular sports novels aimed at the teenage market. These books emphasized the virtues of competitive athletics and featured a modern-day Horatio Alger in the person of the clean-living, scrupulously honest Chip Hilton who, despite the death of his father and the necessity of working part time in a drugstore to help his persevering mother pay the bills, became a self-effacing star in three varsity sports at Valley Falls High School. Bee undoubtedly drew heavily on his own childhood in a depressed West Virginia mill town in creating the legendary Chip Hilton; equally significant, however, was Bee's belief in the myths about good sportsmanship and fair competition in which he enshrouded the blond straight A student, star quarterback, basketball forward, and baseball pitcher from Valley Falls High. In sport after sport, season after season, Bee's Chip Hilton bravely overcame the forces of evil and bad fortune, winning out over dirty tactics by opponents, serious injuries, and jealous teammates to help his team win the championship, usually in a dramatic fashion in the closing minutes of the big game.

Unfortunately for Clair Bee, his star players were not Chip Hiltons. Instead, they admitted they had taken bribes ranging from $500 to $1,500 to shave points in games. Various confessions indicated that the practice had occurred over several seasons. Within a few days Bee's career was shattered. Investigators even learned that he had himself lived a lie by approving illicit payments to his players and by routinely skirting the academic standards of his institution. Even before the basketball season ended, the embarrassed and irate trustees of LIU voted to drop all intercollegiate sports immediately; this onetime national powerhouse disappeared from the nation's sports pages. To his credit, Bee later admitted he had failed his players by not recognizing the danger signs. "Public confidence in college basketball is shattered and the fault is partly mine," he wrote in the *Saturday Evening Post*. "I was so absorbed in the victory grail that I lost sight of the educational purposes of athletics."

Much to the dismay of sports fans and public leaders, it soon became apparent that the cancer of gambling had infected significant segments of the elite of college basketball. Before District Attorney Hogan had finished his investigation, thirty-two players had been indicted; Hogan's widely cast net ensnared players at Manhattan, Bradley, Toledo, and even the University of Kentucky (UK), which had won national championships in 1948 and 1949. Upon learning of the arrests in New York City, Kentucky's autocratic and imperious coach, Adolph Rupp, snorted that "Gamblers couldn't touch my boys with a ten-foot pole." Within a few months the arrogant "Baron" would find out just how much he had to learn about the integrity of his players. Two all-Americans, Ralph Beard and Alex Groza, admitted taking bribes from gamblers throughout their college careers, as did another prominent player on the team, Dale Barnstable. The revelations about Beard and Groza, unquestionably two of the most talented players in the nation, caused special grief across the basketball-crazed Commonwealth of Kentucky where they had become heroes of almost mythical proportions. Between 1947 and 1949 they had led UK to 130 victories, including the NCAA championship in 1948 and 1949; in 1948 they and three other UK Wildcats had helped power the U.S. basketball team to an Olympic gold medal. Kentucky fans were appalled to learn their heroes had actually thrown a first-round NIT tournament game in 1949 to Loyola of Chicago in return for small bribes from a New York gambler, Nicholas "Nick the Greek" Englises. The departure of these three players did not stop the fixing of games at Kentucky: its 7-foot center Bill Spivey, himself a consensus all-American, was also implicated. Although he steadfastly maintained his innocence, Spivey was barred by the university athletic board from competing on the Wildcat team. The board concluded that the evidence clearly indicated Spivey had been part of "a conspiracy to fix Kentucky basketball games" during the 1950–51 season. Groza and Beard, then playing for Indianapolis, were both banned from the NBA in the wake of the revelations.

Most of the thirty-two players indicted by the district attorney were convicted in a New York federal court on bribery, conspiracy, and gambling charges. Although most, but not all, received suspended jail sentences, their lives were severely damaged. As the journalist Charles Rosen reports in his detailed study of the scandals, all were banned for life from playing in the NBA. Several eventually played in semiprofessional leagues in the United States, some sought solace in drugs or alcohol, and all carried a sense of guilt with them for life. The major perpetrator of the scandal, Salvatore Sollazzo, was sentenced to a hefty eight-to-sixteen-year sentence. Ironically, Sollazzo had already suffered, for despite his use of the fix, his wife told reporters that his gambling (which extended to the horses) had resulted in losses exceeding $250,000. She reported that she had had to sell their furniture to pay grocery bills. Many observers believed the scandals ran much deeper and broader than Hogan's investigation revealed—with estimates commonly suggesting two hundred or more players—and he received stinging criticism for not pursuing additional cases after he concluded his Kentucky investigation in midsummer. Whatever Hogan's reasons for curtailing the investigations, it was widely perceived that sufficient damage had been done, the evil had been exposed, and examples had been set for a new generation of athletes which would prevent a reoccurrence. Unfortunately, that did not prove to be the case.

How could such star athletes have been so misguided? A humbled fifty-year-old Clair Bee now understood: "Why did 32 players sell out their schools?" he asked in his revealing *Saturday Evening Post* essay. "They did it for money—the identical motive that impels too many colleges to compromise their standards." Sportswriter Joe Williams of the *New York World Telegram* put the scandal into the broader context of the widespread evils of recruiting: "How much respect do you think a player really has for a school which has outbid six or seven others for his services?" College officials did not care to respond to Williams's observation, just as they sought to overlook Bee's pointed admonition: "Something must be done before all sports are discredited. Nothing will be accomplished until college presidents take aggressive action in cracking down on irregularities in their athletic departments." Many concluded that a sordid "New York influence" was to blame, noting that the 1950 NCAA and NIT finals had been played in Madison Square Garden. As a consequence, the Garden forever lost its premier place in the world of college basketball.

Just as the headlines about the basketball scandals began to fade from public view, another devastating blow rocked college athletics. In August of 1951 the commandant of the U.S. Military Academy announced that ninety cadets had been dismissed for violation of the honor code. They were guilty of "cribbing"—a West Point term for academic dishonesty. To be certain, the academy's honor code was demanding, stipulating not only that all cadets never engage in any form of academic dishonesty but also that they are honor bound to report any cheating that comes to their attention. Approximately one-half of those dismissed were members of Army's nationally ranked football team, including all-American quarterback Bob Blaik, son of head coach Earl "Red" Blaik. Several players charged they were the victims of selective punishment, contending that many others had violated the honor system. They also implied that the rigorous demands of football practices left them too exhausted to tackle their books with the same enthusiasm as their opponents on Saturday afternoons, which somehow justified cutting corners on the honor code. They plaintively argued they had upheld the honor of the academy with their gridiron exploits. One dismissed cadet, angrily denouncing what he believed to be selective enforcement of the code against football players, told the *New York Times* he personally knew that at least one-half of the recently graduated class of 1951 were guilty of having violated the code.

Until the cribbing scandal, Coach Blaik had routinely produced nationally ranked teams and more than his share of all-American players, including such legendary running backs as Glenn Davis and Doc Blanchard. The fame and glory of being a national football powerhouse, it now seemed apparent, had come at the expense of academic integrity. The scandal immediately took on a major political dimension, as President Harry S. Truman ordered a thorough investigation and various congressmen called for harsh punishments. Senator William Fulbright, a former president of the University of Arkansas, went so far as to demand the abolition of the football programs at both military academies. Columnists and editorial writers wrung their collective hands, suggesting that what had occurred at West Point was only the tip of an extremely large iceberg that raised fundamental questions about the integrity of college athletics. Could it be, they asked, that sports did not build strong moral character, as was often contended, but instead created an environment in which the overriding importance of winning caused institutions, coaches, and players alike to live a shameful lie?

The Ethics of College Recruiting

As the popularity of college football grew during the postwar period, so too did the pressures on coaches to produce winning teams. Nearly all institutions established their athletic budgets on revenues generated, relying relatively little on student fees or general funds. Winning teams sold tickets and losing teams did not; winning programs generated important booster donations, losing teams did not. And in order to win, coaches understood that recruitment of top athletes was their most important task. With the NCAA unwilling to provide strong leadership, responsibility for enforcing recruiting and academic regulations fell on the institutions, occasionally on conference officials, themselves the employees of the member schools. The dilemma facing the big-time college football coach was aptly defined by Jim Aiken, head coach at the University of Oregon during the early 1950s: "If you have to choose between breaking the rules and losing games, wouldn't it be better to break the rules?" he asked a journalist with unusual candor. "If you lose your games you're certain to be fired. If you break the rules, you have to get caught to be fired."

The views of one of Aiken's rival coaches in the Pacific Coast Conference are illustrative. After a successful nine years at the helm of the powerful University of Southern California Trojans, during which his team appeared four times in the Rose Bowl, head coach Jeff Cravath was fired in 1953 by the university's president, who bowed to pressure from disgruntled alumni following a 5–2–2 season that included an upset win over top-ranked Notre Dame. Cravath, however, was relieved to be out of coaching, although his frustration and sense of outrage led him to publish an article in *Collier's Magazine*. The rules established by "well meaning but floundering faculty representatives," he complained, were "so impractical and so outdated that a coach has no choice but to cheat if he is to produce the teams demanded by his own administration." Describing the situation as "pure hypocrisy," Cravath described the recruiting of a high school phenomenon, Johnny Olszewski, that led to a bidding war between USC and University of California boosters. Eventually, he alleged, the illicit offers included a promise of $150 cash a month, a new convertible automobile, guaranteed admission and tuition to law school after his playing days were over, and even a junior partnership in a law firm! Such a system, he said, was "rotten and corrupt." (Olszewski, incidentally, chose Cal, which perhaps prompted Cravath's decision to cite this particular example.)

Repeated and flagrant disregard for the rules and ethical standards to which the colleges pledged themselves, Cravath contended, "reduced players to perjurers, scalpers and football gigolos. The alumni demand winning football teams. To get winning teams, colleges must violate the rules they themselves have made." Cravath contended that even most college or university presidents could not clean up the mess and keep their jobs: the president "must know the corrupt practices that are being used to build his football squad. But if he tries to stop them, he runs afoul of prominent alumni, or the board of trustees, or board of regents, or alumni with endowment money." Cravath found his own solution to the ethical dilemmas he faced in coaching; after his firing by USC, he left college football to operate a small farm in southern California.

The near-hysterical cries of outrage that the gambling and cribbing scandals produced, coupled with a rising tide of questions regarding recruiting and academic standards, had little appreciable impact. It is significant that at this time the NCAA modified its policy—long ignored by member institutions—that had required athletes receiving scholarships to demonstrate financial need. No longer. With the athletic directors and coaches of "big-time" programs firmly in control of the association, it established a new policy that eliminated the financial need requirement; athletes now could command a "scholarship" irrespective of their academic abilities or financial need. With the association continuing its reliance on institutional self-control, the stage was set for even greater abuses in the future. So much for reform.

Sports and the Cold War: The Olympics

The last prewar Olympic games had been held in 1936 in Berlin, where Adolf Hitler had masterfully orchestrated the games to generate favorable publicity for his repressive regime. Vast pageants featuring German youth and elaborate torchlight ceremonies presented an image of a powerful and purposeful Reich that obscured to most visitors the dark and sinister side of Nazism. Hitler had demonstrated that the Olympic ideal could be subverted for political and nationalistic purposes. As the 1948 Olympics approached, it became evident the world's premier sports event would once more have heavy political overtones. Because the International Olympic Committee insisted that each country's organizing committee had to be independent of its government, the Soviet Union was not permitted to participate. Most significantly, by the time some five thousand athletes representing fifty-nine nations assembled in a rainy and war-scarred London in late July, the military coalition that had defeated the Nazis had already disintegrated. On March 5, 1946, in a speech in Fulton, Missouri, Winston Churchill denounced the Soviet Union for establishing an Iron Curtain "from Stettin in the Baltic to Trieste in the Adriatic." Stirred to dramatic action by what he considered to be hostile actions by the Soviet Union, on March 12, 1947, President Truman told a joint session of Congress that Soviet aggression threatened the peace of the world and the security of the "Free World." Congress quickly approved his urgent request for financial and military aid to Greece and Turkey to assist in their struggles against communist insurgents. The Truman Doctrine thus officially signaled that a new and bleak era in international affairs—the Cold War—was at hand.

Although the Soviets were not invited to London, the pall of the Cold War hung heavy over the games. During the weeks preceding the gathering of the world's best athletes at London's Wembley Stadium, the tension mounted. The American secretary of state, George C. Marshall, had announced the establishment of the European Recovery Program (popularly called the Marshall Plan), which the Soviets perceived as an economic declaration of war against the communist bloc. They quickly responded by blocking access by western nations to Berlin by closing the Autobahn and shutting off rail and water access. The Berlin blockade added a new and fearful chill to an already Cold War, raising the specter of the very real possibility of armed conflict between nations that had been allies just three years previously.

The American people readily believed their Olympic athletes symbolized the values and virtues of the American way of life. Americans took pride in the supremacy of their athletes as they swept to victory after victory, interpreting those victories as a vindication of the American system. With the Russians and other Eastern bloc nations missing, the United States faced relatively little opposition in London, especially in the centerpiece of the Olympiad—track and field. The sprinter Mel Patton set a new world record of 9.3 seconds in the 100-meter dash, setting the tone for a flurry of American gold medals. The American basketball team (led by the as yet undetected point shavers Ralph Beard and Alex Groza) waltzed to the gold medal with a lop-sided 65–21 win over a "bewildered" French team in the championship game. Although there were many heroes to cheer, the exploits of seventeen-year-old Bob Mathias of Tulare, California, captured the imagination of the American people; his stirring victory in the most demanding of all the Olympic events, the decathlon, was viewed as a dramatic statement about the virtues of discipline, hard work, and individual achievement. Mathias's triumph in this grueling ten-event competition merely highlighted an overwhelming American conquest. In an unofficial point system established by the press, the United States amassed 662 points, with Sweden coming in a distant second with 353. Just as the Yanks had overpowered the Japanese and Nazis, so too did they dominate at the highest level of competitive sports. The Americans might have gloried in their athletes' powerful showing, but the informed sports fan recognized that in future Olympiads, with the Soviets and other communist bloc nations present, the Americans would face a much greater challenge. Thus the London games merely set the stage for a dramatic athletic confrontation between the capitalist and communist powers at Melbourne in 1952.

The Advent of Television

In the summer of 1948 Americans followed the heroic exploits of their Olympians primarily through daily newspapers, whose detailed reports were supplemented by radio newscasts and filmed highlights shown at movie theaters. Lacking the immediacy soon to be created by television, the drama of the Olympics was muted by a sense of detachment produced by the barriers of time and distance. The American people in 1948, however, were at least dimly aware of the potential of television, although no one could anticipate the revolutionary impact this new form of electronic communication would have on American society. Nor could they appreciate just how pervasive the impact of television would be on American sports. The first sports events were broadcast in 1938 and 1939, but not until the late 1940s did the new industry begin to experiment seriously with sports telecasting. The primitive DuMont network broadcast the 1947 World Series between the Brooklyn Dodgers and the New York Yankees to five eastern cities, and during the 1948 baseball season WPIX in New York City occasionally telecast Yankee home games. Public reaction to televised baseball proved to be somewhat less than enthusiastic. The early technology was primitive, the small white ball difficult to see on a black and white screen often obscured by interference (dubbed "snow" by irritated viewers). Announcers and commentators, conditioned to describing action for a radio audience, struggled to find an appropriate format for the new medium.

By the 1949 baseball season, however, television began to demonstrate the immense power it would later command in the sports world. Although the cost of television sets remained prohibitive for most American families, tavern owners discovered they could substantially increase the size of their clientele by perching a television set above the bar to show sporting events. A few business executives now anticipated the day when television sets would sit in the living rooms of most American homes, but the vast potential of commercial sponsorship of televised sporting events still largely eluded television executives and corporate sponsors. A noteworthy exception was the Gillette Razor Company, which had sponsored the limited television coverage of the 1947 World Series; its executives had been amazed by the surge in sales of its new plastic razor that had been featured in its advertisements. Impressed by the potential of sports advertising, Gillette signed a contract to telecast the 1949 World Series for the heretofore unheard of fee of $175,000. In 1950 Gillette began sponsorship of the Friday night fights from Madison Square Garden. As advances in technology soon made it possible to send television signals across the nation, its audiences grew enormously—and so did sales of Gillette products. Recognizing the importance of targeting sports audiences, beer companies moved to tie up local baseball broadcasts. The relatively small Ballantine brewing company in Newark gained remarkable market share by sponsoring regular season telecasts of the New York Yankees; in smaller markets, such local breweries as Burger Beer in Cincinnati and the Busch enterprises in St. Louis established important connections between their product and baseball fans.

As television intruded onto the playing fields, subtle changes in the nature of sports events began to surface. The venerable *New York Times* sportswriter Red Smith noted that umpires became much more demonstrative in making their calls when the television camera was trained on them. Even on routine calls, he complained, "they play every decision out like the balcony scene from *Romeo and Juliet*. On a strike they gesticulate, they brandish a fist aloft, they spin almost as shot through the heart, they bellow all four parts of the quartet from *Rigoletto*." When a foul ball was lofted into the stands, spectators would look toward the camera, waving wildly, the individual who had succeeded in retrieving the ball holding his prize proudly aloft. "Television is making us a nation of hams," this distinguished, if old-fashioned, sportswriter groused.

Perceptive though he was, Red Smith did not know the vast changes that television would soon produce: the transformations in rules and playing times designed to accommodate the particular needs of television, the meteoric rise of boxing only to result in the virtual destruction of the sport as it had once existed, the invention of such "trash" sports as roller derby, the boom in the sham of professional wrestling, the immense popularity and celebrity status accorded broadcasters, the rapid ascension of professional football in popularity, the garish spectacle of the Super Bowl, sports bars outfitted with several large color television sets tapping into games via satellite dishes, an all-sports cable network, college basketball's lavish national tournament culminating in the Final Four, and, above all, the infusion of billions of dollars annually into television advertising, thereby making sports a major growth industry. Within the next few decades, television would modify, distort, and eventually revolutionize the very fabric of American sports.

Conclusion

As America moved into the second half of the twentieth century, it became caught up in an era characterized by rapid growth and pervasive change. Although many characteristics of the prewar era remained, they were each day becoming more and more vulnerable to the imperatives of modernization. These forces had an impact on the once limited and provincial world of American sport. Inevitably, such disparate forces as the civil rights movement, the Cold War, suburbanization, the consumer culture, the baby boom, the new leisure, and the electronic miracle of television transformed the form and function of American sport. In the years to come other major influences would, for better or worse, add substantially to the accelerating rate of change—the feminist movement, the widespread use of illegal drugs and steroids, gambling, the fitness movement. And sports would move to center stage of national life, embodying and symbolizing the dreams, the fears, the frustrations, the successes, and the failures of the American people and their society.

Marion Motley (76) carries the ball for the
Cleveland Browns against the New York Giants
on December 20, 1950. Motley helped break
down racial discrimination in professional
football immediately after World War II.

Chapter 2

The Dilemma of Race

From the first day he set foot on the practice field at the University of Nevada in September of 1940, Marion Motley was recognized as a rare football talent. He also was one of the first black players ever to don the silver and blue colors of the diminutive state university tucked away at the foot of the Sierra Nevada mountains in Reno. When he first registered for classes, Motley carefully followed instructions from budget-conscious coaches seeking to avoid out-of-state tuition charges and listed his home as "Eli," Nevada. This nineteen-year-old youth did not come from the eastern Nevada mining town of Ely, however, but had been brought west by the new head coach, Jim Aiken, who had watched Motley tear up the opposition as an all-state running back at McKinley High School in Canton, Ohio. Motley's dubious academic record had forced most college recruiters to back off, but the lax admissions standards at Nevada, where nearly every prospective student was welcomed enthusiastically, did not pose a problem.

Motley almost immediately became a starter at fullback and linebacker and eventually played three years for the Wolf Pack. His crisp tackling and powerful blocking impressed knowledgeable football fans, but his ball-carrying skills deservedly attracted the

most attention. When coach Aiken initially showed a
reluctance to move his talented new recruit into the
starting lineup ahead of returning lettermen, fans were
quick to pressure the coach to play his explosive new
recruit, the possibility of some hurt feelings among
senior lettermen notwithstanding.

The transplanted Ohioan's blossoming football
career almost ended in tragedy in late October of
1940 when an automobile he was driving while returning from a game in San Francisco was involved
in an accident that resulted in the death of the driver
of the other automobile. A Reno newspaper reported
that the "flashy" freshman running back had spent
several days in the Solano County Jail in Fairfield,
charged with involuntary manslaughter. Concerned
boosters soon dispatched a leading local attorney to
provide legal services pro bono, and several "prominent businessmen" traveled across the mountain pass
to testify to Motley's good character. When the judge
assessed Motley a $1,000 fine after he pleaded guilty
to an involuntary manslaughter charge, student body
president Ray Garamendi, taking note of Motley's "high
character and spotless behavior," spearheaded a fund-
raising drive that raised the money in quick order—
a substantial sum in 1940. The student newspaper
enthusiastically supported the fund-raiser, commenting that Motley was "a clean-living and well-man-
nered boy." Duly impressed by this outpouring of
community and university support, the judge released
the running back to the supervision of English professor and dormitory master Paul Harwood, with the ad-
monishment that Motley repay the money. Two days
after his release from jail, Motley repaid his many
supporters in kind by scoring two first-quarter touchdowns in his team's 78–0 romp over Arkansas A&M.

His legal problems behind him, Motley enjoyed
three banner seasons with the Wolf Pack before he
was called into military service during World War II.
By the end of his first season, a Reno sportswriter correctly observed, "In Marion Motley the ball club has
one of the best backs in the entire nation." Motley
could power his way through the opponent's line with
the brute strength of a classic fullback, but once into

the defensive secondary, could run with the speed and deception of an all-American broken field runner. He returned several kickoffs for touchdowns—his 105-yard return against San Jose State is still a school record. He also starred on defense. In describing a 100-yard return of an intercepted pass against the University of San Francisco in 1942, a Reno sportswriter wrote admiringly, "The 220-pound Nevadan reached into the end zone, snatched the ball and powerhoused his way through a knot of San Franciscans, scattering them in all directions."

Although a contrite and greatly relieved Motley had told the student body upon his release from jail, "I shall try to show my gratification in the quality of schoolwork I do and the service I can render on behalf of the University of Nevada," his classroom efforts proved to be minimal. He left the campus in 1943 without having made significant progress toward a degree, and jokes about his proclivity for sleeping through classes became legendary. One wag even placed a sign above a chair in the back of one classroom that proclaimed, "Marion Motley slept here." His coaches showed little concern. They had brought him 2,000 miles from Ohio to score touchdowns, not earn a degree. Like many a college athlete who appeared on a college campus unprepared for academic life, Motley did not receive adequate counseling and guidance from his coaches or the university faculty.

Motley left Nevada in 1942 for the navy. Like many top athletes during the war, he was assigned to duties where his particular athletic skills could be utilized. Thus he spent most of the war at the Great Lakes Naval Station near Chicago. Coaching the naval station team was one of the nation's most promising young coaches, Paul Brown, recently departed from Ohio State. Among the more notable victories won by the Great Lakes aggregation was a stunning upset over Notre Dame. When Brown signed a contract in 1945 for the lofty sum of $20,000 to coach the Cleveland Browns in the new All-American Football Conference, one of the first players he signed to a contract was Motley. Not only were the Browns challenging the long-established National Football League (NFL) for talented players, they were prepared to break the color line in professional football. The powerful running back from Ohio via Nevada would be one of two blacks who played that first season for the Browns in 1946.

Motley quickly established himself as one of the new league's premier running backs. He joined such stars as quarterback Otto Graham, place kicker and offensive tackle Lou Groza, and receivers Dante Lavelli and Mac Speedie to lead the Browns to the league championship, a feat they would repeat the next three years. The other black initially signed by the Browns, defensive lineman Bill Willis, had played for Paul Brown at both Massillon (Ohio) Washington High School and Ohio State; he anchored the defensive line as an all-conference selection although he weighed only 206 pounds.

Motley played eight years for the Browns. He made all-conference each year in the new league and achieved similar recognition when the Browns joined the NFL after the A-AFC disbanded. The Browns continued their winning ways in the NFL in 1950, shocking football experts by winning the league championship their first year in the league. In fact, the Browns powered their way into the championship game for four consecutive years by utilizing the precision passing of Graham and the slashing runs of their 240-pound fullback. Paul Brown continued to build his reputation as one of the nation's most imaginative and successful coaches, becoming one of the first coaches to send in each offensive play to the quarterback, to use extensive classroom sessions, and to rely heavily on films to evaluate player performance and plan future game strategies. He designed innovative draw plays and trap blocking schemes to spring loose his talented fullback, and also pioneered the short "flat" pass to get him the ball in open field. Motley thrived in Brown's sophisticated offensive scheme, gaining 4,721 rushing yards and scoring thirty-one touchdowns in his eight-season career. On one memorable Sunday afternoon in 1951 against the Pittsburgh Steelers he gained 188 yards on only eleven carries. He averaged an amazing 5.7 yards per carry for his professional career. Motley broke the existing NFL rushing records held by

Bronko Nagurski, although his impressive statistics would soon be exceeded by his successor in the Cleveland backfield, Jim Brown from Syracuse University.

Despite his on-the-field performances, Motley's monetary rewards remained minimal. The days of enormous salaries for professional athletes had not yet arrived. He earned $4,500 in 1946 for a twelve-game season, and despite his impressive performance year after year, his pay never exceeded $15,000. A recurring knee injury, a legacy of his days in Nevada, forced his retirement at age thirty-four in 1954. Reflecting back on his income as an all-league running back, Motley noted that it was more or less standard for the time; in those days teams kept individual salaries secret, although it was widely recognized that white players of less skill received higher salaries than he and other leading black players. When asked to compare his salary to the lofty ones of the late 1980s, he commented laconically, "I guess I was just born 40 years too early."

In 1968 Motley became the second black to be admitted to the Professional Football Hall of Fame, located in his hometown of Canton, Ohio. This and other awards were appreciated, but he left the sport he loved with mixed feelings, expressing bitterness over his inability to land a position as an assistant coach in the NFL. A victim of the unwritten rule that prevented blacks from entering the coaching profession, he was turned down for coaching positions by several professional teams, including the Browns. He later bitterly recalled that when he once inquired of a Browns' executive about a job after his retirement, he was asked, "Have you tried the steel mills?" "I knew the game," he told a *New York Times* reporter in 1982, "but they never asked me to be a coach." Noting that in 1962 Coach Brown encountered criticism for perceived insensitivity from several black players, including Jim Brown and all-conference lineman Jim Wooten, he said, "I could have helped Coach Brown. I would have known how they felt. But they didn't have anybody to talk to."

Excluded from entering the coaching ranks, Motley first found employment as a parking lot attendant, then with the postal service; he eventually took a position as a spokesman for the Ohio State lottery. Lacking an adequate retirement program, he still worked full time at the age of sixty-nine. In the early 1980s he began a movement to include players who had retired before 1959 in the lucrative NFL players' pension plan; he worked hard to get himself and other players of his generation included in the plan, but to no avail. Motley never considered himself a pioneer in the civil rights movement, despite breaking the color line in a major professional sport before Jackie Robinson. But he took justifiable pride in his ability as a football player. "He was a great guy, and one helluva player," a University of Nevada teammate recalled some fifty years after he had played alongside him for the Wolf Pack.

Racism's
Reluctant Retreat

In comparison to the attention that Jackie Robinson generated in 1947, the integration of professional football by Marion Motley the previous year received little notice. Actually, he and Bill Willis effectively "reintegrated" professional football because during the 1920s several blacks had participated; in 1933, however, the NFL became an all-white league, apparently the result of behind-the-scenes pressure applied by Washington Redskins' owner Preston Marshall. The relative lack of public interest in Motley and Willis was understandable for several reasons. First, they performed in a new league, one many observers believed to be inferior to the established National Football League. Football also lacked the symbolic importance of baseball. As the distinguished black sociologist E. Franklin Frazier said, "Baseball is an American sport with American respectability." Moreover, the distance of the spectators from the field, the number of players involved in a football game, and the tendency of the helmets, pads, and protective uniforms to render each player more or less indistinguishable from the other further reduced the impact of the presence of black players. The significance of the pioneering presence of Motley and Willis was also diluted by the decision that same year by the Los Angeles Rams of the NFL to sign two black players who had played with Jackie Robinson at UCLA, Kenny Washington and Woody Strode. Except for the interest they generated in Cleveland and Los Angeles, Motley and the other three blacks played without the glare of national publicity that accompanied the exploits of Jackie Robinson the following year. And they were able to go about their business largely unaffected by the incredible pressure under which Robinson had to perform.

Branch Rickey's decision to put Jackie Robinson in a Dodger uniform unleashed a maelstrom of conflicting attitudes and values—pride, admiration, ambivalence, anger, even extreme hatred and bigotry. But Robinson's presence brought into public focus the emerging civil rights movement in a symbolic way that even President Harry Truman's substantial efforts did not accomplish. The saga of Jackie Robinson was indeed one of immense courage and individual achievement under extremely difficult circumstances.

Despite Robinson's immediate success as a player and his estimable contributions to Dodger National League championships in 1947 and 1949, rival baseball teams were conspicuous for their reluctance to emulate the Dodgers' initiative and tap into the substantial pool of available black baseball talent. The failure of other teams to do so is glaring testimony to the powerful racist sentiment that still infected much of organized baseball's high command. In July of 1947, however, the brilliant if unpredictable president of the Cleveland Indians, Bill Veeck, announced he had signed Newark Eagles' infielder Larry Doby to a major league contract. That this innovative owner became the first to follow Branch Rickey's leadership seemed inevitable; in 1943 Veeck had quietly but seriously pursued the idea of purchasing the Philadelphia Phillies and fielding an all-black team of veteran Negro League players. Interestingly, the Dodgers' efficient scouting system had already strongly recommended to Branch Rickey the twenty-two-year-old Doby, but when Rickey learned Veeck was also pursuing him, he told his scouts to back off: "By all means, let him go over to the other league. It will help the movement." On July 5, 1947, Doby played center field for the Indians against the Chicago White Sox, and shortly thereafter the *Sporting News* proclaimed—prematurely as it turned out—that the issue of race in organized baseball "no longer exists."

By the end of this historic season, a total of five black players had appeared in major league games, but no rush to sign black talent materialized. The color line in baseball did not come crashing down but only slowly disintegrated over the next decade. The attitude of the most successful and powerful franchise in professional baseball, the New York Yankees, carried considerable symbolic importance. President Larry MacPhail's lack of enthusiasm for black players was well known, and it came as no great surprise that the Yankees delayed putting a black into one of their famed pin-striped uniforms for as long as possible. Only after several years of simmering controversy, during which time the Yankees signed several blacks to minor league contracts but then either traded them away or simply refused to promote them to the parent team, did they finally call up the enormously talented Elston Howard in 1955. It was not until 1959 that the last of the major league teams fielded a black player when the Boston Red Sox—its front office long recognized for harboring no enthusiasm whatsoever for black players—finally capitulated with the signing of Pumpsie Green to become the team's second baseman. By this time 15 percent of four hundred major league players were nonwhite.

During the 1950s segregation in professional sports essentially ended. Despite a less-than-elegant record, American sports nonetheless stood well out in front of the U.S. government on racial matters. The example set by Jackie Robinson, Marion Motley, and other pioneers undoubtedly helped provide a changing climate of opinion in which the Supreme Court in May of 1954 reversed the "separate but equal" doctrine with its sweeping ruling ordering the end to segregation in the nation's public schools. Not until another decade passed, however, did Congress act to correct a century of racial discrimination with the Civil Rights Acts of 1964 and 1965; these important laws ended discrimination in public accommodations and voting and greatly strengthened the enforcement powers of the Department of Justice. By then Jackie Robinson had been retired from baseball for seven years and was enshrined in the Hall of Fame.

In 1949 Althea Gibson, a native of Harlem, made her debut on the professional tennis circuit; improving her game with each season, she won both the Wimbledon and U.S. Open tournaments in 1957. Her shyness and reluctance to speak to reporters, coupled with her fierce competitiveness, made her a favorite media target. Not until 1963 did the first black male tennis player, Arthur Ashe of Richmond, Virginia, appear on the men's circuit. Tennis facilities and youth programs simply did not exist in the black neighborhoods of America. Similarly, economics and social discrimination effectively excluded minorities from the opportunities presented by the rapidly growing sport of golf. Professional golf proved highly resistant to nonwhites, although by the late 1960s Hispanic Lee Trevino and blacks Charlie Sifford and Lee Elder regularly played in sanctioned Professional Golf Association (PGA) tournaments. As late as 1990, however, only a handful of blacks had been able to make the tour. In that year, the golfing world suffered an enormous public relations setback when it became known that the country club in Birmingham, Alabama, where the prestigious PGA tournament was scheduled to be played still excluded blacks from membership. Only a last-ditch effort by association leaders, spurred by threats from corporate sponsors to withdraw their television commercials, forced the local club hurriedly to approve a solitary black membership in order to prevent cancellation of the tournament.

The immense popularity of the Harlem Globetrotters during the immediate postwar years complicated somewhat the integration of professional basketball. Founded in 1927 by a white Chicago businessman, Abe Saperstein, the Globetrotters had over the years developed a strong national following for their caricature of the game they presented throughout the United States and in many foreign countries on their perpetual barnstorming tour. The dazzling display of dribbling by Marques Haynes and the comedy routines of Goose Tatum—often using a mystified white referee or a clumsy white player as the straight man—entertained millions of Americans, but in the process evoked demeaning racist themes. From their famous pregame sleight-of-hand ball handling routine choreographed to the sounds of "Sweet Georgia Brown," through the ball hidden under a uniform shirt and the attempted kick of a "field goal," the Globetrotters reinforced stereotypes of black athletes as physically talented but undisciplined and devious— fun to watch, perhaps, but not capable of helping serious teams in competitive leagues win championships. In town after town, night after night, in gymnasiums filled to the rafters with appreciative, and predominantly white spectators, the Globetrotters ran their hapless all-white opponents (usually the so-called Washington Generals) ragged. Even though they made a mockery of the rules and invariably won their well-scripted "games," these talented Sambos in garish red, white, and blue striped uniforms did nothing to advance the cause of racial equality. One black player lamented, "The Trotters act like white people think they should act." But for many years they afforded talented black basketball players their only meaningful professional opportunity. They also made Saperstein a wealthy man, because fans turned out wherever these black vaudevillians took their act.

Although the first black to break into professional basketball did so with the Rochester Royals of the National Basketball League in 1946, it was not until four years later, amid a swirl of controversy, that the New York Knicks lured Nat "Sweetwater" Clifton away from the Harlem Globetrotters. In that same year the Washington Capitols signed

Earl Lloyd of West Virginia State, and Charles Cooper of Duquesne University joined the Boston Celtics. With these three players setting the example, other clubs soon followed suit. For many years, however, NBA teams maintained an unwritten quota system that decreed their rosters would not include more than four black players, and no more than two would be starters.

Ever since its inception in the 1920s, professional basketball had plodded through its lengthy seasons in relative obscurity. Confined to a few cities in the Northeast and upper Midwest, the professional teams attracted relatively little national attention. Each year entailed a struggle for survival. The days of enormous crowds, huge modern arenas, and high player salaries lay in the distant future. Even professional basketball's biggest star during the mid-1950s, the ball-handling whiz of the Celtics, Bob Cousy, received an annual salary of less than $20,000; Cousy and his teammates frequently played before small crowds in dingy civic auditoriums and high school gymnasiums. This situation began to change in 1956 when the Celtics added the 6-foot, 10-inch rebounding and defensive standout Bill Russell to its roster. The following year the Philadelphia Warriors signed the enormously talented 7-foot, 1-inch Wilt Chamberlain. The titanic battles between these two premier centers brought national attention to the NBA, setting off a rapid ascent in fan acceptance. The influx of black talent into the NBA began to accelerate. Soon such leading play-making guards as Oscar Robertson and Lenny Wilkins asserted themselves, bringing an abrupt end to the belief that blacks lacked the intelligence and discipline to provide team leadership. These changes did not come without many embarrassing incidents. To give one example, in 1960, one of the league's outstanding new black players, Elgin Baylor of the Minneapolis Lakers, attracted national attention to the issue of segregation of public accommodations when he refused to play in a regular conference game scheduled in Charleston, West Virginia. He sat stoically on the team bench in street clothes to protest the refusal of a local hotel to permit him to register with his teammates.

The new black players quickly moved the NBA to a superior level of play. Basketball fans came to accept that basketball was truly a game in which black athletes excelled. Basketball had already become the most popular street game in the inner cities, and the devotion of black youth to the game year round revealed itself in the talent they sent on to the college and professional levels. The once carefully observed informal guidelines of the 1950s restricting each professional team to a maximum of four black players disappeared during the 1960s; by 1970 blacks made up more than 50 percent of active players in the NBA, and by 1990 that figure had jumped to 80 percent. Despite management's fear that white fans would not attend games in which a preponderance of the players were black, the popularity of the NBA continued to grow as the number of black players increased. Fans— predominantly affluent professional whites—were apparently not overly concerned that blacks dominated the game. The ratio of white to black players became a point of ironic comment during the mid-1980s when the Boston Celtics featured a black coach (K. C. Jones) with three and sometimes four white starters. Television coverage helped produce a national market that enabled professional basketball to build an enormous following; during the 1980s such players as Michael Jordan of the Chicago Bulls and Earvin "Magic" Johnson of the Los Angeles Lakers became two of the best known and most popular men in the United States. With lucrative product endorsement contracts coupled with their multimillion-dollar basketball salaries, they were also two of the highest paid as well.

College Athletics and Integration

Segregation remained in effect somewhat longer at the college level. During the early 1960s the drama of the civil rights movement often focused on leading southern colleges and universities. Not surprisingly, the teams of southern universities and colleges remained all white, even long after blacks had been admitted to their student bodies. Coaches, typically conservative in their political and social views, were not the type of individuals to initiate racial reform. They were not about to challenge the status quo for fear of alienating university administrators, influential boosters, or state legislators. A black wide receiver at a southern California junior college during the late 1960s later recalled observing a white on his team being recruited to the University of Alabama by the famous coach Bear Bryant. At one point Bryant casually told the black he was the better of the two players and he would like to have him on his team but that Alabama simply was not ready for a black player.

As a result of this powerful racist environment that intimidated even the likes of a Bear Bryant, southern Negro colleges had routinely attracted the best southern black athletes. Although the teams of such institutions as Grambling, Jackson State, Prairie View A&M, and South Carolina State were overlooked by the average fan, professional scouts were quick to recommend the drafting of many of their top athletes. During the late 1950s enterprising coaches at major northern universities began to harvest many blue-chip athletes out of Deep South high schools. In 1960 the University of Minnesota won the Big Ten championship and went to the Rose Bowl, led by a consensus all-American quarterback, Sandy Stephens. A high school standout from South Carolina, Stephens was the first black at the major college level to play this leadership position. Stephens's success sparked a wholesale invasion of the South by recruiters from northern universities.

By the mid-1960s Negro college coaches recognized that this new development had begun to cut into the talent level of their teams; even more worrisome, they recognized that major southern universities had begun to join in the scramble for superior black athletes. Once a few southern coaches defied the long extant "gentlemen's agreement" not to recruit blacks, resistance crumbled and blacks appeared in increasing frequency on the once lily-white teams of major universities throughout the South.

Two important events symbolized this important change. For years the track and field team at Texas Southern University—a small black institution in Houston—had dominated their opponents, with their athletes regularly placing among the nation's best in their specialties. In 1962 Texas Southern accepted a precedent-shattering invitation to participate in the prestigious Texas Relays at Austin. Much to the surprise of casual fans, but not to serious track enthusiasts, Southern's teams not only swept to victory in every relay event, but did so by establishing a new Texas Relays record for each relay event. Their time of 3:09 for the mile relay also set a new NCAA record. Of particular significance to reporters covering the event was the enthusiasm with which the all-white audience cheered Texas Southern's runners; whatever racial views the spectators might have held, they obviously appreciated the athletic ability they witnessed. On that April Saturday, the world of college track and field turned upside down. A writer for *Sports Illustrated* concluded that Texas Southern had "the best all-round relay track team in the nation" and suggested that track coaches everywhere could no longer ignore the black talent that such obscure institutions as Texas Southern had assembled. But this moment of glory also carried a potentially heavy cost: "Integration will probably ruin Texas Southern's edge in the near future," he correctly predicted.

The second event received much more attention. In March 1966 the University of Kentucky played Texas Western College (its name soon to be changed to the University of Texas at El Paso, or UTEP) for what its followers fully expected to be its fifth NCAA basketball championship. For more than thirty years Coach Adolph Rupp and his UK Wildcats had dominated Southeastern Conference (SEC) basketball. Over the years his teams had routinely walked away with the conference championship, on three occasions between 1948 and 1958 winning the NCAA title. That the imperious "Baron" had cut many a corner in running his program was widely recognized, but that mattered little to the adoring fans in Kentucky. Well connected to the political and economic leadership of the state, Rupp enjoyed the status of a genuine folk hero. Representing a state that struggled under a backward hillbilly image, Rupp's basketball teams were an important source of statewide pride. On game night the voice of announcer Cawood Ledford filled the homes and taverns across the bluegrass state as fans eagerly followed the progress of their favorite team. Adolph Rupp's nickname of "Baron" fit him perfectly because he ran his program in an autocratic fashion, caring little what the university faculty, or even its president, thought about his program. Despite the point-shaving scandals that had brought shame to his program in 1951, and subsequent revelations of major recruiting scandals that had compelled the university athletic board to cancel the entire 1953 season, Rupp's position and power had never been threatened.

The Baron had long enjoyed a reputation as a stern taskmaster whose teams played an aggressive man-to-man defense and a controlled, patterned offense that left little to chance. Even though UK had admitted its first black student in 1949, Rupp had adamantly maintained an all-white team. His racial views manifested themselves in a pattern of paternalism not unlike that exhibited by many white southerners of his time. Rupp remained convinced that although black athletes might have impressive physical skills, they lacked the personal discipline and intelligence to play the demanding style of basketball he taught. As long as the SEC maintained its unwritten but ironclad all-white policy, he knew his coaching and recruiting skills would enable him to continue to dominate his opponents.

Prodded by the unfolding national drama of the civil rights movement during the early 1960s, however, the question of race pressed in on the SEC. Between 1959 and 1963, Mississippi State University and Auburn University managed to edge out UK for the league championship.

Each year, despite pleas from students and players, fearful administrations had refused to permit their teams to play in the NCAA postseason tournament because they might have to compete against black players, but by the mid-1960s several SEC teams now played regular season games against blacks when they ventured outside the conference. By 1964 only the two Mississippi schools maintained a policy against playing teams with black players; in 1963 the president of Mississippi State had permitted the Bulldogs to play in the NCAA tournament, but in so doing incurred the wrath of segregationists across the state. In 1964 Tulane University, one of two private institutions in the conference but with its intention to leave in 1965 for independent status already announced, broke the SEC color line when it fielded a black outfielder on its baseball team.

During the 1965–66 season Kentucky returned to its normal perch atop the SEC, its all-white team once again demonstrating the classic Rupp version of disciplined basketball. Despite the lack of a dominating center, "Rupp's runts," as their fans affectionately called them, played efficiently and intelligently. They moved with ease through the early rounds of the sixteen-team field to the NCAA finals held on the campus of the University of Maryland. Kentucky coolly dispatched a strong Duke University team by four points in the semifinals, led by forward Pat Riley. In the other semifinal game, however, unheralded Texas Western College upset the University of Utah. Not only did the Miners come from a school without any semblance of a basketball tradition, but their young coach, Don Haskins, had only a few years of coaching experience. But Haskins had learned his basketball from another legendary college coach, Hank Iba of Oklahoma A&M. Like Rupp, Iba emphasized the virtues of ball control, careful shot selection, and tenacious man-to-man defense. Iba's teams had produced two national championships and enviable winning records.

Along the way Don Haskins had learned the essential rule of successful coaching: superior talent is essential to win basketball championships. So when he assumed the head coaching position in 1963, he immediately began scouring the nation for outstanding players. His aggressive talent search produced a team that included several players from as far away as New York City and Detroit to complement talent available within the state of Texas. More to the point, Haskins brought a large number of blacks to El Paso. Unable to compete with the major Texas schools for outstanding white players, Haskins did not hesitate to recruit blacks.

Thus it was a classic contrast when the two teams took to the floor to compete for the national championship. Not only were all five Texas Western starters black, but so too were the two most frequently used substitutes. From the early minutes of the game the upstart team from Texas took control of the game; most significantly, they did so by outplaying Kentucky at its own game of ball control and defense. Utilizing the disciplined offense that Haskins had learned from Hank Iba, and frustrating the Wildcats with a suffocating man-to-man defense, the Miners controlled the tempo of the game from the opening tip-off. They took the lead and never relinquished it, winning decisively, 72–65. In so doing they gave Adolph Rupp a most bitter taste of his own medicine. The disconsolate Kentucky players and coaches were so distraught by their unexpected loss that they left the runner-up trophy in the locker room!

Shortly after this memorable championship game, Vanderbilt University of the SEC announced it had signed a black basketball player; this opened the floodgates, and soon thereafter several other SEC schools began to recruit blacks. Nonetheless, Adolph Rupp stubbornly adhered to his all-white policy for several more years, but shortly before he retired in 1971 he too relented. That same summer Southern Methodist University of the Southwest Conference signed its first black football player, Jerry Levias, thus putting additional pressure on the SEC and the Southwest Conference. The once impenetrable walls of segregation in southern sports had been forever breached.

The Resilience of Racism

The rapid demise of de facto segregation in American sports took place against the dramatic backdrop of the civil rights movement. Under the incessant prodding of President Lyndon Johnson, Congress finally overcame its entrenched and determined segregationist southern leadership to pass the Civil Rights Acts of 1964 and 1965. At the same time, the dramatic confrontations between civil rights demonstrators and segregationists intensified. On August 28, 1963, a massive demonstration of some quarter of a million people in front of the Lincoln Memorial focused the nation's attention on racial discrimination; capturing the moment perfectly, the charismatic Reverend Martin Luther King, Jr., gave the greatest speech of his career, which culminated in his famous exhortation, "Free at last! Free at last! Great God Almighty, free at last!" King's advocacy of nonviolence, however, did not prevent brutal attacks by segregationists on civil rights workers. In the summer of 1964 local law enforcement officers in Mississippi murdered three civil rights workers (two white, one black) who were working on a voter registration drive. Stories of murders, beatings, intimidations, arson, and bombings became almost commonplace. Eventually, the frustrations long endured by America's blacks spilled over into massive rioting in the streets of scores of American cities. On April 4, 1968, an assassin's bullet struck down Dr. King in Memphis, where he had come to support the city's sanitation workers in a bitter labor dispute.

On the surface American sports seemed to be out in front of the civil rights movement. By the late 1960s, unlike in other major social institutions, segregation in the sports world seemingly had become a thing of the past. At least most whites took such a view. But such a rosy outlook proved shortsighted. On the contrary, just as overt discrimination against black athletes died out, racism reasserted itself within the sports world in new but equally damaging forms. In 1967 Muhammad Ali, the extraordinarily talented heavyweight champion, had his title stripped away by state boxing commissions when he refused to enter the armed forces because of his opposition to the war in Vietnam. That Ali had also become a leading spokesman for the much feared Black Muslim faith contributed significantly to the eagerness of the commissions' actions.

Ali's harsh penalty met with broad public approval. To his many critics, Ali came across as an unpatriotic and ungrateful egocentric individual who did not appreciate his good fortune. In the parlance of the day, he was not a "credit to his race." Ali, however, seemed to be the anomaly. To the casual white fan, witnessing the growing number of black athletes, it seemed natural to conclude that sports had given these individuals a special opportunity in the form of a free ride to a college education. And for the few especially talented, it meant the golden opportunity to earn large incomes as a professional. "Sports," the popular cliché went, "has been good for Negroes."

But black athletes at all levels knew differently. They learned early on that the racial biases and practices long established in American society remained in place as blacks entered the college and professional sports ranks. Black collegiate athletes soon recognized that their coaches and other university officials considered them little more than interchangeable human commodities open to exploitation. Once their eligibility expired, they found themselves quickly discarded and forgotten by the same coaches who had promised them the moon during their recruitment. Those few who made it to the professional ranks discovered that comparable white athletes made higher salaries. College and professional athletes also discovered that many of their white coaches harbored deep-seated racial prejudices that often led to cruel and insensitive treatment. With amazing ease, white coaches and college administrators adjusted to the arrival of blacks by recognizing their athletic achievements while simultaneously isolating them from the broader experiences of university life. On predominantly white campuses, blacks quickly learned they were hired hands, expected by their coaches to help win games, but not expected to move in the mainstream of campus life. Once the black had performed during the game, he was expected to know his proper, deferential place. Harry Edwards, a track athlete at San Jose State College who later became a sociologist and black activist, angrily charged that the black athlete was "expected by the honkie to play the role of the responsible Negro, the good Negro, no matter what else was going on in the black world." Within the new era of integrated sports competition, Edwards contended, whites expected the black athlete to remain "the institutionalized Tom, the white man's nigger."

At all levels of competition black athletes discovered the insidious new racist tools of racial quotas and position "stacking," and the widely believed myth that blacks lacked the discipline and mental capacity to provide team leadership. Coaches often assumed blacks could not compete in the classroom and routinely advised them into marginal courses that would enable them to maintain their athletic eligibility but not necessarily lead toward a degree. Many black athletes arrived on campus without adequate academic preparation, the result of the urban ghetto or rural southern backgrounds from which they came. Many lacked basic language, reading, and mathematical skills. An academic counselor at a major midwestern university who took a special interest in the problems of black athletes on his campus gloomily observed in 1968 that many had the ability to overcome their initial handicaps, but had themselves come to believe the popular myth that they lacked the requisite brainpower: "The saddest cases of all are the ones who could pass their courses but just can't believe it. They are so bowled over by the white kids and the big words and the academic atmosphere that they give up." Thus the result was that only a very few black collegiate athletes graduated. Like Marion Motley at the prewar University of Nevada, they learned they had been brought to the campus to win games, not get a college education. When pressed to reveal graduation rates of black athletes, universities revealed an extreme reluctance to do so; when forced to reveal these depressing and embarrassing statistics, they frequently sought to put the best possible light on them by manipulating the criteria and standards used. Even then, the announced graduation rates of black athletes during these early years of racial/sports integration at most major athletic institutions seldom exceeded 15 percent.

The successful basketball coach at Kansas State University during the 1960s, Tex Winter, candidly admitted his profession deceived and manipulated these young men. "We're getting ourselves into a situation where outstanding Negroes with talent are being exploited," he said. "We go out and look for the exceptional Negro basketball player, and without regard to his background, education, intelligence, morals and character we bring him into a white college environment with one purpose in mind—to get what we can out of him as a basketball player."

Alienated by the academic life on campus, black athletes also learned they were not expected to participate in the social life of their institution. Fraternities and other social organizations were strictly off-limits. They also lamented the limited number of black women students on campus, and if they sought to date white women they were immediately subjected to not-so-subtle "guidance" against such behavior by their coaches. If they persisted in breaking this taboo, they found themselves subject to various forms of team discipline, even the cancellation of their athletic scholarship. The case of the outstanding running back Junior Coffey of the University of Washington is instructive. When in 1964 he refused to stop dating a white student, the coaching staff unceremoniously demoted him to the second team. At the time of his removal from the starting lineup he was the third leading ball carrier in the nation! And he never again started a game for the Huskies.

Many black athletes complained that they found the college campus a hostile environment. Harry Edwards confirmed that the lack of a normal social life intensified the sense of alienation from the college environment. "For four years black athletes live on the playing field. . . . After the season is over they go back to the dormitory. They live for the vacations, to get back to L.A. or Chicago or Philadelphia. When they're not thinking about vacations they're thinking about sports. This is the only part of campus life in which they take part."

Even on the playing field or court, the black college athlete encountered intriguing forms of racism. Football coaches routinely stacked their squads, assigning black players to certain positions while reserving other positions for whites. The most glaring example of stacking was the position of quarterback, a position that demands not only exceptional athletic skills but also mental acuity in calling plays—especially in changing the call at the line of scrimmage to take advantage of defensive alignments. Equally important for quarterbacks is the intangible quality of providing team leadership. Not surprisingly, then, few blacks received an opportunity to compete for quarterback positions. Sandy Stephens of Minnesota's Rose Bowl team was an early exception to this almost universally accepted rule. Coaches even reassigned outstanding black high school quarterbacks to positions stacked for blacks—wide receiver and defensive back. Anticipating a similar mind-set in the professional ranks, as a freshman at Stanford University in 1977 Gene Washington asked his coaches to move him from quarterback to wide receiver, a position he knew he would be permitted to play in the professional ranks (as he did at an all-pro level with the San Francisco 49ers). Although James Harris of the Los Angeles Rams became the first starting black quarterback in the NFL in 1978, more than a decade later only Warren Moon of the Houston Oilers, Doug Williams of the Washington Redskins, and Randall Cunningham of the Philadelphia Eagles had established themselves as premier NFL quarterbacks—who just happened to be black.

Quarterback was not the only position reserved for whites by college and professional coaches. They seldom assigned blacks to the offensive line positions of center and guard, which require players to read defenses and to respond in a variety of prescribed maneuvers; likewise, on defense blacks seldom played linebacker because of the cerebral aspects of identifying offensive plays. Conversely, large numbers of blacks found themselves stacked in such positions as running back, defensive back, and defensive lineman.

During the early days of the integration of teams, the practice of position stacking protected white coaches from criticism for playing too many blacks at any one time. On the basketball floor this translated into the standard practice of seldom permitting a black to play point guard, which is roughly equivalent to the quarterback in football. It also stipulated the informal rule that coaches not play more than three blacks at any one time. The first major power to defy that custom was Loyola University of Chicago, which regularly started four and sometimes five blacks enroute to the 1964 NCAA championship. However, it was the dramatic confrontation between Kentucky's all-white team and Texas Western that attracted the most attention. When Kansas University coach Dick Harp occasionally played four or five blacks simultaneously, he received pointed criticism from white Jayhawk fans. Rather than submit to this criticism, he resigned as coach in 1963. When teams traveled, coaches routinely made roommate assignments based on race. When the eminently successful football coach at USC, John McKay, sought to break down racial divisions within his team by assigning blacks and whites to room together, it was considered a radical departure from accepted procedure.

By the 1980s even such once defiant all-white athletic programs at such institutions as the University of Mississippi, the University of Texas, and the University of Arkansas recruited blacks. Their basketball teams had become predominately black, and their football squads approached 50 percent minority students. Position stacking had been relegated to the pages of history books. Even the appearance of a black quarterback no longer attracted comment. In 1988 a survey revealed that fifteen of the thirty-four starting quarterbacks in the bowl games were black. On New Year's Day in 1990 when the University of Notre Dame and Colorado University met in the Orange Bowl to play for the mythical national championship, both teams were led by black quarterbacks, Tony Rice and Darian Hagen.

Stacking also existed in the antediluvian social order of professional baseball, although enough early cracks developed so the concept had broken down by the 1970s. Although exceptions existed, it was apparent that not only blacks but the sizable number of Hispanic players (mostly from the Caribbean and Latin America) were subject to the practice. Management routinely assigned the preponderance of minorities to first base or the outfield, positions that required the least leadership and decision-making qualities. Seldom did a nonwhite become a team's regular shortstop—such star players as Ernie Banks, Luis Aparicio, and Maury Wills won their positions because of their truly exceptional skills—and only slowly did blacks establish themselves as second and third basemen. The crucial positions of catcher and pitcher seemed especially off-limits to blacks; pitchers Don Newcombe and Joe Black and catchers Roy Campanella and Elston Howard were major exceptions to the position stacking that characterized professional baseball. Between 1969 and 1973, for example, whites pitched 87 percent of all major league innings. Clearly, such racial practices benefited fringe white players. For a black or Hispanic player to make the team, he almost certainly had to beat out competing white players for a starting position. The composition of team rosters clearly indicated that few blacks or Hispanics ever made a team as utility players; these substitute positions routinely went to whites. Not until the 1970s did the practice begin to decline.

Baseball statisticians were quick to point out that from the pivotal season of 1947 until the present, minority pitchers had significantly better earned-run averages and won-lost records, and that nonwhite batters also posted significantly higher batting averages than their white counterparts. Minorities were clearly superior at the art of stealing bases. These telling statistics do not lead to the conclusion that blacks were necessarily better players; rather, they point conclusively to the policy that reserved most substitute positions for whites. Since minorities had to be clearly better than white competitors to make the team, the preponderance of white marginal players tended to drag down the cumulative performance statistics of their fellow white players. That racial stacking had staying power in organized baseball was made clear when *Sports Illustrated* reported in 1988 that 78 percent of all minority major leaguers were either first basemen or outfielders. Further, few teams had more than one black coach, thereby making the elevation of many blacks to managerial positions unlikely.

At the top, however, the success of minorities in baseball was indisputable. Between 1949 when Jackie Robinson won the most valuable player award and 1990, of the eighty-two such awards made by the nation's sportswriters in the two major leagues, thirty-six went to nonwhites. Similarly, minorities walked away with league batting titles at a rate of 52 percent. Not since Jackie Jensen of the Boston Red Sox led the American League in stolen bases in 1954 has a white player done so. Blacks also have dominated the much publicized leadership in home runs. During the forty-year span between 1950 and 1990, black sluggers won their league home run derby precisely 50 percent of the time.

Black Coaches and Managers

Black coaches faced perhaps even greater obstacles than athletes. Even in the early 1990s the number of black head coaches at all levels remained minuscule. Apologists contended qualified blacks were not available, but clearly they were victims of the same racial stereotyping that had for so long applied to black athletes. Those largely responsible for hiring assistant coaches—white athletic directors and head coaches—often shared the belief that blacks lacked the organizational and intellectual skills necessary for success in coaching. When blacks were appointed to college staffs as assistant coaches, they almost invariably were assigned two major responsibilities—recruiting more black talent to the campus, and serving as special counselors for black athletes once they enrolled.

In many instances the first appointments of black assistant coaches came only after heavy pressure had been placed on the university administrators by civil rights groups and black athletes. Despite many such protests and continued criticism from the media, the number of black assistant coaches at the college and professional levels increased at a perceptively slow rate. This action led inevitably to a classic catch-22 situation. When it came time for athletic directors or professional team owners to appoint new head coaches, they looked to the ranks of leading assistant coaching for candidates. Or they decided to "go with experience" by hiring a coach who had head coaching experience at another institution. Whichever, the result was that very few blacks became head coaches. Most college athletic directors had been head coaches themselves—often before racial barriers had fallen—and they brought the prejudices of their coaching experiences with them to their administrative positions. As a group they seemed unwilling to take a chance on an untested minority applicant. Thus it was not until the 1980s that the first blacks were appointed to Division 1-A head coaching positions in football, and these were at institutions whose programs were not expected to compete for national recognition: Northwestern, Tulsa, Ohio University, and the University of Nevada Las Vegas. As late as 1990 the number of black head coaches at the 160 Division A and Division 1-AA schools remained less than ten. The appointment of Dennis Green as head coach at Stanford University in 1989 remained the single exception to standard hiring practices by major football programs. (He had earlier served as head coach at perennial Big Ten cellar occupant Northwestern.) As late as 1991 such premier football conferences as the Southwest, Southeastern, Western, Big Eight, and Atlantic Coast Conference had yet to appoint a black head football coach.

The acceptance level of black coaches in college basketball—a sport that had come to be dominated by black players—was somewhat better, with such pioneers as George Raveling (Washington State, Iowa, and USC), John Thompson (Georgetown), Clem Haskins (Western Kentucky, Minnesota), John Chaney (Temple), Charles Coles (Central Michigan), and Randy Ayers (Ohio State) demonstrating conclusively that blacks could succeed at the highest levels of the college sport.

Thompson, in fact, moved to the top of his profession. A graduate of Providence College who had played for a time with the Boston Celtics, Thompson guided his Georgetown University team to the NCAA championship in 1984, and he received the very high honor of being selected to coach the 1988 U.S. Olympic basketball team. Perhaps most significant were decisions in the mid-1980s by two southern universities with strong athletic traditions—Tennessee and Arkansas—to appoint blacks to lead their high-profile basketball programs. In his fifth year at Arkansas, Nolan Richardson led his team to the semifinal game of the 1990 NCAA tournament, and the Razorbacks enjoyed the prestige of being routinely ranked among the nation's top teams. These notable success stories greatly reduced opposition to hiring black basketball coaches. In 1992, when that once most defiant bastion of segregation, the University of Mississippi, appointed a black head basketball coach, the announcement created virtually no national attention.

A similar pattern existed in professional basketball. In 1966 Bill Russell became the first black professional basketball coach when he assumed the role of player-coach of the Boston Celtics. This premier NBA star led his team to championships in two of his first three years as a coach. Russell later served as the head coach for the Seattle Super Sonics (1973–1977) and briefly as vice president of the Sacramento Kings. Russell's immediate success with the Celtics, coupled with the increasingly large number of blacks on NBA teams, led to the appointment of several other black coaches. Among the most noteworthy for their success were Al Attles of Golden State, K. C. Jones of Boston, and Lenny Wilkins of the Cleveland Cavaliers. Many others came and went, as is the norm in this high-pressure environment. Nonetheless, at no time did the number of black coaches even approach 25 percent although the number of black players had reached the 80 percent level.

The record of professional baseball and football in selecting black leadership paled in comparison to the record of the NBA. It was nearly thirty years after Jackie Robinson's debut in 1947 before the Cleveland Indians finally defied tradition and appointed baseball's first black manager, Frank Robinson. A highly competitive Hall of Fame player for the Cincinnati Reds and Baltimore Orioles, Robinson endured three frustrating seasons with this weak franchise before moving on to managerial stints with the San Francisco Giants and the Orioles. Recognized as a demanding manager and able strategist, Robinson was respected for the aggressive play of his teams. But only a handful of other blacks were given the opportunity to manage. Burdened by teams with notoriously inferior talent, both Larry Doby with the Chicago White Sox and Maury Wills with the Seattle Mariners lasted only short periods of time before being fired. In 1993 only four of twenty-eight major league teams had black managers. Interestingly, all of the major league black managers had enjoyed outstanding careers as players; the major leagues have yet to see a black manager in the tradition of Walter Alston and Tommy Lasorda of the Dodgers or Sparky Anderson of the Cincinnati Reds and Detroit Tigers—talented managers who rose to the top of their profession solely on their managerial skills without the benefit of a previous career as an outstanding major league player.

A similar pattern of systematic discrimination against black coaches existed in the NFL. In the midst of a losing season in 1989 the maverick owner of the Los Angeles Raiders, Al Davis, fired his youthful head coach, Mike Shanahan, and replaced him with Art Shell, who had earned all-pro honors while playing on the offensive line for the Raiders during the 1970s. Like several other blacks who sought careers in coaching, Shell had become an assistant coach with the Raiders, but unlike several other highly recognized black assistant coaches, he got his opportunity. The NFL's first black head coach quickly reversed his team's fortunes, leading the Raiders to a divisional championship in his first full season at the helm, an achievement that prompted the Associated Press to name him coach of the year. In 1992 the Minnesota Vikings lured Dennis Green away from Stanford University, bringing the NFL's cumulative total of black coaches to the resounding total of two.

The Saga of
Henry Aaron

Although blacks suffered from persistent discrimination in their quest to compete as coaches and managers, from the pioneering days of Marion Motley and Jackie Robinson there was no question about their ability to compete on the playing fields and courts. Once the opportunity came, black athletes immediately became recognized as stars. Examples of these achievements are endless. By the 1970s the majority of the college all-American football teams were made up of blacks, and it became almost a rarity when a white basketball player was able to break into the top ten college players drafted each year by the NBA. Between 1980 and 1990, no college team that made the final four of the NCAA national tournament had a majority of whites on its starting five. Most of these teams started four or five blacks. Experience often demonstrated, however, that even superstar performances could not remove the sting of racism

Such was the case of Henry Aaron. A native of Mobile, Alabama, he signed a professional contract as an eighteen-year-old batting prospect in 1952. Aaron immediately demonstrated impressive skills and was promoted to the Milwaukee Braves after just two years in the minor leagues. In his first year in the major leagues Aaron hit 13 home runs, and his pursuit of Babe Ruth's seemingly unreachable record of 714 home runs was on. In 1957 he played a major role in the Braves' World Series championship, hitting 44 home runs en route to winning the league's most valuable player award. Year after year "Hammerin' Hank" continued his prodigious power hitting, leading the league four times in batting average. When the club ownership moved to Atlanta in 1966 he continued his impressive batting performance.

Much to his dismay, however, Hank Aaron quickly learned that despite Atlanta's claims to be a progressive southern city, many fans did not appreciate his achievements. Unlike the popular Willie Mays of the San Francisco Giants, who refused to speak out on racial issues, Aaron had never been reluctant to condemn racial prejudice and discrimination. He also found that, like black stars everywhere, local or national advertisers seldom came to him for lucrative endorsements, preferring instead to use white players of lesser talent. In fact, he discovered that many fans even resented his high salary: "The Atlanta fans weren't shy about letting me know what they thought of a $200,000 nigger striking out with men on base," he recalled in his illuminating, if not embittered, autobiography. Even worse, his fan mail routinely contained a large number of hate letters. As he closed in on Babe Ruth's record in 1973, the amount and hostility of the racial comments increased. In that year the U.S. Post Office reported that Aaron received more mail than any other American except President Nixon—some 930,000 pieces. Substantial numbers of these letters indicated that many baseball fans across the country were not pleased the immortal Babe's record was soon to be eclipsed, as many correspondents indicated: "Dear Hank Aaron, How about some sickle cell anemia, Hank?" or, "Dear Nigger, You black animal, I hope you never live long enough to hit more home runs than the great Babe Ruth." In 1974 when he finally surpassed Ruth's record, Aaron knew that millions of Americans deeply resented his achievement. The commissioner of baseball was noticeably absent that historic April day; even a congratulatory telephone call from President Richard Nixon was inexplicably cut off in mid-conversation.

Thus this proud man discovered that even at the moment of his supreme accomplishment, his feelings were distinctly mixed. "It should have been the most enjoyable time in my life," he recalled, "and instead it was hell." But his relentless quest of Ruth's record was his way of responding to his racist critics: "I had to break that record. I had to do it for Jackie [Robinson] and my people and myself and for everybody who ever called me a nigger."

Can White Men Jump?

The increasing black presence on the playing fields and courts of America produced many responses, as indicated throughout this chapter. One persistent myth often cited was that blacks enjoyed special physical advantages that enabled them to leap higher and run faster than whites. Many self-appointed "experts" suggested that black athletes benefited from selective breeding practices during slavery and from a "survival of the fittest" process during the slave trade—only the strong could have survived the horrors of the "middle passage" on the slave vessels. Basketball fans routinely talked about "white man's disease," which prevented white players from jumping as high or running as swiftly as blacks. A popular 1991 movie, *White Men Can't Jump*, developed that theme in a more or less humorous fashion. In 1971 the nation's most respected sports magazine, *Sports Illustrated*, brought this issue to the forefront when it published a major article by Martin Kane which argued that blacks had major advantages over whites because of different bone structure and musculature. This highly respected sportswriter even drew on the long-standing stereotype from the slave days about the "happy-go-lucky" Sambo to suggest that blacks had a greater ability to relax under intense competitive situations than whites did.

A fire storm of protest ensued following the publication of Kane's provocative article, producing a great deal of heat and occasionally some light. The most perceptive of those who entered this field was a young sociology professor from the University of California, who had already established himself as a leading sports sociologist as well as a black activist leader. In an important article in *The Black Scholar* and in his 1973 textbook, *Sociology of Sport*, Harry Edwards correctly dismissed Kane's article as essentially racist, noting the evidence presented in the article simply did not stand up to rigorous scrutiny. Blacks, Edwards noted, come in all sizes and shapes, and to generalize about musculature or bone structures as absolutes is absurd. Instead, he argued that the real force leading to impressive levels of black achievement in a few select sports—football, baseball, basketball, track and field—actually results from the pervasive nature of American racism. These sports are the ones in which young blacks have an opportunity to develop skills, primarily on the streets and playgrounds of America's cities, and that are available to students throughout the nation's public school system. These sports require little equipment and little or no expense. Private tennis lessons are beyond the means of almost all black families, but a nearby city park offers basketball hoops. With so few other opportunities available to them and stimulated by television coverage, young blacks with inherent athletic abilities naturally gravitate toward such sports as basketball, putting in incredible numbers of hours playing and practicing on neighborhood playgrounds. However, Edwards noted, economic and racial barriers also mean that blacks only rarely appear in tennis or golf championships at the high school through the professional levels. Social and economic factors mean that while blacks can compete at the highest levels in boxing or football, they are almost never evident in swimming and diving championships or among the leaders of automobile racing or skiing.

Conclusion

The pervasive pattern of racism in postwar American sports accurately reflected the larger American society. Thanks to such leaders as Marion Motley, Jackie Robinson, and Muhammad Ali, the history of blacks in sports includes stories of incredible courage and immense achievement. Yet, as the years rolled by racism has persistently manifested itself in many and often surprising new ways—as Hank Aaron's bittersweet experience so aptly demonstrates. As certain barriers came tumbling down, other more subtle forms of discrimination, such as the selection of head coaches, the stacking of positions, or the allocation of endorsement money by advertisers, invariably took their place. The truth remains inescapable: the American dream of equality for all remains as elusive as ever in the world of American sport. In the 1990s, as in the 1940s, the playing fields of America have not yet become level.

Sportscaster Howard Coswell became one of America's most controversial public personalities as sports television came of age during the 1960s.

Chapter
3

"The Thrill of Victory, the Agony of Defeat"

American sports fans had never before encountered anything like him. He was, beyond
question, the most unlikely person to become
the nation's leading sports broadcaster one could
imagine. But sports journalism would never be the
same after Howard Cosell galvanized the American
sports scene in the 1960s as a television commentator
on ABC's "Wide World of Sports." His aggressive and
irreverent style shocked sports fans long conditioned
to broadcasters who portrayed athletes in heroic terms,
rarely criticizing their performances and never touch-
ing on questionable aspects of their private lives. Unlike any broadcaster before him, Cosell emphasized
the social and political implications of an athletic
event. Not surprisingly, there quickly swirled around
Cosell a maelstrom of controversy unprecedented in
the small and clubby fraternity of sports journalism.

Born in 1918 to immigrant Jewish parents, Cosell
grew up in Brooklyn, graduating from Boys High School.
After serving at the rank of major in the army during
World War II, Cosell—he had changed his legal name
from Howard Cohen—earned a law degree from New

York University. Extremely ambitious and possessed of high intelligence and a great memory, Cosell soon developed a successful legal practice in New York City. Despite his considerable success as an attorney, he chafed under the slow pace at which the wheels of justice turned and yearned for a more dynamic field of endeavor.

He found the perfect outlet for his energy and ambition as a sports reporter for a New York radio station. Always an enthusiastic sports fan who had amazed friends and acquaintances with his incredible ability to recall sports history and trivia, Cosell had provided legal services for such sports figures as Monte Irvin and Willie Mays of the New York Giants. It was his work as an attorney for a newswriters' union, however, that made him familiar with the communications industry and prompted him to explore professional opportunities in the media. Thus in 1954 Cosell abandoned his substantial $30,000 annual income to take an entry-level sports reporting position at just $250 a week. His was indeed an inauspicious beginning—moderating a local radio program that featured Little League players asking questions of major leaguers. Undaunted by a program format that forced him to take a backseat to twelve-year-olds, Cosell soon demonstrated he could create his own opportunities. Within a decade he had become one of the nation's leading sports broadcasters.

In so doing Cosell had to overcome considerable inherent liabilities. For one thing, he had an unpleasant voice, its corrosive qualities further exacerbated by an accent that resonated with the sounds of his native Brooklyn. Cosell's voice grated on many listeners, not unlike the sound of fingernails being scratched across a blackboard. Balding and with sloping shoulders and an awkward presence, he lacked the handsome physical appearance viewers had come to expect from television personalities. Although he kept his feelings to himself, he often suffered the sting of anti-Semitism. Cosell's enormous ego, which seemingly grew exponentially with his expanding fame, naturally invited searing criticism. Unlike most sportscasters, Cosell had never enjoyed a career as a successful athlete, even at the public school level. As he entitled one of his four—yes, four!—autobiographical books: *I Never Played the Game*. His many and voluble critics did not hesitate to complain that only someone who had paid his dues on the field of play could dare criticize the performance of others, a point of view he dismissed as insipid.

Cosell succeeded in part because the time was right for his new style of sports journalism. He introduced what he termed his "tell it like it is" style of sports reporting at the onset of a new era in American journalism. Just as a new breed of investigative reporters exposed Lyndon Johnson's "credibility gap" and relentlessly pursued the Watergate burglary story despite Richard Nixon's efforts to stonewall their investigations, so too did Cosell bring a new toughness and a higher set of professional standards to sports reporting.

At a time when sports reporters served more as boosters and public relations emissaries for local teams than as unbiased reporters, Cosell introduced the tools of a tough investigative reporter. He had occasionally enlivened his Little League show by slipping tough questions to the youngsters to ask of unsuspecting major leaguers. Cosell also shocked his listeners by drawing relationships between sports news and the broader issues of American society, frequently making important connections between sports and such touchy issues as free agency, corruption, gambling, and discrimination against women and minorities. His ability to recall the details of even the most obscure sports event and to relate that information to current issues produced perspectives never before encountered by intrigued listeners. His interrogatory skills developed during his legal career enabled him to generate explosive stories. Many of his uncomfortable interview subjects often found themselves essentially being cross-examined before a live network audience. Blessed with the gift of being able to ad-lib under intense pressure and to present on-the-air commentaries of amazing coherence without the benefit of a written script, Cosell quickly moved to the top of his new profession. As his career soared, Cosell even turned his nasalized Brooklyn accent to advantage, making it a trademark that many comedians sought to imitate.

His voice—so dramatically different from the mellifluous intonations of most radio and television reporters —simply *demanded* the attention of the listener.

By 1956 Cosell had his own ABC radio program, "Sports Focus," and he invaded the Florida baseball spring training camps, lugging an enormous tape recorder on his back, pursuing new angles with the tenacity of a pit bull, asking baseball players penetrating, news-generating questions. His listening audience grew rapidly, but he received only scorn from his sports broadcasting brethren because of his brashness and eagerness to expose the underside of the sports world. His interview subjects quickly grew cautious, or responded angrily to his style. "You're just like shit," New York Yankee manager Ralph Houk once snapped at the feisty Cosell, "you're everywhere." In 1959 Cosell made his debut as a commentator on national television for ABC, but his abrupt style led to his termination the following year. His friends charged he was a victim of anti-Semitic prejudices, but Cosell put a more glorious face on his temporary removal from the national airwaves, suggesting it was a result of "prejudice against truth in the sports world."

Howard Cosell's exile from the living rooms of America lasted only briefly. He had caught the attention of another creative and ambitious New Yorker seeking to make his mark in the rough-and-tumble world of television—Roone Arledge, the youthful new head of ABC sports, then in the early stages of a meteoric career as a television producer and executive. At this juncture ABC television lagged far behind rivals NBC and CBS in its programming and viewer ratings and was desperately seeking ways to close the gap. Much to the surprise of most observers ABC succeeded by having the temerity to elevate sports coverage to a position of central importance in the network's programming. Among Arledge's many innovations was a new program, "Wide World of Sports," which he launched in 1961. Arledge sought to attract weekend viewers by presenting an eclectic assortment of events. Among these was boxing, a sport that had fallen onto hard times during the late 1950s because of plummeting ratings and revelations by federal investigators about the considerable influence exerted over the sport by organized crime. A lifelong boxing fan possessed of a detailed knowledge of the sport, Cosell quickly became "Wide World's" resident boxing expert.

Cosell's new assignment coincided with the emergence of an exciting new heavyweight by the name of Cassius Clay, a lightning-fast boxer from Louisville, Kentucky, who had won a gold medal at the 1960 Olympics. Soon the rising careers of this brash black heavyweight and the equally brash TV announcer became closely intertwined. Unlike most famous black fighters, who had carefully avoided controversy, Clay demonstrated a shrewd sense for attracting immense amounts of publicity. During interviews he often recited short poems he had written, most of which predicted the early demise of his next foe. When Clay had the temerity to predict he would knock out the reigning champion, the fearsome Sonny Liston, boxing's resident experts almost universally dismissed Clay as an immature loudmouth. Scarcely anyone expected him to last more than a round or two against Liston when they met in Miami in February 1964. Cosell, however, was one of a very few reporters who took Clay seriously and produced a series of revealing prefight interviews with the challenger. When Clay stunned the sports world with his embarrassingly easy domination of Liston, Cosell's reputation soared.

But the real action occurred outside the ring. When the new champion announced his conversion to the Black Muslim faith, renouncing his "slave name" of Cassius Clay, Cosell became almost singularly conspicuous among sports journalists for his vigorous defense of the champion's actions. And when the leaders of the boxing world stripped Muhammad Ali of his title in 1967 after he refused to register for the military draft, Cosell again stood virtually alone in defending the defiant ex-champion. It would be Cosell's finest moment as a broadcaster, and he demonstrated immense personal courage in the face of an enor-mous national groundswell condemning Ali for his refusal to serve in the military for religious reasons. The resulting flood of mail to ABC demanded Cosell's removal from the airwaves. Many of these letters denounced him as "a nigger-loving Jew bastard" or worse, but Arledge supported his controversial announcer.

When ABC took a major gamble in 1970 by launching its "Monday Night Football" series, Roone Arledge determined early on that Howard Cosell was ideally suited to help him pull off the dramatic new approach to the televising of professional football that he envisioned. Now one of the longest running programs in the history of television, "Monday Night Football" was anything but a sure thing when it was introduced. Both NBC and CBS had turned down invitations to broadcast football during a prime-time weeknight slot. But unlike his competitors, Arledge viewed his role not as broadcasting football games but as entertaining his audience. He introduced many new technological gimmicks to make the broadcasts more colorful and even included the people in the stands in his coverage. By "casting" Cosell as an analyst whose role was to be the heavy and focus attention on the errors and foibles of coaches and players, Arledge demonstrated his genius. And when he paired Cosell with ex-quarterback Don Meredith, a folksy, down-home Texan given to wry humor and a sardonic irreverence for the sport in which he had starred, Arledge hit on a combination destined to propel his Monday night gamble to the pinnacle of the TV ratings. The action in the broadcasting booth seemed to attract more viewers than that occurring on the field below.

During the initial "Monday Night Football" telecast, Cosell adeptly demonstrated his ability to antagonize many in his audience when he sharply criticized New York Jets' star quarterback Joe Namath for throwing an untimely interception and Cleveland's premier running back Leroy Kelly for failing to have "a compelling night." Unaccustomed to hearing a broadcaster criticize star players, fans assailed Cosell, deluging ABC with calls and letters demanding his removal from the program. *TV Guide* referred to Cosell as "the man America loves to hate," but Arledge was delighted—each week the audience grew, causing ratings and advertising revenue to increase. Everyone wanted to know what Howard or "Dandy Don" would say next. Cosell remained a mainstay of "Monday Night Football" for fourteen years.

A man of immense contradictions who frequently suffered from attacks of insecurity despite his immense talent, Howard Cosell had become one of America's best known personalities. His relationship with the "Monday Night" production crew and his fellow announcers fluctuated wildly over the years. He "resigned" over real or perceived slights so often that no one could recall the number. As the years went by, however, Cosell became increasingly disenchanted with the program, reflected in an intensification of his focus on the negative. His friendship with Pete Rozelle chilled because of his occasional critical commentary on league policies. His relationship with fellow "Monday Night" broadcasters Meredith, Frank Gifford, and O. J. Simpson became strained to the point where they could barely speak to each other. In 1984 Roone Arledge, his own relationship with Cosell now reaching the breaking point, received yet another resignation from Cosell. This time, much to Cosell's surprise, Arledge quickly accepted it. As one chronicler of "Monday Night Football" observed, "Their relationship, once so close, had become so twisted around their Olympian egos that they could no longer communicate at all."

Cosell moved on to other ABC assignments—more boxing, an occasional World Series, many commentaries. But he would always be most closely associated in the public's mind with "Monday Night Football." He had played a central role in introducing an immensely entertaining, and more honest, form of sports broadcasting. His absence was immediately apparent. "It isn't the same without him," a Dallas sports columnist wrote. "Now it's just another football game on Monday night." Even the longtime talented producer of the program, Chet Forte, who had his own major disagreements with the mercurial Cosell, conceded, "When Howard left, it was the end, in a way, the end of Monday Night Football. . . . He could make two eighty-five year olds playing marbles sound like the most exciting thing in the history of sports."

By dint of his personality, his intelligence, and his passion to "tell it like it is," Cosell introduced a new level of seriousness into sports journalism. But old ways die hard, and by the time he retired in 1992 at the age of seventy-three, television sports journalism remained in the clutches of too many intellectually shallow ex-jocks who blabbered away without either coherence or meaning; too many "team-approved" broadcasters remained fearful of saying anything controversial or critical of the home team. That sports journalists scarcely noticed his retirement no doubt confirmed Cosell's own low estimate of the standards of his profession. But Cosell had made an impact on sports journalism; he left a small but dedicated group of professionals, most notably Bob Costas, in his wake who continued to challenge the status quo. By his example, Cosell forced sports broadcasters to pursue important story lines beyond the final score. He made social and political relationships central to sports reporting, forcing fans to place their interest in sports in a much larger and more meaningful context. In so doing, he transformed the way Americans perceived the role of sports in their society. In the process, the controversial Howard Cosell became a unique American icon.

The Early Years of Television

The immense popularity of "Monday Night Football" stunned both the sports world and the television industry. It constituted, truly, a revolution in the worlds of sports and communications. It vividly demonstrated the immense power of the medium. Certainly no one could have conceived of the potential inherent in television when the first sports contest—a baseball game at Columbia University —was televised to a studio audience on May 17, 1939. The reaction of the few hundred persons who watched the fuzzy small screen that day was one of disappointment. Except for a few plays near home plate, they could not even see the ball. A reviewer in the *New York Times*, definitely not impressed, complained that the players seemed like "white flies" on the screen and the viewer could not follow the action. In the few remaining prewar years the pioneer New York City station W2XBS telecast several other sporting events—an Eastern Grass Courts tennis championship, a Fordham University-Waynesburg College football game, a Brooklyn-Cincinnati baseball game, a heavyweight fight between Maxie Baer and Lou Nova, even a professional football game between the Brooklyn Dodgers and the Philadelphia Eagles. Most of the audiences were tiny at best, for there were just four hundred television sets in the New York viewing area. Only the fight proved to be a technical success; the huge Iconoscope camera, which could not capture the action on large surfaces, demonstrated a capacity to produce vivid images from within the 20-foot-square boxing ring. World War II ended these experimental broadcasts, but interest returned with the growth of commercial television broadcasting following V-J Day.

During the postwar years Americans eagerly embraced television as picture quality improved and local stations and networks began airing entertaining programs. By 1955 fully 75 percent of American homes contained a television set, a figure that would grow to over 90 percent by 1970. As a twisted maze of television antennas appeared over American neighborhoods, social commentators soon detected that the new media had an immediate and profound effect on American life. An enormous postwar boom in suburban housing and commercial construction provided the catalyst for a restructuring of American society, producing a dynamic new lifestyle featuring an enormous consumer appetite. Central to the new consumer culture was television. Americans—primarily middle- and upper-class whites—moved away from the urban core in search of a more pleasant, less stressful environment in which to raise their families. Middle-class family life increasingly revolved around the home and the backyard. The once dominant attractions of the central city—the theater, restaurants, music halls, museums, movies, ballparks, and sports arenas—no longer held the powerful allure they once enjoyed. Increasingly concerned about urban crime, fearful of unpleasant encounters with minorities and the poor, and unwilling to make an unnecessary automobile commute into the central city in the evening or the weekend, America's new suburbanites turned to new pursuits. With the arrival of the suburban shopping center and the relocation of many offices and factories to the city's outskirts, millions of Americans found the central cities irrelevant to their lives. Those who had to commute to downtown for work did so primarily on the new urban expressways and immediately left the city after work for their suburban refuge. They enthusiastically embraced the less structured life of suburbia, becoming willing slaves to their yards and gardens, involving themselves in an endless round of do-it-yourself projects in and around their heavily mortgaged split-level houses.

One of the major lures of the suburbs—the "crabgrass frontier," to use historian Kenneth Jackson's terminology—was the perception that they provided the best environment in which to raise children. It is not surprising that the explosive growth of suburbia coincided with a baby boom which increased America's population by 47 million between 1940 and 1960. Parents became absorbed with the process of rearing their children, seeking to provide for them the meaningful experiences they had been denied as children of the Great Depression. They consequently became ensnared in an endless round of PTA functions, Little League practices, gymnastics lessons, and Girl Scout outings. With increased leisure time adults also found themselves involved in a myriad of social and community events—church socials, the Tuesday night bowling league, the Rotary Club's entry in the slow-pitch softball league, and the March of Dimes fund-raising drive. Suburban family life required the presence of both parents. Unlike in the central cities, husbands were much less likely to seek relief from the tensions of home at a nearby neighborhood tavern. Instead they took on new roles, including the much satirized role of expert backyard barbecue chef. The new suburban father was also expected to coach the Pop Warner football team or to lead the annual camping expedition of the Campfire Girls. His wife was busy with an equally demanding schedule, monitoring car pools for the children, serving on innumerable committees, playing in the Friday morning doubles round-robin at the tennis club, organizing the end of the bowling season potluck dinner, keeping the house neat, and preparing the meals for her busy family.

An Economic Bonanza Beckons

Central to this new lifestyle was the ubiquitous television set. It received priority treatment, inevitably placed in a prominent spot in the living room or, as housing design adapted to the casual suburban lifestyle, the den or family room. Families routinely gathered together in a semidarkened room to watch the evening's fare—often eating their evening meal from a TV tray. Traditional forms of relaxation and entertainment no longer commanded the same attraction. Attendance at movie theaters plummeted, as did the use of public libraries. Teachers complained of unfinished homework. Downtown stores and restaurants fell on hard times; the once flourishing neighborhood taverns in the central cities now struggled to keep their clientele. Families everywhere seemed to withdraw into their homes, and even traditional forms of visiting with friends became less common. Because of the relatively high cost of a television set—which in the early years also frequently required costly repairs—families sought to save money by reducing entertainment expenses outside the home. The doings of Jackie Gleason or Lucy and Desi, the comedy of a youthful Jerry Lewis, or the musical fare of Lawrence Welk more than filled the void.

Despite the immediate and overwhelming popularity of television, networks and local stations introduced sports programming at a slow pace. Sports executives, not yet aware of the enormous economic potential to be gleaned from selling television rights, believed that "giving away" their games to stay-at-home television viewers adversely affected ticket sales. Attendance figures confirmed their fears. Paid attendance at major league baseball games plummeted 32 percent between 1948 and 1953, from a record high of 20 million to just over 14 million. With the option of staying home to watch a game for free, casual fans found the trip over congested city streets through deteriorating urban neighborhoods to an aging inner-city ballpark less and less appealing. College football also felt the sting of television at its gates. After wholesale televising of college football games during the late 1940s reduced attendance by nearly 1.5 million, a panicked NCAA in 1951 adopted a drastic plan that severely restricted the availability of televised games. The damage had been done, however; it took nearly a decade before college attendance returned to its 1948 level. A much different attendance pattern existed in the National Football League, whose commissioner, Bert Bell, had anticipated the potential for disaster and had imposed a firm rule blacking out all home game telecasts. The NFL enjoyed a steady increase in paid attendance. When Bell died in 1959, the league sold 90 percent of its seats.

Even more damaging to sports attendance were the many new activities now available that competed with spectator sports. Although many business managers placed the blame for the slump in sports attendance during the 1950s solely on television, the new suburban lifestyle seems to have been the primary cause for the disaffection by fans. Individuals, who earlier would have gone to the ballpark, now flocked to public golf courses, piloted their new boat over a nearby lake, enjoyed a weekend family camping trip in their new mobile home, or resolutely attacked the crabgrass encroaching on their suburban domain. And, perhaps, they might also catch a few innings of a ball game on the black and white tube between other weekend activities.

During these formative years sports executives never anticipated the enormous fees that would begin to flow to their franchises during the 1960s. Baseball's television revenue did increase from $2 million to \$12 million during the 1950s, although a select few teams located in the largest media markets garnered the lion's share of these dollars. This lack of vision regarding the potential of sports television resulted from the primitive nature of telecasts; they simply failed to convey to the viewer the excitement of a live game. Producers used few cameras and lacked the capacity for close-up shots. Producers and broadcasters in the 1950s failed to develop an appealing format that could capture the sports fan's imagination. Not until the 1960s did the technology develop to the point where the camera could transmit the excitement and flow of the action. The introduction of color, instant replay, deployment of multiple cameras, close-up pictures, hand-carried minicams, "rifle" microphones to pick up on-field sounds, and better picture definition eventually opened up new vistas for sports telecasting.

The Power of the Tube

During the 1950s, however, television sports conclusively demonstrated its enormous power to shape consumer tastes. In the process the new medium gave ominous indications of its inherent tendency to demand substantive changes in the character of the sports it covered. That power was vividly demonstrated in the sports that best served the needs of television during its early years. After decades of surviving outside of the law and beyond the limits of accepted social standards, boxing had carved out a unique niche for itself in the American sports world during the early decades of the twentieth century. Promoters such as Tex Rickard had produced exciting championship fights during the 1920s with such personalities as Jack Dempsey and Gene Tunney, bringing to the sport a modicum of respectability. Across the country in cities large and small, promoters worked through local boxing clubs to present regular fight cards for fans, many drawn to the action by their gambling interests. Most young fighters came from the lower rungs of American society—recent immigrants, the poor, minorities—with dreams about the large purses being paid by promoters for championship fights. They willingly entered into long apprenticeships in hundreds of dank storefront gymnasiums.

Unlike baseball or football, the action in boxing is concentrated within a small area, making it possible for a television camera to vividly transmit the violence of the bout to the television viewer. Advertisers appreciated that the action stopped every three minutes, making it possible to insert beer or shaving commercials between rounds.

By the early 1950s boxing had become the most popular sport on television. Most sports fans in the United States had never attended a live fight, and their previous exposure to the sport had been limited to listening to Don Dunphy describe the feature NBC Radio fight from Madison Square Garden on Friday evenings. They now became instant boxing experts. Tavern owners attracted customers by placing a television set above the bar to show the fights, but as the cost of television sets declined many of their once loyal patrons preferred to watch the matches from the comfort of their own living rooms and to swill their beer at a lower cost.

For a time during the 1950s interest in boxing seemed insatiable. Two networks and many local stations increased the number of telecasts to meet the demand; the Gillette Razor Company moved its popular Friday night fights to NBC Television and Pabst Blue Ribbon Beer countered with its Wednesday night cards on CBS. But as happened later with other sports that came under the influence of television, the market soon became saturated and public interest dropped appreciably. Even more troubling, traditional boxing fans began to protest the changes being forced on the sport. They complained that the new generation of television fans simply did not understand or appreciate the many subtle nuances of the art of boxing. In fact, many of the more sophisticated techniques of the sport—slipping punches on the ropes, the use of a slow but calculated strategy designed to expose weaknesses or to wear down an opponent, counter punching, the persistent long-range jab, the clinch from which short but telling body punches (often not discernible to the television viewer) could be thrown— so obvious and important to the savvy fan at ringside, proved to be tedious and unexciting to the television viewer. Instead, the camera best portrayed the wild slugger who threw long-range punches; to the new TV fight fan, the subtle techniques of boxing appreciated by the ringside regular now seemed to be boring, even suggestive of a lack of courage. Style and technique now gave way to a simple, mindless brutality with emphasis on the sensational knockout punch.

Television executives seeking market share and advertisers paying the fare essentially changed the very nature of the sport by demanding that boxers abandon traditional boxing styles. They also perceived that television viewers did not want to see fighters who had lost many bouts, thus creating a constant demand for new fighters who would help generate a high viewer rating. This forced promoters to place inexperienced boxers into highly publicized featured fights for which they were often not prepared. Such was the tragic case of Chuck Davey, a promising welterweight who defeated a series of inferior opponents selected by television-wise promoters. In 1952 the left-handed Davey became an extremely popular fighter because of his flashy style that translated into large TV audiences. He was also a white athlete in a sport dominated by blacks and Hispanics, his blond curly hair and his dancing style making him a video version of the Great White Hope. Announcers further enhanced his mystique by repeatedly emphasizing that he had attended Michigan State University. Thus the new imperatives created by television prematurely thrust the popular Chuck Davey into a championship fight in 1953 with the talented and experienced champion from Cuba, Kid Gavilan. Much to the dismay of a television audience estimated at 40 million, Gavilan systematically savaged Davey, eventually knocking him out in the tenth round after administering the former college student both a serious boxing lesson and a brutal beating.

Chuck Davey retired shortly thereafter. Overnight, he had gone from being one of boxing's brightest attractions to a virtual nobody. Now damaged goods, Davey could no longer generate high television ratings. Longtime boxing insider Chris Dundee aptly summarized this harsh new reality of the television age:

> TV made him and it ruined him. Davey had everything going for him, he was a nice clean college kid. The audience loved him. A real comer. Then they signed him against Kid Gavilan. . . . Gavilan gave him some going over. Davey never came back. One bad fight, see, ruined that poor kid and it was a sin. But that was true of a lot of fighters then. Off TV a guy could lose a fight and people would have a few doubts. But a bad fight on TV would kill a guy because everybody—I mean everybody—could see it.

Like the meteoric career of Chuck Davey, the startling rise of boxing's popularity was surpassed only by its even more sudden demise. As it attracted high viewer audiences to its boxing cards, television in the process virtually destroyed the traditional training grounds for future champions—the several hundred small boxing clubs scattered in cities large and small across the land. These clubs provided newcomers opportunities to develop their talents in apprentice fashion, but they could not compete with television. With major bouts featuring the nation's best fighters being telecast into America's homes and bars at no admission charge, boxing fans abandoned the local clubs. The rapid demise of the local clubs severely reduced the flow of new talent into the sport. No longer could a promising young fighter earn a marginal living in the clubs as he developed his skills.

Television also oversaturated the market. By the late 1950s ratings indicated that the casual fan would watch only a major highly publicized bout; consequently, network executives, ever conscious of audience share, began to look elsewhere for more attractive programming to attract viewers and advertisers. In addition, sensational congressional investigations into the world of organized crime revealed a close relationship between boxing and the underworld. These hearings raised serious questions about the integrity of the sport and produced widespread public disaffection. Thus in 1961 an era began to come to an end when NBC announced a cessation of its Friday night fight program. Although ABC continued its weekly fight card for a time, boxing never regained the popularity it enjoyed for a few short years during the early days of network television. It continued to exist on the fringes of respectability in the world of American sports, finding itself increasingly reliant on the giant hotels of Las Vegas and Atlantic City, which staged much ballyhooed championship bouts to attract high roller bettors to their big-stakes casino tables. But the "fight game" as it had existed was no more. It had been knocked out by television.

TV Spawns the Era of Junk Sports

Boxing's early success inevitably spawned interest in even more dubious sporting events, soon labeled "spin-offs" in the vernacular of the television industry. The practice began shortly after the war in Los Angeles when an imaginative small-time promoter and part-time actor, Dick Lane, staged wrestling matches in a movie studio for station KTLA. These matches were anything but true sporting events, as the grapplers faked injuries, used "illegal" tactics, and engaged in other staged semivaudevillian routines that played well to a gullible local television audience. These spectacles usually featured a contrived contest between good and evil, invariably ending in a wild flourish of action as the heroic underdog bravely overcame the nasty tactics of such notorious characters as The Destroyer. Exploiting racial and ethnic animosities, the matches often featured such villains as a cruel Middle Easterner (The Iron Sheik) or such fiendish Japanese as Dr. Fugi and

Mr. Moto. As long as wartime sentiments remained strong, many wrestlers also posed as vicious Nazis, but as anti-German and anti-Japanese feelings declined so too did the number of Nazi and Asian wrestlers. They were swiftly replaced by America's newest enemy, the Soviet Union. As the Cold War grew ever more frigid, a number of alleged Russian wrestlers appeared, posing under such names as The Mad Russian or Ivan the Terrible. They entered the ring to a resounding chorus of catcalls, wearing bright red costumes, complete with the hammer and sickle insignia on their robes. After they had employed all sorts of dirty tactics on a clean-cut all-American victim, they would be ultimately dispatched in a heroic last-minute comeback by a Jack Armstrong imitation amid the wild cheering of fans. It was a charade, of course, a simplistic good versus evil morality play posing as a legitimate sporting contest. This made-for-television spectacle—confined to an easily viewed ring—proved enormously successful; television viewers seemingly could not get enough of this new form of entertainment.

The sociologist Michael Smith cut to the core of wrestling's appeal when he wrote that it "exemplifies the need for simple-minded answers: black and white, good and evil, based on sexual and ethnic stereotyping, the Arabs, the Nazis, Orientals, gays versus the Captain America types. It reinforces underlying hostilities in a blatant, outrageous way." At the KTLA microphone during the early days of TV wrestling, the clever Dick Lane recognized as much, and through his commentary created a contrived sense of moral drama, devoting many of his comments to creating anticipation for upcoming matches. Soon local announcers across the country began imitating Lane's style. For their part, the actors/wrestlers pandered to the television audience, grimacing in feigned pain, applying their "secret" sleep-inducing headlocks and life-threatening choke holds, occasionally flying through the air with spectacular kicks to the opponent's head, often ending the match with acrobatic "body slams."

It was all show, of course, as evidenced by the spectacular ascent to television stardom of Gorgeous George. For several years George Wagner had sought in vain to establish himself as a legitimate wrestler; failing that, he decided to add a large measure of showmanship to his bona fide wrestling skills. He let his brown hair grow long, dyed it a luxuriant blond and wore it in a coif of long curls. What this former Nebraska farm boy recognized was that many individuals were attracted to wrestling by its sexual connotations. When his new character of Gorgeous George swished into the ring in an exaggerated walk draped in a bedazzling array of satin outfits complete with gold-sequined capes and accompanied by a tuxedoed valet who sprayed the ring with perfume, he evoked a variety of responses about homosexuality. The television announcers, an integral part of the performance, pointedly let the television audience in on speculation that he wore a fur-lined jockstrap. George's meteoric rise to prominence produced a bevy of imitators, but none could capture the public's fascination like Gorgeous George.

Having discovered the financial rewards to be derived from sexual exploitation, the wrestling cards soon also featured heavily muscled women, whose strength and violent performances were designed to play on the erotic sexual fantasies of viewers. These would-be Amazons often wrestled in "tag team" style, which inevitably resulted in the staged mayhem of four women grappling at each other at the end of the bout, titillating many viewers with fantasies about group sex, lesbianism, and sadomasochism. In an endless search for new gimmicks to keep the viewers before their black and white screens, promoters even stooped so low as to present midget Indian wrestlers with such ring monikers as Sky Low Low and Little Beaver.

This made-for-television version of wrestling destroyed whatever legitimacy professional wrestling might have enjoyed before World War II. It was spectacle, not sport. Not surprisingly, television viewers soon tired of the patently fabricated matches; by the late 1950s wrestling had largely faded from the television screens of American homes into a much deserved obscurity. In the 1980s, however, it made a return of sorts under the guise of the World Wrestling Federation (WWF) as a means of providing the proliferating number of cable television networks with inexpensive fare to fill their schedules. Popular performers of the 1950s like Gorgeous George and Don Mohawk had long since retired, but the format remained the same. The WWF presented such new heroes as Andre the Giant, who at 7 feet, 4 inches and 520 pounds claimed he had never been pinned. The brightest new star was a native of Venice, California, who stood 6 feet, 8 inches and weighed a solid 300 pounds. The personification of the good guy, all-American giant, Hulk Hogan entered the ring to the sound of his rock theme song, "The Real American," his long blond hair flowing down his muscular back as he flexed his 24-inch biceps, which he breathlessly described to the TV audience as his pythons. His dedicated fans remained unfazed when media speculation intimated that his pythons were probably steroid induced. His opponents, of course, reflected modern trends in an age of sophisticated marketing, their names registered as trademarks by the WWF. Among the more notable of these modern-age villains was the despicable Million Dollar Man, a less-than-transparent takeoff on the much publicized and widely condemned speculations of such real-life financiers turned felons as Ivan Boesky, Michael Milken, and Charles Keating. Another contrived evil character, the kilt-clad Scotsman Rowdy Roddy Piper specialized in racial and ethnic insults in his contrived prematch hype.

Utilizing the newest technologies and effective marketing techniques, the WWF generated more than a million paid attendance each year, but it kept its major focus on the cable television audience. Its shows routinely enjoyed rankings among cable television's top ten weekly shows. But it was not competitive sport. When appearing for a license before the New Jersey Athletic Commission in 1989, the president of the WWF carefully defined his product as a "staged spectacle" and not a legitimate athletic contest so as to avoid the regulations of that body. "We are the wonderful hybrid of sports and entertainment," the WWF marketing director told *Forbes Magazine*. "When you walk into an arena that has WWF on the bill, the pictures, the show, the music, is all part of a bigger goal to entertain you from the minute you walk in. We want to be like Disney." And indeed it tried, reporting revenues in excess of $145 million in 1987 from television fees and ticket sales, supplemented by income generated by the sale of "Hulkmania" videos, T-shirts, and posters. But the intentions of the WWF notwithstanding, even Hulk Hogan never became as popular as Mickey Mouse.

Riding the rising tide of wrestling in 1949, an irrepressible Dick Lane also foisted an even less believable "sport" on an unsophisticated viewing America—his incredible concoction of roller derby. Once again KTLA in Los Angeles was the first to put this made-for-television spectacle on the air. Within a couple of years a makeshift eight-team league had been fabricated, featuring such exotic team names as the New York Bombers, the Texas Outlaws, and the Los Angeles Thunderbirds. Its male and female performers, outfitted in outlandish uniforms and padding, skated around and around a small wooden track, performing various acts of mayhem on their opponents while the audience shrieked in anger at dirty tactics by the opponents and cheered whenever the locals retaliated. Those who watched the faked violence of roller derby came from the same socioeconomic groups that had been attracted to wrestling. As Lane remembered the customers attracted to the short-lived spectacle of roller derby, "Violent? Oh, my God yes, they were violent. . . . They were like the wrestling fans. I'd look at them out there in the seats, sometimes, screaming and yelling and throwing things, and I'd say to myself, 'My goodness—they must eat their young.'" Even these fanatical souls soon tired of this patently staged show, and except for an occasional abortive attempt at resuscitation, roller derby mercifully disappeared from the airwaves, scarcely remembered and definitely not lamented.

The Lure of TV Lucre

The examples of boxing, wrestling, and roller derby, however, proved to be most instructive, even prophetic. Television executives and canny promoters had learned a new truth: properly promoted, television could in a short span of time generate enormous revenues from marginal, even nonexistent sports. If it could perform such miracles with trash sports like roller derby and wrestling, what could it do with a real sport product? Yet the early years of sports television had already given even the most enthusiastic sports executive reason for caution. The new medium had also demonstrated it had the capacity to destroy if its powers were not used cautiously. Such were the cases of such traditional mainstays as college football and professional baseball. The leaders of these two lucrative enterprises did not manage the new medium carefully, and the results were a severe decline in paid attendance not offset by television revenues.

In the case of baseball, the initial impact of television proved devastating. Not only did attendance for the sixteen major league teams go into a sharp decade of decline, but the advent of network major league telecasts severely undercut the minor leagues. In 1949, just as national network television arrived, paid attendance at minor league games reached a new high—an incredible 42 million. Most major league teams had a dozen minor league teams in their elaborate farm systems, with the more aggressive Dodgers and Cardinals supporting even more. Independent or affiliated teams also thrived. From top to bottom, the health of professional baseball never seemed better, the future very promising. Within a very few years, however, commercial television had not only undercut major league attendance but had dealt the minor leagues a near mortal blow. The greed of major league owners, compounded by fear of antitrust suits by a few television stations, permitted the destructive—and unnecessary—electronic incursion into the hinterlands that destroyed the backbone of professional baseball, its extensive minor league system.

By the mid-1950s baseball fans, even in the most remote areas, could watch—for free—the greatest stars of baseball. Equally significant, while they watched the likes of Jackie Robinson, Stan Musial, or Ted Williams they could also enjoy the entertaining commentary of the legendary Jerome "Dizzy" Dean. This ex-pitcher's savaging of the English language ("he slud into third") became a national delight, much to the despair of high school English teachers. Dean's unexpected new stardom as an announcer even outstripped his popularity as a pitcher for the St. Louis Cardinals during the 1930s and gave an early indication of a new sports phenomenon—the journalist as performer and news maker. The minor leagues could not compete with the deadly combination of Dizzy Dean and Mickey Mantle on CBS's Saturday "Game of the Week," and neither could they overcome the televising of large numbers of major league games within their region. Consequently, fans abandoned the minor leagues in catastrophic numbers. Between 1949 and 1959 minor league attendance fell 70 percent to just 13 million. During the 1960s the collapse continued, the number of minor league teams declining from a postwar high of 488 to just 155. Between the late 1940s and 1960 the number of minor leagues fell from 59 to just 21.

Baseball's short-sighted television policy also severely damaged many major league teams as well. Cleveland provided the extreme example. In this industrial city located on the shore of Lake Erie, the dynamic leadership of Bill Veeck had produced a 1948 World Series championship. New attendance records were established as more than 2 million fans paid their way into Memorial Stadium. Veeck's successors in Cleveland, however, permitted extensive televising of home games, and despite continued success on the field (including a 1954 American League championship), attendance had plunged 66 percent by 1956. Correctly blaming television for baseball's falling attendance, the aging Branch Rickey, now the president of the Pittsburgh Pirates, called for a drastic new approach. Long an advocate of the use of radio broadcasting because he felt it created images in the listeners' minds that produced a desire to attend a game, Rickey complained long and loud, but with little success, that television gave the entire product away—and for free!

Not satisfied with these errors, organized baseball compounded them with a severely flawed policy that permitted each team to develop its own local radio and television markets. Consequently, baseball soon realized it had a monster on its hands that it could not control. This led not only to the electronic invasion of minor league territories but also to the relocation of major league franchises. During the 1950s five of the sixteen major league teams departed their longtime homes for lucrative new markets, each of which had been a leading minor league baseball town. In several instances the motivation for relocation was not the lack of local fan support, but rather the attraction of a potentially lucrative television market. This trend intensified during the 1960s, which witnessed the expansion of the major leagues with the creation of eight new franchises.

Some relocation was inevitable and desirable, of course, because such relatively small cities as St. Louis, Philadelphia, and Boston had teams in both the American and National leagues. Thus in 1953 the struggling Boston Braves moved to Milwaukee, and the following year the perennial cellar-dwelling St. Louis Browns became the Baltimore Orioles. In 1956 the Philadelphia Athletics, their attendance now sagging below 250,000, departed for the promised land of Kansas City. Sports fans everywhere supported these moves because of sagging attendance and the warm welcome accorded them by fans in their new homes. But this was not the case when two highly successful franchises departed New York City. For several years the president of the Brooklyn Dodgers, Walter O'Malley, had fretted about the small seating capacity of aging Ebbets Field, lamenting especially the lack of adequate parking and the deteriorating neighborhood in which it was situated. He understood that changing metropolitan demographics threatened the future of his team if it remained in Brooklyn. Instead of moving to a new location within the New York metropolitan area, however, O'Malley decided to capture the lucrative media markets of distant Los Angeles. In so doing, O'Malley had decided to join the rival New York Giants, whose owner, Horace Stoneham, had apparently already made a decision to move to the San Francisco Bay Area.

The soaring populations of the Los Angeles basin and the Bay Area—and the vast potential of controlling their television markets—proved irresistible to such unsentimental bottom-line businessmen as O'Malley and Stoneham. O'Malley's brazen move can be justified only if one condones raw greed. His Dodgers were the most successful postwar franchise in the National League, winning the pennant seven times and posting enviable attendance records despite the many liabilities of Ebbets Field. The intense loyalty of the Dodger fans proved inconsequential to O'Malley; the prospects of exploiting the nation's third largest media market mattered much more. Intrigued by similar opportunities in the nation's sixth largest metropolitan area, as well as continuing the longtime rivalry with the Dodgers in California, Stoneham uprooted a Giants team that had enjoyed nearly the same level of success as the Dodgers, although drooping ticket sales gave him some justification for his move. The Giants had won pennants in 1951 and 1954 and had a strong team featuring such premier players as Willie Mays. The possibility of developing subscription cable television coverage provided Stoneham and O'Malley with yet an additional attraction. This possibility failed to materialize when voters in Los Angeles refused to support an initiative to permit pay-for-viewing television. Nonetheless, the Dodgers reaped enormous media income in Los Angeles —second only to the Yankees—by blacking out home games and carefully controlling the televising of selected road games.

The Stoneham family found the Bay Area to be something less than the promised land, especially after the Athletics moved from Kansas City to Oakland in 1968. Only in the 1980s did the Giants eventually produce a modified form of pay-for-view home television, with only modest financial rewards. Saddled with the worst stadium in the major leagues—windblown and often cold Candlestick Park—and its media and fan markets divided with the more successful Athletics, the Giants suffered through many losing seasons with predictable poor attendance and television ratings. During the 1970s the Giants came close to moving the franchise again to locations where the fan base and the media market seemed more attractive—Toronto, Denver, or one of several Florida cities. Only the sale of the Giants in 1976 to a local executive, Robert Lurie, for $8 million prevented their departure for Toronto. But in 1992 when San Francisco and Bay Area voters rejected four ballot measures to authorize public funding of a new stadium, the Giants once more appeared on the verge of departing the golden West for St. Petersburg, Florida. Only a last ditch effort by a group of local millionaires prevented the team's move when they purchased the team from Lurie for $100 million.

The impact of television on the Milwaukee Braves is especially instructive. Abysmal attendance caused the Braves to leave Boston in 1953. During their thirteen years in Milwaukee, the team attracted over 2 million fans four times, leading the league in attendance in six different seasons. But the new economics of television decreed to a new ownership that Milwaukee simply would not do. They took a careful look at a map and discovered a hopelessly constricted broadcasting territory: the Braves were, or so it seemed, hemmed in by the recently arrived (from Washington, D.C.) Minnesota Twins to the north and west and the Chicago teams to the south. Atlanta now beckoned with an alluring $1.5 million radio-TV package; the lack of other southern teams meant the Braves would enjoy a lucrative broadcasting hegemony over an eight-state area. Thus in 1966 the Braves abandoned a group of loyal and supportive fans because of this new driving force in franchise location. Broadcast revenues had become more important than paid admissions; fans sitting before their television sets had become more important than those in the bleachers. A new era in professional sports had arrived.

Pete Rozelle and the Promised Land

It is agreed by most students of television sports that December 28, 1958, signals the day when sports television arrived as a major force in American life. On that day professional football took a quantum leap forward toward its envied position as the most popular of all American sports when the Baltimore Colts staged a thrilling drive to tie the vaunted New York Giants in the championship game of the NFL with a field goal on the final play of regulation time. In the ensuing sudden death overtime period, while a national NBC television audience of 30 million viewers watched in suspense, quarterback Johnny Unitas calmly led the Colts down field in a classic thirteen-play drive that was capped by a short run for the winning touchdown by fullback Alan Ameche, giving the Colts a 23–17 victory. More than three decades later, many fans still believe it to be the greatest football game ever played. Perhaps, but it undoubtedly was sports drama at its best. Almost overnight professional football had gained millions of fans—including the leaders of the New York City advertising and broadcasting professions. In the wake of this exciting championship game, professional football grew rapidly in stature and popularity.

The announcement of the formation of a competing professional football league in 1959 indicated the immense economic power now wielded by television. The new American Football League resulted from the irritation of two young multimillionaires from Texas, Lamar Hunt and Bud Adams, who had been rebuffed by the NFL in their quest for franchises for their hometowns of Dallas and Houston. Relying on an initial $2 million contract from ABC television, they lined up six other teams and initiated play in 1960. Without the prospect of substantial television revenues, Adams and Hunt would never have launched the new league. For several years the nation's two dominant networks, CBS and NBC, had broadcast NFL games on Sunday afternoons with home games blacked out as a means of protecting and expanding the local fan base. At this juncture ABC lagged far behind its two competitors in all respects, but its aggressive president, Leonard Goldenson, and sports director Roone Arledge were convinced that ABC could gain on its competitors by emphasizing sports broadcasting. It was assuredly a major gamble when Goldenson agreed to pay the new American Football League $2 million for its 1960 broadcast rights, a huge sum at the time. Of course, within a few years this seemingly chancy investment would seem downright piddling in comparison to the escalating fees being extracted from the networks.

Despite the essential funding provided by ABC, the new league barely survived its first year; its teams lost an estimated $3 million and the intended flagship team in New York City, the capital of the television industry, floundered because of a lack of capital and inept management. Game attendance was often so small that ABC's camera operators received special training in covering games without unduly revealing the embarrassing sight of row upon row of empty seats.

As a rival league loomed on the horizon, the NFL faced the difficult problem of selecting new leadership following the death of longtime commissioner Bert Bell. In mid-January of 1960 the owners of the twelve NFL teams sequestered themselves for several days in the Kenilworth Hotel in Miami to pick a new commissioner. This meeting, which came close to failure because of an inability to reach a consensus, now stands out as the league's defining moment. For several days none of the dozen or so candidates failed to gain the necessary eight votes. *Sports Illustrated* reported that the mood at the deadlocked meeting was one of "stalemate and despair." The owners finally turned in near exhaustion, and some suggested, near desperation to an individual who had initially received only scant attention—the relatively inexperienced and untested thirty-three-year-old general manager of the Los Angeles Rams.

The owners apparently made the compromise selection of Alvin "Pete" Rozelle for all the wrong reasons, but in retrospect the decision seems to have been one of almost divine inspiration. When Rozelle was named the new commissioner on January 26 the NFL had existed for thirty-nine seasons, most of them played before small and indifferent crowds. During that time the league had undergone more than sixty major changes in franchise ownership or team location. Now that it had finally captured the attention of the nation with the thrilling 1958 championship game, it faced the threat of a rival league, whose rules promised a more wide open and exciting brand of football. Although a healthy growth in attendance during the 1950s provided reason for optimism, the future of the NFL was anything but assured.

Bert Bell's leadership since 1946 had enabled the league to grow slowly but steadily; he had brought to the league the confidence that derived from increased stability and occasional profits. But as late as 1952 one team had declared bankruptcy, and as Rozelle assumed office few owners had any realistic dreams of ever turning a substantial profit. The NFL, soon to become an incredible money machine thanks to television, still remained a small-time operation in every sense of the word. The winning members of the Baltimore Colts in that epochal game of 1958 had each received the wondrous sum of $1,500; most player salaries remained well below $20,000, and the value of most franchises hovered around the $1 million level. When Bell died, league offices occupied a few rooms in the back of a small branch bank in suburban Philadelphia. For several years Bell had actually operated the league out of his kitchen! He had, however, enabled the league to withstand the challenge of the All-America Football Conference, ultimately absorbing three of that upstart league's most lucrative franchises in 1950 (Baltimore, San Francisco, and Cleveland), and he had maintained the integrity of the game. But most important, unlike the leaders of baseball, Bell had protected the league from the potential ravages of unrestricted television.

Rozelle's expertise was not in football but in public relations. He had begun his professional career as a public relations staffer for the Los Angeles Rams, moving up to the position of general manager at the tender age of twenty-seven. On football matters he largely deferred to his coaches, concentrating instead on increasing the Rams' income by hyping ticket sales and marketing team memorabilia—beer mugs, T-shirts, sun visors, and the like. But most important, Rozelle had become intimately familiar with the arcane world of television in the aggressive Los Angeles market. It was Rozelle's mastery of the unique business of television that propelled the NFL to a level of power, prestige, and riches that league owners could not have imagined in 1960. Significantly, one of Rozelle's very first decisions was to move NFL headquarters to the nation's media capital, New York City.

It is among the greatest of ironies that Rozelle produced an enormous capitalist bonanza by imposing on the league the essential truths of socialism. Recognizing that the future of the league depended on maintaining the competitiveness of each of the league's teams—"parity" he called it—Rozelle convinced the owners of teams in the major media markets that it was essential to divide all television revenues equally. In Green Bay, the smallest city in the league, the impact of revenue sharing made it possible for that team to remain competitive with teams located in the biggest of media markets; in 1956 the Packers had received just $35,000 from the sale of its TV rights. Having gotten begrudging approval for his plan from such football barons as George Halas of the Chicago Bears, Wellington Mara of the New York Giants, and Dan Reeves of the Rams, who stood to lose the most, Rozelle then spent the summer of 1961 lobbying the U.S. Congress for legislation exempting the plan from federal antitrust prosecution. Congress complied with the Sports Antitrust Broadcast Act, which permitted professional leagues to pool revenues and to sell their television rights as a single entity.

Thus properly armed, Rozelle orchestrated an elaborate plan that placed the three networks under intense pressure from viewers, advertisers, and, especially, their local station affiliates to secure the new television rights for the 1964–65 season. He made certain that the network decision makers fully understood the rapidly growing popularity of the game as he announced the rules for what would become a highly publicized bidding process. Rozelle shrewdly created a scenario placing the three networks in an intense, highly publicized competition with each other; ABC recognized an opportunity to gain credibility as a major network, while NBC and CBS perceived that their prestige was at stake. When Rozelle opened the sealed envelopes the size of the bids astounded even the most seasoned of reporters assembled at NFL headquarters. Rozelle shuffled the three envelopes, opening them at random. He first opened the NBC bid, and he produced gasps of shock when he announced it to be $10.4 million for *each* year! The league's total TV revenue for 1963, in comparison, had totaled just $4.6 million. Rozelle next opened the bid from upstart ABC—it eclipsed NBC's by nearly $3 million! Rozelle recalled, "I thought, based on rumors, that we might get over ten million bucks." But after he had announced ABC's blockbuster, Rozelle found his mind spinning. "My God, the ABC bid was beyond any of my dreams. Even figuring the wildest sort of thing they might do . . . I never thought it'd go as high as $12,000,000." As he opened the CBS bid, Rozelle recalled he was in a state of near shock: "I figured the CBS bid had to be anticlimactic. . . . So I opened their bid kind of lackadaisically. The thing was two pages long—all that fine print. The number itself was sitting way down toward the bottom on the second page. I looked at it, and . . . Goiinnnnnnngggggggg! 'Good God,' I thought, its for $14,100,000 a year!"

It was, by far, the biggest contract in the history of sports. Euphoria swept through the league. When Rozelle called the chair of the NFL television committee, Art Modell of the Cleveland Browns, to report the good news, the conversation went something like this: "Art, Art. CBS got it for fourteen million." A disappointed Modell responded, "We-e-e-ll it could be worse. I did expect a little better, but hell, Pete, seven million a year isn't half bad. We can make it." The ecstatic Rozelle retorted: "Art—Art—Fourteen million a year. Twenty-eight million for two years." After a long pause, Modell replied, "Pete, you've got to quit drinking at breakfast."

The Vision of Roone Arledge

This seemingly amazing breakthrough proved to be only the beginning. In future years the staggering figure of $14 million would seem like a bargain basement price. Those who commanded the boardrooms of network television had become aware that sports—properly produced—could generate high viewer ratings, which in turn produced increased advertising revenue. Early in the 1960s the creative Roone Arledge at ABC Sports had discovered an essential fact that had escaped everyone else: viewers in large numbers could be lured into watching sports on television even if they were not much interested in a particular event *if* the program itself was entertaining. Arledge's genius as head of ABC Sports stemmed from his basic premise that he should furnish viewers with entertainment, not merely sports.

When ABC launched its coverage of NCAA football in 1960, Arledge provided viewers with the sounds and excitement of the game unlike anything they had experienced before—picking up crowd noise and the collisions on the field with special microphones, weaving shots of spectators, cheerleaders, and excited coaches into the coverage of the game itself. He instructed announcers like Keith Jackson to present the game in a format that appealed to the casual fan. ABC became known in the business for its "honey shots," pictures of pretty coeds in the stands, dancing cheerleaders, or scantily clad baton twirlers. Color technology made the show much more attractive even to those indifferent to football. Dedicated football fans, however, were enthralled with the introduction of such innovations as the instant replay, slow-motion recreations of important plays, and the many new viewing angles provided by the nine cameras Arledge placed around the stadium. He provided coverage of football as an event, an exciting spectacle. "What we set out to do was to get the audience involved emotionally," Arledge emphasized. "If they don't give a damn about the game, they still might enjoy the program." College football ratings soared under Arledge's artistry.

Arledge also proved the accuracy of his philosophy when he launched "ABC's Wide World of Sports" in 1961. Using the catchy slogan suggested by announcer Jim McKay, "the thrill of victory, the agony of defeat," Arledge broke most of the accepted rules of sports broadcasting, including giving network coverage to sports events of limited importance because they could be used to fill airtime at little cost. The program featured track meets from Des Moines, rodeos from Cheyenne, golf from Scotland, bowling tournaments from Little Rock, mountain climbing from the Alps, baseball from Japan, surfing from Maui. His staff went in quest of almost anything remotely connected to the accepted definition of the word *sport* to fill the hour-long weekend program. Arledge even resuscitated boxing from its well-deserved TV limbo, and in so doing thrust Howard Cosell on an unsuspecting nation. Announcer Jim McKay demonstrated the special gift of being able to light a fire under even the most inconsequential of events by emphasizing the story line—colorful personalities, feuds between competitors, possible physical danger, and especially, given the wide world theme, the remote or exotic location of the event. ABC crews logged stupendous numbers of air miles as they circled the globe searching for events to televise.

Arledge was also the first producer to recognize that an event need not be broadcast live to attract an audience; he and his associates discovered the delightful fact that a taped replay, properly edited, could actually increase the entertainment value of an event. Thus a 200-mile automobile race could be compressed into a few minutes, enough time to show a spectacular accident, the leaders jockeying for position, a grimy pit crew changing tires, and the inevitable waving of the checkered flag. Similarly a 26-mile marathon could be encapsulated into a few minutes with careful editing: brief glimpses of the start of the race, a few sympathetic shots of agonizing runners hitting the dreaded "wall," and coverage of the near-exhausted leaders straining for the finish line.

Critics complained—with good reason—that Arledge stretched the definition of sport beyond the breaking point. By the time the program had reached its thirtieth anniversary in 1991, more than two hundred different so-called sports had been covered. Events never before considered for broadcasting appeared, if only briefly, on "Wide World": jai alai, triathalons, archery, dog sled racing, cat shows, bicycle racing, badminton, wrist wrestling, lumberjacks chopping down trees and balancing themselves on floating logs, horse shows, truck pulls, water skiing, chess, ice figure skating. You name it, and ABC probably proclaimed it to be a sport and put it on the tube. Arledge's blending of sport and entertainment occasionally led to the absurd: automobile demolition derbies, motorcycle jumps, Eiffel Tower speed climbs, Mexican cliff divers, computerized boxing matches, high wire walks. "Wide World" probably reached one of its most fatuous levels when it featured Evel Knievel's near-fatal motorcycle jump over the large fountain located in front of Caesar's Palace in Las Vegas in 1967. For his efforts Knievel ended up with a broken spine and a crushed pelvis, but the ratings were high and the intrepid daredevil returned to "Wide World" several more times. Entertainment? Apparently for some. Sport? Definitely not. Good TV ratings? Absolutely.

The Success of Monday Night Football

It was inevitable that such pioneering souls as Roone Arledge and Pete Rozelle would combine their talents. For several years Rozelle had tinkered with the idea of placing professional football on prime-time evening television, but he met resistance from tradition-bound television executives who could only conceive of professional football on Sunday afternoons. CBS, fearing women would not watch football, and more than satisfied with its high Monday night ratings, expressed no interest. NBC toyed with the idea for a time, only to back off for fear of angering late-night star Johnny Carson by having to air his show somewhat later than the traditional 11:30 EST start.

ABC's Arledge, however, viewed the concept as an opportunity to demonstrate his conviction that sport as entertainment could attract the casual fan, including women. For starters he decided to deploy numerous cameras around the stadium, instead of stationing three or four near midfield as had long been the norm for coverage of professional games. ABC staffers roved the sidelines with hand-held cameras in search of the unusual shot; cameramen mounted on motorized platforms followed the ball up and down the sidelines to provide graphic pictures of the violence on the line of scrimmage. Special microphones picked up sideline noises (including a coach's occasional curse). Between plays, director Chet Forte frequently cut to a homemade sign draped around the stadium (which invariably mentioned ABC or one of its announcers), or to outrageously dressed fans (sacks over heads in New Orleans, a man wearing only a blue and orange barrel in subfreezing Denver, dog masks in Cleveland). If none of these were available, Forte could always fall back on the time-tested shot of an attractive woman.

Football fans had never before witnessed such coverage. Instant replays from several angles became common, as did extensive use of "isolation" cameras. Dramatic visual effects resulted from an in-close picture of the football being smacked off the tee by a kicker's foot, a vivid shot of a player's bloody face, the gut-wrenching slow-motion pictures graphically showing the severe break of quarterback Joe Theisman's leg, or several replays of a referee's blown call. All of this and more was accompanied by Cosell's biting commentary or the irreverence (and frequent irrelevance) of Don Meredith's down-home observations. On occasion Meredith, fortified by a cocktail or two, would break into dubious song.

"Monday Night Football" was one of Roone Arledge's greatest technical and artistic achievements. But it was, above all other things, a financial triumph of the first order. Immediately following the first Monday night game between the New York Jets and Cleveland Browns in September of 1970, the all-important Neilson ratings soared. "Monday Night" jolted the television industry with the force of a powerful California earthquake. As eager advertisers rushed to get aboard, NBC and CBS glumly watched from the sidelines. "Monday Night Football" took on the aura of a special social event. Bars and restaurants lured patrons into their establishments on what had previously been a slow night with large-screen television sets and food and beverage specials. For his part, the iconoclastic Cosell happily pricked sacred cows everywhere he went, denouncing the performances of all-pro players, second-guessing coaches, and teasing "Dandy Don" Meredith. The former Dallas Cowboy quarterback, in turn, scored points with his rural Texas humor, especially when he turned it on Cosell. While these two characters jousted with each other, the third man in the broadcast box, Keith Jackson and (beginning with the second season) former all-American and all-pro halfback Frank Gifford, attempted to report the action on the field. It was new, it was controversial, and it was superbly entertaining. Millions who had never before evidenced much interest in football became ardent "Monday Night" devotees.

Howard Cosell's performance, especially, delighted Arledge because it created controversy and sparked high ratings; but the sensitive Cosell seemed unprepared for the deluge of criticism he received. To his discomfort ABC's cameras showed anti-Cosell banners between plays, and several bars across the country attracted large crowds by inviting customers to enter contests for the right to throw a chair through a television screen when Cosell's image appeared. Howard Cosell dart boards became a temporary craze. More ominously, his mail contained many death threats and innumerable anti-Semitic comments. The combination of high ratings and critical praise for his journalism, coupled with the "hate Howard" phenomenon, sent Cosell on an emotional roller coaster, his moods often fluctuating between euphoria and depression.

"Monday Night Football" rewrote the rules about sports television and assured Roone Arledge a central place in the history of broadcasting. The program became an American institution, and although the fascination slowly wore off as the cast of characters in the broadcast booth changed, its ratings steadfastly remained high after both Cosell and Meredith had departed. As the show reached its twenty-second anniversary in 1992 with the broadcast team of Gifford, Dan Dierdorf, and Al Michaels, "Monday Night Football" still enjoyed good ratings. Would it become television's longest continuous program?

America's Special Holiday: Super Bowl Sunday

While Roone Arledge revolutionized the way America spent its Monday nights, Pete Rozelle used television to create a new American national holiday—Super Bowl Sunday. The power of television inspired this uniquely American institution, although at the time of its creation in 1967 no one, not even the creative Pete Rozelle, could have anticipated the impact of the game. Born of the merger of the American and National Football leagues—for which Rozelle successfully lobbied Congress for another exemption to antitrust laws—it became within a few years the most single important sporting event in the United States, easily surpassing the World Series in popularity. By the early 1980s more than 50 percent of the American people watched the game. Rozelle gave the game an initial aura of grandeur when he decided to number the games with Roman numerals (e.g., Super Bowl XXII), and he and the television executives of NBC and CBS (which alternatively broadcast the game until 1982) provided immense public relations hype during the two weeks leading to the game.

The first two games were less than exciting, with coach Vince Lombardi's powerful Green Bay Packers soundly defeating the American Football League representatives, the Kansas City Chiefs and the Oakland Raiders. The advertising rates of $35,000 per minute reflected the game's early tenuous stature. But in 1969 the New York Jets of the upstart AFL, led by quarterback Joe Namath, who had rashly "guaranteed" a Jets victory, defeated the heavily favored Baltimore Colts. The irreverent Joe Namath and the Jets contributed greatly to the mystique of the Super Bowl; thereafter the game became a national obsession, much of it created by heavy network promotions and lavish media coverage. On a Sunday late in January upward of 2,500 reporters descended on the Super Bowl site to squeeze every ounce of news out of player interviews and to gorge themselves at the lavish buffets and cocktail parties provided by corporations.

The Super Bowl became the quintessential made-for-television event. Newspapers published suggested menus and recipes for Super Sunday parties. Estimates on the total amount of money bet on the game, legally in Nevada or illegally everywhere else, reached to several hundred million dollars. Rozelle's legendary pregame reception hosted six thousand very important people. It became a spectacle of spectacles. Many felt the pregame hype and media overkill overshadowed the game itself because most of the games proved to be boring, lopsided affairs, but few people cared. By the mid-1980s advertisers willingly paid upward of $400,000 to broadcast a thirty-second commercial, a staggering figure that nonetheless doubled by 1993. When Rozelle admitted ABC to the network rotation to televise Super Bowl XVI in 1982 it had to pay the NFL an "admission fee" of $18 million!

TV Discovers the Olympiad

Only the Olympics inspired as great an effort by television as the Super Bowl. Again, it was Roone Arledge who provided the imagination and creative genius. He viewed reporting the Olympics as the greatest challenge of his career because of the complexity of covering a multitude of events over many days of competition. Except for the occasional Cold War–inspired drama of head-to-head competition between American and Soviet athletes, the Olympics had never attracted sustained attention in the United States. Only a relative handful of Americans had much interest in the Winter Olympics, and except for track and field and basketball the Summer Olympics struck most Americans as a big bore. But in 1960, CBS telecast the winter games from Squaw Valley in California with Walter Cronkite anchoring the coverage; CBS also did the summer games that year from Rome, using delayed-tape summaries of the day's events. CBS succeeded in conveying the human drama of these competitions to the television audience, and Americans began their quadrennial love affair with the Olympiad. CBS secured the rights to the 1960 winter games for only $60,000; the summer games rights cost slightly more than half a million dollars. Based on the high ratings, however, in 1964 NBC had to ante up $1 million to cover the summer games in Tokyo, while ABC paid $200,000 for the winter games in Innsbruck.

From a technical standpoint, the Olympics presented enormous problems for television. With events spread out over great distances, and scheduled for more than a week in duration, the games clearly did not easily lend themselves to the special requirements of television. And with the 1964 games located in Austria and Japan, the time differences created even greater logistical problems. By the winter of 1964, ABC had already had three years' experience telecasting ice skating, skiing, and bobsledding on "Wide World." Arledge thought the 1964 Winter Olympics presented an opportunity to showcase ABC's advanced technical skills. Indeed. Facing a six-hour time difference with the East Coast, producers air-expressed four-hour videotapes of each day's events to New York each night in time to become the prime-time feature the next day. Americans thrilled to the beauty of the figure skaters, the high drama of ski jumpers, the reckless speed of the bobsleds. And they stayed glued to the evening shows even though only one American athlete—Terry McDermott in the 500-meter speed skating—won a gold medal. The new technology of videotape made possible a technical and commercial success. But even more significantly, as a harbinger of things to come, the first use of a communications satellite made it possible to show fifteen minutes of the gala opening ceremonies live before the satellite moved out of range.

Having demonstrated the potential inherent in his approach, Roone Arledge threw himself into preparation for the 1968 games with a special passion. The cost had gone up considerably: the network had to fork over $2 million for the winter games in Grenoble, and $4.5 million for the Mexico City summer games. During the winter games a team of 250 ABC staffers moved into the small French city in the Alps and produced incredible stories and pictures. The athletes did their part to excite the stateside audience—the incredible beauty and skill of American figure skater Peggy Fleming, skiers flying down the mountain at speeds over 70 miles an hour, the courage and skill of the ski jumpers, the scary spills of racers tumbling head over heels down the treacherous Casserousse run after a fall. The use of carefully placed microphones took the sounds of the skaters and skiers into American living rooms, and the use of slow motion and replays underscored the stunning skills of the athletes. Americans became infatuated with the Olympics as television once again demonstrated it could transform a sporting event into something with enormous mass appeal. Under Roone Arledge's special touch, the Olympics had been elevated to a major event that both fascinated and entertained.

The technical and commercial success that ABC enjoyed at Grenoble was merely a prelude to Mexico City. More than 450 ABC staffers descended on the city in September, a "team" larger than those sent to compete by all but three countries. They produced forty-seven hours of coverage spread over ten days. Using fifty cameras located at as many as thirteen venues at one time, Arledge and his associates in the enormous control room switched with aplomb from one event to another—from boxing to gymnastics to fencing to track, even to an equestrian event—with a sure sense of drama and anticipation. Always alert to new possibilities, Arledge even hung a camera from a 250-foot crane to get a unique angle on the running track.

In Quest of the Golden Goose

Sports coverage entered into its golden age in the 1960s. Promoters and leagues extracted enormous sums from competing networks. Sports promoters created new leagues and teams based solely on anticipated television revenues. When the hoped-for television rights were not forthcoming, such enterprises as World Team Tennis, the World Football League, the World Hockey League, the American Basketball

Association, and the United States Football League folded. Interestingly, when the latter football league was established in 1984, it was no coincidence that it named Chet Simmons, a former ABC television sports executive, as its first president. The enormous amounts of monies generated by successful programs undoubtedly stimulated new initiatives. For example, in 1977 the NCAA signed a four-year contract with ABC for $120 million to televise college football, and by the early 1980s it had extended its contract to include the new Turner Broadcasting cable system; its annual revenues now approached $75 million. Competition intensified with the creation of the Mizzlou TV sports network, which sought to reap its own reward from the new golden goose of sports, focusing its attention on live events that major networks declined to telecast. The establishment of an all-sports cable station, the Entertainment and Sports Network (ESPN), in 1980 added another important dimension to the commercialization of sports. Within a few years ESPN had penetrated 60 percent of the nation's homes and with its flair for using satellites and other advanced communications technologies, took sports broadcasting in significant new directions. Its entertaining and informative evening Sports Center news summary attracted a large and dedicated audience, and although it had to fill the many hours with reruns of golf matches, body building competitions, demolition derbies, and a seemingly endless parade of mind-numbing automobile races, it became a major force in the mid-1980s by signing large contracts with organized baseball and the NCAA to cover regular season basketball and several rounds of the postseason tournament.

The escalating size of contracts was staggering. Pete Rozelle, capitalizing on continued increased ratings, negotiated a five-year contract in 1982 with the three major networks that produced $2 billion—or $14 million per team per year—for the NFL. In 1986 the growing interest in the NCAA inspired CBS to pay out $166 million for the rights to televise the finals of the NCAA tournament for three years; in 1989 it stunned the sports world by shelling out $1 billion for the rights to televise the tournament for seven years. Television rights for the 1988 Winter Olympics cost $309 million, and NBC expended more than $500 million for the rights for the summer games in 1992. ESPN moved aggressively in 1988 to compete with the major networks when it signed a $75 million contract to broadcast major league baseball five nights a week throughout several seasons, having previously enjoyed success with its telecasts of a few selected Sunday evening NFL games.

The broadcasting industry justified these enormous costs because of the ratings they received. Between 1980 and 1985, for example, advertisers paid up to $120,000 for a 30-second spot on a regular season NFL game, $71,000 for a similar spot on baseball. Super Bowl telecasts, which annually have set records for viewer share, escalated to unbelievable levels. In 1987 advertisers paid NBC $600,000 for each 30-second spot, and the following year ABC increased that to $675,000! Super Bowl XXVII in 1992 extracted a mind-boggling $850,000 for a 30-second commercial. Despite such revenues, the networks often reported substantial losses from their sports divisions; they justified these loses as the cost of doing business. Not to offer their local affiliate stations major sports programming would have led to very serious network problems. As the 1980s drew to a close, the new owners of ABC, Capital City Communications, put cost-saving regulations into place, even replacing the free-spending Roone Arledge with a budget-conscious administrator. But such economies were scarcely noticed by a public now inundated with sports television.

The Rules of the Game

Although various leagues and sports enterprises benefited from the television revenue bonanza, they also had to pay a stiff price in return. By paying out enormous sums, television producers were in a position to demand major changes in the sports they covered to make them more palatable to their viewing audience. More significant, the requirements of commercial television even forced the rewriting of the rules and policies of the sports it covered. The importance and value of the television audience—and in particular the advertisers paying enormous sums—far outweighed that of the fans who paid money to attend the event in person.

Examples of the changes produced by television are seemingly endless. For example, because of the popularity of the forward pass with television audiences, professional football changed its rules on blocking and defensive play to give the passing offenses new advantages. It even moved the hash marks toward the middle of the field to give the quarterback a wider area to attack. Names were placed on the backs of players to help announcers and viewers identify players. One-minute time-out periods were extended to two minutes and their frequency increased to accommodate the growing number of commercial breaks. Professional football introduced the nonsensical two-minute warning—an additional break for commercials with two minutes left to play in each half. The impact on other sports was similar. Tennis, which enjoyed a spate of interest in the mid-1970s, rewrote its rules to include the tie-breaker as a means of determining the winner of a tied set instead of the frequently lengthy former means of requiring the winner to take two consecutive games. Women's professional tennis received an enormous financial boost when the makers of Virginia Slims cigarettes decided to sponsor a series of tournaments as a means of getting its name before the viewing public after the Federal Communications Commission forbade cigarette advertising; in return the women's tour had to endure charges of hypocrisy for accepting enormous sums from a company whose product was deemed harmful to the health of its users. In response to the dictates of television, professional golf dropped its eighteen-hole playoff (held on Mondays) as a means of settling ties for the more dramatic one-hole playoff that could be televised live before the high-revenue Sunday evening programs commenced. The NBA, discovering that only playoff games could generate decent television audiences, thereupon expanded its postseason playoffs to include two-thirds of all the teams; what was once considered to be a "winter" sport now ended its interminable championship marathon in mid-June.

Even the game most steeped in tradition was not immune. In 1969 major league baseball opted for a playoff between the new "division" champions for similarly greedy reasons—increased television revenue. It also horrified baseball purists by moving the World Series from the traditional autumn afternoon to prime time to increase television ratings. In all sports, traditional fans complained that starting times for televised contests were determined by network requirements; fans on the West Coast became accustomed to important games beginning at the inconvenient and illogical hour of 5 P.M. so the networks could target a prime-time 8 P.M. audience on the eastern seaboard. College bowl games, traditionally held on or near New Year's Day, now began in early December and were scheduled throughout a three-week period, the number of bowl games increasing fourfold, each of the newcomers enticed by television revenues. One of these TV-spawned events, the Fiesta Bowl in Phoenix, became one of the most important and lucrative bowl games during the 1980s. The NCAA increased its annual postseason basketball tournament from sixteen to thirty-two and then to sixty-four teams; more teams meant more games, which meant more revenue.

Television also served to nationalize sport. Premier sportscasters like Joe Garagiola, Curt Gowdy, Dick Enberg, John Madden, and Jim McKay now commanded six- and even seven-figure salaries; some, like Howard Cosell, became news makers in their own right. New and often unusual loyalties sometimes resulted: a visitor in the 1980s to the small isolated mining town of Austin, Nevada, was bemused to learn that most of the town's residents were ardent Atlanta Brave fans. They followed the Braves because their new satellite dishes picked up Ted Turner's Atlanta "super station," which broadcast the Braves' games. Similarly, the sale of Chicago station WGN programming to cable companies created a national fan base for the Chicago Cubs. The Dallas Cowboys became known as "America's team," a result of their sustained high profile on national television. College basketball coaches in western states loudly cried foul in the 1980s when the Big East Conference negotiated major television contracts that placed their teams on national telecasts with greater frequency. Much to their dismay, these coaches found they were losing many top West Coast recruits to Big East teams, the primary reason being the lure of increased national television exposure.

With the development of satellite technology, sports bars flourished, offering their patrons several large-screen television sets that showed several different sporting events simultaneously. Television commercials even took on lives of their own. Setting the standard in this regard was the often humorous use of former sports stars by the Miller Brewing Company to promote beer. Winning, always important to Americans, became even more important as fans everywhere dreamed of becoming "number one." College basketball coaches found lucrative incentive clauses in their contracts if their teams reached certain levels of the NCAA basketball tournament; football coaches were similarly rewarded if their team appeared in a postseason bowl game because television rights to these games helped increase the revenue for participation in a major bowl team to several million dollars—for one game. Coaches now felt extreme pressure to take their team to a postseason tournament or bowl game; athletic directors even included such hoped-for income into their annual budgets. "The college game is just like the pro game," one disgruntled veteran college basketball coach complained. "It all changed with all that big TV money. The need to win is tremendous. A monster has been created that people just can't keep feeding."

Conclusion

Monster or munificent benefactor? Television has been both of these and much more. On one hand it has brought sports to the nation, producing an endless parade of enjoyment in the form of athletic competition at all levels. On the other hand it has converted both professional and amateur athletics into major business enterprises, exploiting higher education and individual athletes in a shameful fashion. It has also demanded and received major changes in the sports themselves. Not surprisingly, television has produced a new set of values and attitudes among spectators and participants alike. For better or worse, television has been a dominating force in American sports in the second half of the twentieth century.

Bobby Plump, Indiana's "Mr. Basketball" of 1954, remains one of the state's most famous residents. His exploits became the basis for the popular 1987 movie, *Hoosiers*.

HARBRACE
BOOKS
ON AMERICA

SINCE 1945

Chapter 4

Win! Win! Win!

Even Professor James Naismith, who invented the uniquely American game of basketball while teaching at a small college in Springfield, Massachusetts, in 1891, recognized the special appeal the sport enjoyed in the state of Indiana. "Basketball really had its origin in Indiana, which remains today the center of the sport," he said shortly before his death in 1939. Indeed, in this midwestern state, high school basketball has long taken on special significance in the general order of things; for more than three-quarters of a century high school games have been routinely treated by newspapers as front-page stories. Anthropologists Robert and Helen Lynd, while researching their much acclaimed ethnology of the mid-sized city of Muncie during the 1920s, were struck by the basketball fever that gripped the community: "During the heart of the basket-ball season when all the cities and towns of the state are fighting for the state championship amidst the delirious backing of the rival citizens, the dominance of this sport . . . is all-pervasive."

The Lynds were amazed to see the Muncie city council approve construction of a new 9,000-seat arena in the euphoric afterglow of the Muncie Central High School Bearcats winning the 1929 state championship; at the same meeting the city fathers slashed the library budget. The Lynds also lamented, as would many others, that otherwise mature adults treated outstanding players, just sixteen or seventeen years of age, like royalty. Such behavior was not unique, however; in small towns and big cities, for nearly a century Hoosiers have exhibited an acute case of basketball mania. Successful coaches have frequently received new automobiles from appreciative fans, whereas those who suffered through losing seasons have found themselves ostracized, the subject of malicious phone calls and incessant criticism. Local politics has often revolved around bond elections to pay for the construction of gymnasiums larger than most college arenas. The hiring and firing of coaches has bitterly divided communities, and the election of school board members has often hinged on issues related to boys' basketball. On game nights in the many small towns that dot the Indiana map, restaurants and bars are routinely closed because nearly everyone in town will be at the game. Several Indiana high school gymnasiums have seating capacities exceeding 8,000. It is not surprising that eighteen of the nation's twenty largest high school gymnasiums are located in Indiana.

Many have likened Indiana's obsession with high school basketball to a quasi religion, and few natives would dispute that assertion. One longtime observer of this unusual phenomenon wrote, "In Hoosierland, the pulse of winter life is the high school team, the Sabbath is Friday Night, and the temple is your home gym." When the postseason tournament starts in late February, the suspense begins to build across the state, ultimately reaching a frenzy when the surviving four teams meet in Indianapolis in mid-March. Attendance for all tournament games has frequently approached 2 million, even though many of the games are broadcast on statewide radio and television networks.

Of all the state champions that have been crowned in this curious midwestern spectacle, none has enjoyed the lasting attention of the team that emerged triumphant in 1954. Many communities have memorialized a championship team with a large sign at the city's limits, but only the 1954 victor has endured in the collective consciousness of Indiana basketball fans. In that year a gritty team from a small rural community tucked away in the southeastern corner of the state fought its way to the state championship, in the process defeating several heavily favored teams from much larger schools. The triumph of the team from the small village of Milan (pop. 987) was the classic story of the underdog overcoming enormous obstacles. Unlike most other states, Indiana does not classify its teams by enrollment; thus a team from an obscure hamlet, with no player taller than 5 feet, 11 inches and representing a school that had only seventy-three boys enrolled in its upper four grades, rallied for one improbable victory after another against schools with enrollments ten or fifteen times as large.

The "Mighty Men from Milan," as newspaper writers referred to them, pulled off their fabled triumph in such dramatic fashion that their exploits became the basis for the popular 1987 movie *Hoosiers*. This film touched the hearts of moviegoers everywhere because it depicted the struggle of the team and its coach (actor Gene Hackman) to combat community criticism while defying all odds to win the state championship on a dramatic last-second shot. But for Hoosier basketball fans, this motion picture was special because it reinforced the legend surrounding Milan's triumph and the star of its team, Bobby Plump. This self-effacing senior guard was indeed an improbable candidate to become Indiana's fabled "Mr. Basketball" that year. Standing a mere 5 feet, 10 inches and weighing only 150 pounds, he was a soft-spoken young man who had grown up in the tiny crossroads community of Pierceville some three miles from Milan. There he and teammate Gene White had learned to play the game of basketball outdoors, braving cold winds, rain, and snow in winter and the heat and humidity of summer to shoot baskets at a hoop nailed over a barn door. Ever since their early grade school days, they logged endless hours in pick-up games on the dirt surface. From the beginning Bobby stood out as a player of substantial talent. Even by stringent Indiana standards, his dedication to the game was unusual. He spent countless hours alone each week perfecting his skills, dribbling with either hand, practicing free throws, and working on the newest trend in the game—the one-handed jump shot.

Unlike the storyline in *Hoosiers*, Milan did not appear out of nowhere in 1954 to win the champion-ship; the previous year the team had won sectional, regional, and semifinal tournaments enroute to the final four in Indianapolis. There Milan had lost to pow-erful South Bend South High School in the first elimina-tion game. The following season four starters returned, including senior Bobby Plump. Using a traditional zone defense (contrary to one of the subplots of *Hoosiers*) and a cautious, controlled offense, they lost only two regular season games. Their coach, Marvin Wood, was no stranger to Indiana basketball, having been a star high school player before becoming a guard on vet-eran coach Tony Hinkle's teams at Butler University in Indianapolis. Wood, in fact, had decided to take the Milan coaching position in 1952 over better paying jobs at larger schools because of the talent he recog-nized on the squad. Despite Milan's 20–2 season record and its surprising showing in the previous tournament, sports writers did not include the Indians in their rank-ings of the top teams as the state tournament began.

Seven hundred and seventy-three teams entered the single elimination tournament that year. Milan easily trounced Cross Plains and Versailles in the sectional and proceeded to capture the regional tour-nament with a come-from-behind win over Aurora, one of the two teams to whom the Indians had lost during the regular season. The following week they encountered the state's top-ranked team, the powerful Tigers of Indianapolis Crispus Attucks High—the city's all-black school. Leading the Tigers was a multi-talented sophomore, future college all-American and NBA star Oscar Robertson. Bobby Plump, however, was unfazed, connecting on nine of thirteen shots from the field, most of them on his accurate jump shot from beyond 15 feet, as he led the Indians to a surprisingly easy victory over the heavily favored Tigers, 65–52. "There is nothing synthetic about Milan's powerful triumph," an appreciative Indianapolis sportswriter conceded. "They have a world of experience and an abundance of cool, calm confidence."

They would need all of that, and more, the following Saturday night in the state finals against perennial power Muncie Central Bearcats. After his team methodically dispatched the Black Cats from favored Terre Haute Gerstmeyer in the Saturday afternoon semifinal game, Coach Wood returned to his hotel room to plot his strategy for Muncie Central. He faced a formidable challenge. For starters, Muncie Central had tradition on its side. It had won the state championship four times previously, a record no other school could match. But Wood's major problem was not tradition; it was simply that while his center Gene White stood less than 6 feet tall, Muncie's starting team averaged 6 feet, 4 inches. Wood opted for a strategy he had used occasionally during his coaching career—his "cat and mouse" offense, a patient, slow-paced offense that would keep the score close and perhaps help negate the height advantage the Bearcats enjoyed.

While 15,000 fans in Butler Field House shouted themselves hoarse and a statewide television audience estimated at 2 million watched, Wood's team resolutely passed the ball for minutes at a time before taking a shot. When the larger but increasingly frustrated Bearcats sought to disrupt this strategy with an aggressive pressing defense, Bobby Plump or one of his teammates would drive to the basket for easy shots. This strategy worked to perfection during the first half, but in the third quarter the Indians missed several attempts and only scored one point while Muncie closed the gap. The final quarter began with the score tied at 26–26. After losing the lead for the first time, Plump followed his coach's improbable instructions and stood at midcourt holding the ball as the game clock ticked away. When Muncie's defense refused to take the bait, he continued to hold the ball . . . and hold the ball. For nearly five minutes he stood resolutely near midcourt, the ball tucked under his arm with the score-board showing his team trailing by two points. Finally, with less than two minutes remaining, Coach Wood gave the word to attempt to score; the Indians tied the score and then traded baskets with the taller Bearcats. With just eighteen seconds remaining and the score tied at 30–30, Wood called time out and gave his final instructions. While Plump set up near the sidelines, his four teammates cleared out the center of the court. With five seconds left on the clock and the population of an entire state holding its collective breath, Plump made his move. He had done it thousands of times before in front of the barn in Pierceville—and he did it once more. He released his 15-foot jump shot over the desperate outstretched hands of a Muncie defender, and just as if scripted by a Hollywood writer, the ball nestled softly into the net as the final buzzer sounded.

In that instant, an enduring Hoosier legend was created. The next day an Indianapolis newspaper's front-page headline screamed only one word: PLUMP! Incredibly, when the team returned home to Ripley County the next day, an estimated crowd of forty thousand people crowded into the town to greet the conquering heroes. All along their route home, crowds had stood along highway 101 to cheer and wave. A motorcade several miles long stretched out behind the automobiles carrying the team home. Bobby Plump could not quite comprehend it all, but he remained his typical modest self. Even after he was proclaimed Indiana's "Mr. Basketball," the much coveted designation as the best high school player in the state, he continued to give credit to his teammates. "Bobby Plump overwhelmed Indiana," an Indianapolis sportswriter observed a few weeks after that historic final basket created instant immortality for the seventeen-year-old. "No other high school player ever had a season like the one he just completed. He completely captured the heart of Indiana's basketball fans, a discriminating audience, which chooses its heroes carefully and treasures them forever."

More than thirty-five years later Bobby Plump remained an Indiana celebrity. After graduation from Butler University, where he enjoyed a good basketball career, he established an insurance agency in Indianapolis, his enduring fame undoubtedly helping to attract clients. Over the years he has been invited to speak to several hundreds of audiences, each of which wants to hear once more about "the shot." His special moment, captured on fuzzy black and white film, is played over and over each day by visitors at the Indiana Basketball Hall of Fame. He often has served as a television commentator during the state tournament. As Indiana basketball chronicler Philip Hoose has noted, the single-division concept to which Indiana has stubbornly adhered has provided many thrills and its share of upsets. But only once, in 1954, when Bobby Plump and his fellow mighty men of Milan marched out of the hills of Ripley County to outfox and outplay the likes of such giants as Indianapolis Crispus Attucks and Muncie Central, did this tournament provide such an enduring moment. In Indiana, where high school basketball is indisputably king, Bobby Plump is indeed immortal.

The High School Powerhouse

The good people of Indiana, however, have not been alone in their obsessive attraction to high school sports. Several midwestern and southern states have approached Indiana's zeal in support of basketball or football. Minnesotans have demonstrated a similar enthusiasm for boys' hockey, and Iowans have long been known for their curious attraction to an antiquated version of girls' basketball played with rules established during the 1920s that require six players per team, three each playing either offense or defense exclusively. The Iowa girls' state tournament has often attracted greater attendance and media coverage than the boys' tournament. Only in 1993, after much controversy, did the state high school athletic association bring an end to this popular anachronism.

During postwar America, youth sports assumed a prominent role in the life of American society. The changing role and structure of the American family contributed to this phenomenon. Powerful new social and economic conditions placed extreme pressures on the traditional nuclear family—mothers now worked outside the home and fathers often confronted long commuting times from their suburban homes. Divorce rates skyrocketed and responsibility for rearing children increasingly fell on community agencies. Schools now offered courses in drivers' training and sex education, assuming important responsibilities previously expected of parents. Within this context, it is not surprising that the play of youth became more structured. The coach, for better or worse, helped fill the void left by a father consumed by his career in a large corporation. Organized youth sports were the logical consequence of the conditions of postwar society.

The major justification for the emphasis on youth sports has been consistent—sports build character and foster an appreciation of good sportsmanship. But although examples of dedicated coaches and program administrators can be readily found, far too many of their peers have been consumed by the goal of winning championships to the neglect of other, more lofty goals. The National Federation of High School Associations, which establishes game rules and presides over state associations and officials' organizations, has for years identified the behavior of coaches (basketball and football in particular) as its most serious problem. Those close to high school athletics have been all too familiar with school officials fudging grade reports to keep top athletes eligible, or pressuring teachers to pass athletes in their classes. In metropolitan areas, high school coaches have even become ensnared in the repugnant business of recruiting junior high school athletes to attend their schools. One major research effort by a team of social scientists in 1978 reached a conclusion which challenges the popular myth that sports fosters good character and teaches sportsmanship. They concluded, "There is little, if any, valid evidence that participation in sports is an important or essential element in the socialization process, or that involvement in sport teaches or results in . . . character building, moral development, a competitive and/or cooperative orientation, good citizenship or certain valued personality traits." A substantial body of literature leads to the same conclusion: certain personal characteristics are requisite for success in sports, and sports are so designed as to attract individuals with such traits.

Central to the youth and high school sports craze has been the quest for victory. The comment of famous professional football coach Vince Lombardi, "Winning is the only thing," has been all too widely used as the guiding principle for youth sports programs: all of the professions about the building of character and the teaching of sportsmanship notwithstanding, sports in America has always been preeminently about winning. The pride of a community has often been placed firmly, if not uncomfortably, on the shoulders of impressionable teenage athletes.

Occasionally this emphasis has led to long-term success, even the creation of veritable high school dynasties. Muncie Central High School, the victims in 1954 to tiny Milan, has been a perennial powerhouse in

Indiana since the 1920s. In Georgia, Valdosta High School, representing a small city with a 1990 population of only 40,000, has enjoyed twenty-one undefeated football seasons since beginning play in 1913; the Wildcats have captured eighteen state championships since 1947 and have a historic winning percentage of 83 percent. Between the 1960s and 1990s basketball fans everywhere recognized DeMatha High School of Washington, D.C., as possessing one of the strongest high school programs in the nation. This private Catholic school offered its student-athletes a strong college preparatory academic program and the talent of its veteran coach, Morgan Wooten. This appealing combination encouraged parents of promising athletes to enroll their sons at DeMatha. They appreciated that nearly every year Coach Wooten sent several well-schooled basketballers off to college with a lucrative scholarship in hand.

One recent example of athletic supremacy is provided by the football program of Moeller High School in Cincinnati. Ever since its establishment in 1963, its administration established budget priorities to support the program, while an active booster club provided important supplemental funds. Not constrained by school district lines like its public school rivals, Moeller has been able to attract students (and talented athletes) to its thousand-member all-male student body from throughout thirteen Catholic parishes encompassing a wide swath of the Cincinnati metropolitan area. Its coaching staff was as large as most universities; its athletes benefited from weight lifting and training facilities that were the envy of rival coaches. Moeller's coaching staff informally used many of the parochial elementary and junior high schools throughout the metropolitan area as a feeder system, where carefully supervised coaches taught football fundamentals and offensive and defensive systems similar to those used at Moeller. Between 1963 and 1979 the Fighting Crusaders won 173 games and lost just 17, winning twelve city and five state championships.

Orchestrating this enormous program, which included a dozen assistant coaches, seven volunteer team physicians, twenty-five student managers, and more than two hundred players on the freshman, junior varsity, and varsity teams, was coach Jerry Faust. Emphasizing "precise execution" of his elaborate play book, the energetic and charismatic Faust dominated the high-powered world of Ohio high school football. His Crusaders also won much publicized games over top teams from Michigan, Pennsylvania, and New York, which were played before crowds exceeding 35,000 in Riverfront Stadium. Each year several of his players were identified by college recruiters as blue-chip prospects; even players who were not members of the starting lineup won scholarships! During Faust's seventeen-year tenure at Moeller, more than three hundred of his players received college football scholarships. In 1979 Faust moved from Moeller High School to one of the nation's most coveted college head coaching positions at Notre Dame, but the winning tradition he established at Moeller continued.

DeMatha and Moeller benefited greatly from the inherent advantages provided by unquestioning support from their predominantly middle-class parent groups as well as from their school's religious foundation and ability to attract students from a wide geographic area. Public high schools that have maintained winning programs over a long period of time have generally been located in smaller cities that support only one public high school. In this environment a winning tradition is the product of a sustained and often unrelenting commitment by the entire community. Local politics often turns on issues affecting the team, administrators and boards of education are careful not to offend public sensibilities when establishing budgets, teachers are often placed under pressure to keep star players academically eligible, the selection and evaluation of coaches takes on major political significance, and school life revolves around team membership, the selection of cheerleading squads, postgame dances, and the marching band. Team members frequently enjoy the role of student body leaders, and within the town are often elevated to the status of conquering hero; influential booster clubs, dominated by business and professional leaders, carefully watch over the team's fortunes while providing financial support and political clout.

When not properly channeled, community involvement can distort the intended educational purposes of high school athletics. Simply having winning seasons is no longer acceptable; only undefeated seasons capped by a state championship can placate demanding fans. The age of specialization has also reached the high school level, as many athletes are pressured by coaches into making a year-round commitment to a single sport; offseason weight training has been accepted as a condition for playing football; attendance at demanding summer camps has become the norm for dedicated high school basketball players. Writing during the 1960s about high school football in Texas, the journalist Myron Cope concluded, "They play football as though it were a matter only slightly less important than life itself." Cope detailed an environment where coaches were routinely paid more than the most senior teachers and where the quest for the state championship became an all-consuming community goal.

In his revealing study of one Texas community where the local high school football program had become an obsession, Philadelphia journalist H. G. Bissinger discovered an "intensity more than I could have ever imagined." In his book *Friday Night Lights*, Bissinger detailed the pervasive—and frequently detrimental—impact that football had on the community, the school, its coaches and players. At Permian High School in Odessa, Texas, he discovered an educational budget that neglected academic programs to support such luxuries as air travel by the team and the construction and maintenance of state-of-the-art football facilities—artificial turf, a 20,000-seat stadium, plush locker rooms, and well-equipped weight and training rooms. He discovered young athletes under intense community pressure to perform at near impossible levels, and coaches subjected to incredible public scrutiny and second guessing. He also uncovered a vicious strain of racism within the community directed toward black players. After Bissinger's insightful and well-researched book was published in 1990, he received several threats of physical violence from Odessa and prudently cancelled a trip to the community to promote book sales.

Bissinger concluded that a false sense of reality pervaded the football environment of Odessa. He discovered parents and boosters who lived their lives vicariously through the athletic achievements of teenagers, thereby placing unjustified demands on them. "It became obvious that these kids held the town on their shoulders," he concluded. One perceptive father, who unlike most Odessa residents found much to question in its football obsession, told Bissinger, "Athletics lasts for such a short period of time. . . . But while it lasts, it creates this make-believe world where normal rules don't apply. We build this false atmosphere. When it's over and the harsh reality sets in, that's the real joke we play on people. . . . Everybody wants to experience that superlative movement, and being an athlete can give you that. It's Camelot for them. But there's life after it." That life after football, Bissinger found, often proved difficult for many former Permian Panthers. He described several discouraging stories of disillusioned former players whose absolute devotion to football had prevented them from preparing for adulthood.

Conventional wisdom has long held that the states of Texas, Pennsylvania, and Ohio produce the greatest number of powerful high school football teams and more than their share of outstanding players, but those reputations may result more from public enthusiasm than the actual talent of their top teams. A cursory glance at the rosters of major college and professional teams indicates that other populous states—California, Florida, New York, New Jersey, Illinois—are equally productive in turning out large numbers of outstanding players and, presumably, teams of equal ability. Because public school educators have had the good sense to avoid a system of national high school playoffs, the debate has never been resolved.

Although Cincinnati's Moeller High School has received considerable public acclaim during recent years, its achievement pales in comparison with the much longer tradition of a high school located in northeastern Ohio. Ever since the 1920s high school football in Ohio has been virtually synonymous with the small steel mill town of Massillon. This gritty blue-collar town of 35,000 people has endured many an economic downturn, but has always found solace and immense pride in its high school football juggernaut. As early as the 1920s the sons of the city's steel workers had developed a reputation for their gridiron prowess, but it was not until the school board appointed a youthful Paul Brown as head coach in 1932 that the tradition began in earnest. Between 1935 and 1940 Brown's meticulously coached teams won fifty-eight of sixty games. He established the Tiger Booster Club to provide supplemental funds. An exceptionally innovative coach, he was one of the first high school coaches to use film to critique the team's performance and to prepare for upcoming opponents. He also insisted on having the authority to appoint the coaches at the city's three junior high schools, thereby creating a pipeline of players already well versed in his offensive and defensive systems. On Friday nights 22,000 fans filled Tiger stadium to cheer the home team against such powerful rivals as Warren Harding and Canton McKinley. In 1941 Brown moved on to become head coach at Ohio State University. He would later coach the highly successful professional Cleveland Browns and ultimately become the coach and president of the Cincinnati Bengals. Several of his successors at Massillon also enjoyed substantial professional success; Chuck Mather, Earle Bruce, Leo Strang, Lee Tressel, and Bob Commings took head coaching positions at major colleges. Sixteen players became college all-Americans; former Tigers dotted the rosters of NFL teams, and hundreds became high school and college coaches. For example, the coach of the 1991 national champion University of Washington Huskies, Don James, began his football career as a quarterback for the Massillon Tigers in the early 1950s.

This tradition has endured because of the priority placed on a winning football team by the entire community. The Tiger Booster Club has sustained community interest and raised important funds to provide the team with the best of facilities and equipment. In the 1960s the Booster Club boasted more than 2,200 dues-paying members. Coach Earle Bruce, later to become the head coach at Ohio State, insisted on a year-round weight training and conditioning program for all players. The school board gave primacy to the program in its budgets and personnel decisions. Impartial observers conceded that the Tiger Swing Marching Band was the best in the state, and girls engaged in major rivalry to become a member of the prestigious cheer squad. At the local hospital each new baby boy received a miniature black and orange football as an indication of the community's future expectations. The feeder system begun by Paul Brown now reached into elementary schools, where supervised programs of touch football provided the major extracurricular activity for boys. Eager-to-please businesspeople provided squad members summer jobs, and rival coaches occasionally groused that Massillon employers helped supplement the available talent pool by offering lucrative jobs to the parents of promising middle school players in other communities. In 1945 the Tigers attracted 187,000 fans to eight home games; only football attendance at Ohio State University exceeded that of Massillon High in the buckeye state that year. Between 1933 and 1947 the Tigers won 127 games while losing only 14, during which time they claimed eight state championships. Over the years the tradition begun by Paul Brown continued, as the teams averaged more than eight wins each season through 1990 while claiming more state championships than any other school. On September 13, 1985, Massillon won its 600th game, the first school in the nation to reach that level.

One journalist visited Massillon in 1949 and came away a true believer, dazzled by the community's intense dedication to the team. Football had become, he wrote, "a communal hobby which has upgraded an educational system, buttressed family life by stimulating greater interest in kids, and eliminated much of the juvenile delinquency generally identified with industrial towns." This euphoric evaluation came without supporting data, but it was an accurate summary of the view held by most citizens of Massillon. The unmatched success of their Tigers undoubtedly became the major source of community pride. It also created an atmosphere in which criticism of the program was tantamount to subversion. Membership in the Booster Club became a prerequisite for social acceptance: "If you are a member of the solid blue collar class in Massillon the odds are that you are also an official booster of football," one journalist reported. And the pressure on the players was immense. During Earle Bruce's tenure as head coach, Vince Lombardi's famous dictum, "Winning isn't everything. It is the only thing," was plastered in large letters across the locker room; in Massillon that phrase had a special meaning. Winning was what it was all about. "Visiting teams are crushed before kickoff by the Tigers' record, confidence, spirit, the town's booster pride and noise, their conditioning and training," an *Esquire* magazine reporter concluded in 1965.

The beat goes on in Massillon. In 1991 more than 125,000 fans piled into Paul Brown Tiger Stadium to watch their teenage heroes play on the most modern and expensive of artificial turfs. A slick 100-page media guide was issued to the press, compete with color photographs and detailed analyses of the team and its opponents; few college publications were larger or more complete. The team now benefited from four separate community support groups—the Tiger Boosters, the Touchdown Club, the Sideliners, and the Orangemen—each with its own special mission. And lest anyone forget the tradition of "The Greatest Show in High School Football," the Massillon Chamber of Commerce maintained a Massillon Tiger Football Museum. In 1991 the football staff numbered twenty-two, including the sophomore, freshman, and three middle school teams.

In the tradition of Paul Brown and other head coaches who came before him, in the spring of 1991 youthful head coach Lee Owens notified his team that he expected an unquestioning, year-round dedication to football. In a revealing letter sent to his squad after a "disappointing" 8–4 record in 1990 which included a second-round loss in the state playoffs, Owens said, "We are not asking for perfection, we are demanding it!" He reminding his young charges of the heavy weight of community expectations they carried: "There are thousands of people who live and die with Massillon Tiger Football." Owens promised that the 1991 team "is going to be tough, it is going to be physical, it is going to be relentless." To achieve his goal of winning the state championship, he informed his squad, "Your social life must be nonexistent during the season." He also announced that his team would be the "most disciplined" team in history, and he detailed strict regulations on personal dress and behavior that most teenagers would find repugnant. The 1991 version of the Massillon Tigers fell just short of their coach's lofty goal, losing to the eventual state champion, Cleveland St. Ignatius, by one point on a last-minute touchdown in the semifinal round of the playoffs. The Tigers ended the season with a 10–3 record. For most teams this would have been a banner season, but it was a distinct disappointment in the community that proclaims itself "Football Town USA." But there is always another season bright with hope, and with the feeder system Paul Brown established in the 1930s still grinding away, there will be more than enough players ready and eager to take on the challenge in the seasons to come.

Little League Baseball

Behind the high profile of high school sports lay a series of fundamental changes in modern American society. With the decline of the nineteenth-century agrarian society and its replacement by an urbanized and industrialized one, Americans needed new ways to express traditional values of individualism and community. "Win or lose, good or bad, the team has become the embodiment of the new urban identity," the historian Peter Reisenberg has observed. The link between sports and community thus took on important meaning in modern America. Small communities everywhere have angrily resisted the closing of small and often inferior rural school districts to form larger consolidated districts. The educational and economic arguments on behalf of consolidation were persuasive, but they threatened something very important to many citizens—their own sense of identity. The obsession with high school football in Massillon or Odessa makes little sense in and of itself, but when examined within the larger context of the values of community and an individual's sense of belonging, such behavior becomes both understandable and logical.

Each year an estimated 10 million middle and high school youth participate in organized athletic activity. Most of these youth, fortunately, do not fall victim to the high-pressure programs found in such communities as Odessa or Massillon. But some of the negative factors of the high-powered programs are evident everywhere. Feeding these interscholastic programs is a broad base of athletic programs that provide organized competition for children as young as seven or eight years of age. The most prominent of these programs has been Little League baseball, a highly structured program for boys ages nine to twelve. In many participating communities, however, "minor league" programs introduce would-be Mickey Mantles to the rigors of lengthy practices and the discipline of adult coaches as early as seven years of age. For those boys who want to continue their baseball careers after Little League, obliging adults have offered such programs as PONY League, Senior Little League, Babe Ruth, and American Legion, which provide organized baseball for boys up to age eighteen.

Youth sports programs have their roots in the nineteenth century, when such organizations as the YMCA sought to inculcate religious and moral values in young people thorough the medium of athletics. The first efforts to organize competitive youth sports occurred in the 1920s, but the movement did not gain strength until after the Second World War. Although the programs expressed the simple desire to teach athletic skills—"It is a sports truism that boys who intend to be good athletes must start young" an approving *Life* magazine said in 1947—the motivation ran much deeper. In an age when fears about disloyalty and communism gripped a society, and when it became increasingly evident that in order to succeed adults had to make their peace with big government and corporate organizations, the values that middle-class parents wanted to instill in their children were those of patriotism, discipline, acceptance of authority, and the primacy of the group or organization to which one owed allegiance. Teamwork not only did win ball games, it also swept corporations to the promised land of increased market share and greater profit margins. One of the most perceptive observers of postwar American life, the social psychologist David Riesman, has noted, "In the context of corporate life in America the road to the board room leads through the locker room."

Little League baseball had an inauspicious beginning in the small community of Williamsport, Pennsylvania, on June 6, 1939, when a team sporting the name of the Lundy Lumber Company bested Lycoming Dairy by a score of 23–8. The founder of this small three-team league was a worker in a local sandpaper factory, Carl Stotz. Many of the principles he established in 1939 have remained, including the nine to twelve age group, the importance of uniforms and other "official" paraphernalia, the scaled-down size of the playing field, the establishment of each team's roster by a "draft" conducted by each team's adult coach(es), strict adherence to a large set of rules and regulations concerning competition and eligibility, and the stipulation that each team must compete in a league which adheres to rules and regulations established by Little League, Inc.

During and immediately after the World War II the number of Little League teams began to spread throughout eastern Pennsylvania and into neighboring states. In 1948 the United States Rubber Company underwrote the cost of a national championship tournament—the Little League "World Series"—and the following year provided funding to establish a central office in Williamsport with Stotz as the first full-time paid commissioner. The next year 867 teams competed in 197 chartered leagues in twelve states. In 1952 the program went international when a league in Montreal received a charter; shortly thereafter military personnel stationed in the Far East established leagues in South Korea and Japan. In 1953 fledgling sports announcer Howard Cosell described the Little League World Series on ABC radio, and ten years later Roone Arldege incorporated the championship game into his "Wide World of Sports." By that time the number of leagues had mushroomed to some 6,000 leagues and 30,000 teams playing on four continents. In 1990 the program boasted 16,000 leagues located in forty countries with 2.5 million participants. Little League, Inc., has become, indeed, very big business.

Many forces fueled the enormous growth of Little League baseball. Central to its success were the massive suburban boom and an expanding postwar economy. Increased leisure time, a prosperous and growing middle class, and the new emphasis on youth fostered by the baby boom all helped provide an environment conducive to the growth of Little League. Structured play helped prepare youngsters for the structured life of adulthood. Much of the early public reaction to the program was quite positive because its stated objectives neatly blended sportsmanship, patriotism, and religious faith with the quest for victory. The Little League pledge required each season of the players aptly summarized the program's objectives: "I trust in God. I love my country and will respect its laws. I will play fair and strive to win but win or lose I will always do my best." Former president Herbert Hoover pronounced that the program was "one of the greatest stimulants of constructive joy in the world," and the growing bureaucracy in Williamsport, including as of 1955 a full-time public relations staff, cranked out a blizzard of information promoting the positive aspects of Little League. Among the many benefits that advocates identified were adult supervision and player safety (e.g., Little League introduced the protective helmet later adopted by professional baseball). Little Leaguers, they contended, learned many important lessons that would prepare them for adulthood, including good sportsmanship, the nature of competition, and the importance of the team over the individual.

But many of the benefits ticked off by Little League enthusiasts were precisely the same items singled out by others for criticism. The

bureaucratic organization, complex rules regarding eligibility and competition, discipline, adult domination, and the implicit emphasis on winning produced a flurry of criticism that did not go away. Americans
everywhere shook their heads in disbelief over reports of bizarre parental
behavior at games. These disturbing antics included abusive comments
hurled at umpires, angry criticism of volunteer coaches, even brutal
criticism of their own children who might have struck out with the
bases loaded. Physical violence directed toward umpires occasionally
made the local news, and the term *Little League mother* took on a
universal negative connotation.

Criticism increased as the Little League program swept toward
national prominence during the mid-1950s. Skeptics identified an underlying hypocrisy in the program, contending that Little League actually encouraged questionable behavior by coaches who were consumed
by a "win at any cost" mentality. Critics contended that the program
placed fragile youth under too much emotional stress—often provided
by adult coaches—and produced an environment in which sportsmanship received only lip service. Observers noticed with concern that the
boys playing the game seldom smiled or laughed, that they approached
what was supposed to be a game with an attitude indicating they were
engaged in serious business. Some concluded the joy and learning that
comes from spontaneous play had been stolen from young boys.

Opponents of this new form of "play" also pointed with concern
to the detrimental effect of rules that permitted the best players to
dominate the games while those with minimal athletic abilities had to
endure the humiliation of sitting on the bench much of the time. Youngsters soon learned important lessons about class and status in American
society when they pondered why the "star" players ended up as pitchers
and catchers with the most playing time, while those with limited skills
were ostracized to right field for only the required minimum number of
innings. The chair of the commission on school health of the American
Academy of Pediatrics ominously warned, "Undue pressures from highly
organized programs are undesirable and may be dangerous." An educational psychologist from New York University told *Sports Illustrated*,

> The drive to win is traditional in America and must be
> preserved. But a boy will absorb that lesson soon enough
> in high school. In his grammar school years it is more
> important that his recreation be guided toward other ob-
> jectives: the fun of playing rather than winning; the child

rather than game; the many rather than the few; informal
activity rather than the formal; the development of skills
in many activities rather than specialization.

A housewife from Connecticut suggested in *The Atlantic Monthly*
that Little League was really about preparing youngsters for the corporate
world. "He's sold his independence for security at the age of ten.
Exhorted by crowds, fed by publicity, clothed in impersonal uniforms,
he has forgone the joys of the cheerfully unorganized individual boy
whose every summer day should be a little bit different than the one
before." Lorraine Hopkins lamented that "kids have been organized
into battalions of anonymous little boys who take orders from grownups
and owe their allegiance to the team." She concluded that "the worst
has happened" to the Little League player: the lure of trophies, of
headlines, of making the all-star team, had triumphed over the special
pleasures of unorganized play. "Little League is a long and dreary dress
rehearsal of children acting out roles which grownups have not only
assigned but, worse still, have written."

Critics charged that the Little League experience robbed boys of
the valuable learning experience to be derived from organizing their
own games and setting their own rules. They found much to criticize
in the tendency to force a premature specialization on youngsters; the
sports sociologist Jay Coakley aptly summarized this viewpoint:

> It is sad when a 12-year-old has played three years of or-
> ganized football and never touched the ball or never played
> on the defensive line. It is sad when a Bobby Sox player
> goes an entire season without ever starting a game or play-
> ing a position other than right field. In organized games
> sitting on the bench is an all-too-frequent experience—es-
> pecially for those most in need of playing time. Even when
> everyone is required to play, the substitution process is a
> constant source of problems for the coach and pressure for
> the players.

Interestingly, one of the most outspoken critics of Little League
was a major league baseball pitcher, Jim Brosnan. Writing in *The
Atlantic Magazine* in 1963, this member of the Chicago Cubs complained that Little League "is rapidly becoming a status symbol replete
with too much aggressiveness, competitiveness, and emphasis upon

winning. It is not a world the kids made." He denounced the "drafting" of players by coaches as "a sordid business"; the obvious negative impact on those boys not selected in the preseason draft (referred to as "free agents" in the Little League vocabulary borrowed from organized baseball), Brosnan said, could damage a child's self-image. "Putting a price on a boy's ability is obviously adult business." He also called attention to a continuing criticism of the program—the quality of the coaches. "The people who run Little League . . . are usually on the lower part of the sociological curve, guys who can't quite make it in their business, marriage or social life. So they take it out on the kids." He contended that the overwhelming emphasis of Little League, its proclamations to the contrary, was on winning. If not, why the maintenance of league standings, the declaration of champions, the naming of all-star teams to complete in the annual tournament that leads to the highly publicized Little League World Series? Such an emphasis, Brosnan snorted, constituted a compound idiocy. "Preadolescents are immature and can't be expected to live up to the physical and emotional guidelines of older children—parents included. Winning games should not be given the importance that exists in the Little League age group."

In 1963 *Life* magazine featured a photographic essay on Little League, showing the deadly earnest with which boys in Danville, Indiana, went about their games. Several pictures revealed the tense, unsmiling faces of young boys locked in what seemed mortal combat. One especially telling photograph showed a small uniformed boy slumped on the end of a dugout bench, tears running down his face. This devastated young boy had just been "chewed out" by his coach, who told the reporter that he routinely berated his players because, "Sometimes it helps." For reasons such as these, the successful college football coach Joe Paterno of Pennsylvania State University denounced youth sports: "Kids want the opportunity to do things for themselves. I think they're just sick and tired of having adults organize things for them. . . . We destroy their initiative by arranging things for them. I am unalterably opposed to leagues and summer camps for boys under fourteen. They should be abolished."

Such criticism, however, had little if any impact. Little League and its several emulators continued to grow. Parents across the nation and in many foreign countries willingly supported the program with their time and money. How many boys felt compelled to participate because of parental pressure, however, is unknown. A comparable program for girls, Bobby Sox and American Girl softball, claimed more than half a million young participants by 1990. This program placed less importance on national tournaments and tended to provide local leagues much more flexibility in its organization than did Little League. But that could not be said about the Junior Olympic national championships for teenage girls sponsored by the Amateur Softball Association. Each year parents forked over hefty participation fees and paid the cost of travel for their daughters to compete in their local leagues and tournaments, demonstrating in the process value judgments identical to Little League parents.

And then there was Pop Warner football for boys ages nine through thirteen. "If there is anything more unprincipled than regimenting children's summer," Lorraine Hopkins wrote, "it is lining them up on autumn Saturdays, ensconced in leather and shoulder pads, to send them smashing into each other." Begun in 1929, Pop Warner football grew rapidly in the postwar period with the increased popularity of football at the college and professional levels; by 1980 more than 185,000 players in thirty-nine states participated in the program. Parents had to pay upward of $100 to meet the costs of the expensive protective equipment and other operating expenses. After two months of local league play, selected all-star teams vied in playoff games, with two teams eventually being selected to play in a "bowl" game to determine the national champion. Many high school coaches viewed Pop Warner as a training ground for their programs and willingly offered clinics for the volunteer coaches to instruct them in the basics of blocking, tackling, and team strategy.

Many youth football coaches, however, approached their responsibilities with little knowledge about the fundamentals of the game; they were schooled in their craft only having played the game in high school or from watching the behavior of college and professional coaches on television. Some unfortunately emulated the behavior of such stern taskmasters as Indianapolis Colts' coach Frank Kush, running their own version of violent "hamburger" drills in practice and preaching the glories of "smashmouth" football to their preadolescent charges. The warnings of pediatricians that young growing bodies were not prepared for the physical pounding of contact football were brushed aside by enthusiastic parents and their gung ho coaches. Their games, of course, included adult referees in striped uniforms, cheering parents, even cheerleading squads composed of young girls who had competed for their places.

If anything, adult domination of youth football exceeded that evident in Little League; coaches set the team rules, selected the players, and assigned them to a position (larger boys become linemen, the quicker and more agile ones running backs), designed the plays, and determined game strategy. The journalist John Underwood took a careful look at Pop Warner football during the 1970s and came away concerned, even angry. He reported incidents where parents put their children on health-threatening diets so they could make the required weight limits or even falsified birthdates so their boys could play. He witnessed coaches becoming "wild men" when they walked on the practice field, describing one Dallas coach who "rendered his team to tears daily. I've seen him, and others too, manhandle kids, pick them up and throw them around. He'd yell things at them like, 'You're gonna block if I have to kick your ass all afternoon!'" A psychologist in suburban Washington, D.C., was disturbed by parental behavior at games: "You've never heard such vile language. With clenched fists and lurid faces those parents goaded their children with nasty needling and yelled at the referee as if he were a criminal." Underwood concluded that the game as operated was "a rat's nest of psychological horrors" which defied rationale explanation. Former University of Michigan all-American Chuck Ortman, after observing parental behavior in a suburban Detroit Pop Warner program, wistfully concluded, "If kids' football does not turn boys into men, it certainly turns men into boys."

The Special Case of Tennis

One of the obvious, if usually unstated, purposes of youth programs was the desire of parents to make their offspring into athletic stars. Little League certainly made a point to emphasize the number of its former participants who became major leaguers, making much of such illustrious alumni as Boog Powell, Mike Schmidt, Gary Carter, Nolan Ryan, Orel Hershiser, and Steve Garvey. Official Little League publications during the 1980s emphasized that more than half of players in the annual major league all-star game were former Little Leaguers.

The emphasis on winning that some parents were willing to place on their children was most glaringly evident in the incredibly pressure-packed world of competitive tennis. In part enamored of the lucrative incomes being earned by the top tennis professionals, and caught up in the tournament successes of their children, some parents guided their young daughters and sons into a rigorous year-round regime of tennis lessons and nerve-wracking tournament play. Chris Evert came to the sport naturally because of her father's guidance; he was a teaching tennis professional who understood the pressures of the sport, and he prepared his daughter for them as she developed as a young star. But the demanding expectations exhibited by many parents led to deserved criticism. The lure of the success they could enjoy through their children induced them to spend tens of thousands of dollars for lessons, private tennis tutors, and travel to prestigious national junior tournaments. Because girls mature physically earlier than boys, several teenagers as young as fourteen found themselves competing as professionals for national and world championships. In 1991 sixteen-year-old Monica Seles, born in Yugoslavia but living in Florida, earned more than $5 million on the women's tennis circuit. The success of such young players as Chris Evert, Pam Shriver, and Jennifer Capriotti provided incentive for many youngsters (and their parents). Capriotti turned professional at the age of thirteen and immediately signed product endorsement contracts exceeding $1 million. The tragedies of other promising teenage stars, such as Tracy Austin and Andrea Jaeger, however, should have raised the caution flag. Their promising tennis careers were cut short by serious injuries caused, most likely, by excessive practice and training regimens that their youthful bodies could not tolerate. Austin suffered a severe back injury and Jaeger was forced into retirement by emotional burnout and a debilitating arm injury. Before they were eligible to vote, their promising professional tennis careers had already ended.

For potential tennis stars and their parents, it seemed that no price was too great. The ultimate commitment for promising tennis stars was the Nick Bollettieri Tennis Academy in Florida, where boys and girls with an average age of fifteen attended a private school while honing their tennis skills under Bollettieri's strict supervision. Parents forked over tuition and fees exceeding $1,000 a month and sent their young teenagers away from home for nine months a year in hopes of producing a future Wimbledon champion (as Bollettieri, in fact, did on occasion). The tennis curriculum featured three hours or more of tennis drills each day, supplemented by required weight training and long-distance running. Bollettieri made clear that his goal was to produce world-class tennis players. At a minimum he expected his graduates to earn a college tennis scholarship; for those with special talent he held out the lure of a professional career. A student had to be willing to agree not to watch television except on weekends and to forgo driving an auto-mobile and other normal teenage behavior while adhering to demanding rules. Bollettieri told a reporter that the philosophy of his program was derived from his experiences as a paratrooper. He contended that his system was essential to success as a serious tennis player: "I think it [the academy] will go down in sports history as starting a precedent. It shows what it takes to get to the top in sports today."

Was the sacrifice of a normal teenage life worth it? Apparently so, because his school flourished and most students interviewed ex-pressed approval. And for former students like Monica Seles, Jim Courier, and Andre Agassi, the result was a ranking among the top ten players of the world, Grand Slam tournament championships, and multimillion-dollar contracts for endorsements of tennis rackets and apparel.

Psychologists complained that parents sought to achieve through their children's activities what they themselves were unable to accom-plish. Many prudent and concerned parents, to be certain, recognized the dangers and acted in a mature manner, giving unselfishly of their time and energy to help mitigate the possible undesirable effects of organized sports on their children. But the behavior of some parents who placed incredible physical and psychological demands on their children illustrates how the lure of sports fame and fortune could distort parental judgment in a society that placed an overwhelming emphasis on winning at any price. The cautionary words of Larry Csonka, an all-pro fullback for the Miami Dolphins in the 1970s, pointed up the dangers of turning a game into an obsession. "Take a little kid, put him under pressure of a big championship game before his parents and his entire world, and it can be very bad for him. Especially if he loses. Parents don't stop to consider all the things that can go wrong for a young fellow pushed into that kind of pressure."

Conclusion

It is ironic that one of the results of organized youth sports has been that by the time young athletes reach high school many have already reached a state of burnout. A high school basketball coach in suburban Cincinnati criticized organized youth sports as he watched in dismay as potentially outstanding athletes turned their back on their high school teams—they simply had had enough of competitive sports as young-sters and now turned to other interests. Sports no longer held an attrac-tion for them. Although the case of Minnesota Vikings' center Scott

Anderson was unusual, it is illustrative of the hidden dangers of youth sports. In 1975 Anderson announced he was retiring at an early age, his lucrative salary notwithstanding. His explanation: he had simply lost all interest in playing the game, citing the fact that ever since he was eight years old football had dominated his life each autumn. To Anderson, and untold others like him, sports has become something much more than a game played for fun.

Curt Flood, shown here making a difficult catch at Wrigley Field, caused a major change in the way organized baseball did business when his legal suit challenged the reserve clause.

Chapter
5

The Business
of Sports

At first glance he seemed an unlikely rebel.
For twelve years Curt Flood had been a mainstay of the St. Louis Cardinals. At just 5 feet, 9
inches and 165 pounds he did not hit with power, but he
regularly ranked among the league's leading hitters.
During his lengthy tenure as the Cardinals' center fielder
he batted over .300 in six seasons and had an enviable
career batting average of .293. He also patrolled center
field with aplomb, his quickness and strong arm earning him recognition as one of the league's premier defensive outfielders. Consensus among baseball experts
at the time held that only Willie Mays exceeded him
as a center fielder. Flood had played important roles
in helping the Cardinals win three National League
pennants and two World Series championships. In 1968
he had eight hits in one of the more exciting World
Series ever played, which the Cardinals lost to the
Detroit Tigers in seven games. Not surprisingly, in 1969
Flood commanded one of baseball's highest salaries—
$90,000. But he had obtained that enviable amount
only by deeply irritating the Cardinal management by
rejecting an offer of $77,500, refusing to sign a contract
until several weeks after spring training had opened.
Several other star Cardinal players, including Tim
McCarver, Bob Gibson, and Lou Brock, also negotiated

hard that spring, eventually gaining their demands; as a consequence, the Cardinals that season had the highest player payroll in organized baseball.

Flood had another solid year in 1969, batting .285 and committing only four errors while playing in 153 games. By baseball's standards, he had more than earned his $90,000. But it was not a happy year for Flood and his teammates. Management was upset about the growing militancy of its star players. Beginning in spring training, the Cardinals' autocratic owner, beer magnate August A. Busch, Jr., did nothing to conceal his unhappiness. According to observers, Busch "had a fit" over his players' salary demands. For days his profanity "rattled the windows and turned the air blue." An increased payroll was only one reason for his discontent. Busch, and several other baseball owners, had reacted angrily when the recently organized Major League Baseball Players Association, now under the skilled leadership of former union official Marvin Miller, had successfully negotiated substantial improvements in the players' retirement program. These monies came from enhanced television revenues, monies that would otherwise have gone into the pockets of management. A skilled negotiator who always had a firm grasp of the relevant facts and figures, Miller had overwhelmed management's negotiation team. Within a few months after assuming command of the Players Association, Miller had become management's enemy number one. Miller's threat of a players' strike might have led to enhanced retirement programs for the players, but it also earned him the eternal enmity of owners like Augie Busch.

Consequently, on March 22 at the Cardinals' St. Petersburg, Florida, spring training facility, Busch called a special meeting of his team, to which he invited the press and several other baseball executives. For more than an hour he lashed into his team for its ingratitude and militancy, accusing them of using strong-arm tactics in obtaining retirement and salary concessions, ultimately accusing them of threatening the future of baseball with what he considered to be their greed. The fans, he said (incorrectly, as it soon became apparent), were unwilling to support the new demands:

"Fans are telling us now that if we intend to raise prices to pay for the high salaries and so on and on, they will stop coming to games, they will not watch and will not listen. . . . It doesn't take a crystal ball, gentlemen, to realize that with so many fans being so aware of the big payrolls in baseball, they will become more and more critical of us."

Busch's lengthy tirade, which included many comments that Curt Flood and his teammates felt were not only factually wrong but also insulting and humiliating, set the tenor for the 1969 season. Flood later recalled that he and his teammates sat in quiet shock, because they knew Busch failed to take into consideration that even with their recent salary increases, baseball players remained well behind the salary curve of other sports professionals and entertainers. They also knew that most franchises made substantial profits, especially from television and radio revenue, which the owners were not willing to share with their players. The baronial August Busch had never tolerated union activity at his brewery, and he was loathe to accept it from his baseball team. Busch knew that his players had little choice but to accept his verbal assault because they could not quit the team and seek employment elsewhere in baseball. Because of the special considerations that professional baseball had received from the federal courts and Congress, the players were in effect "owned" by the Cardinals. Baseball's reserve clause meant that a player became the sole property of the team when he signed his initial contract; he could not move to another employer (team) unless his contract was transferred in a trade. No other workers in American society had their freedom to change employers so constrained. As he listened to Busch's verbal assault Flood angrily contemplated his unique legal status in the American work force. "In no other industry of the Western world could an employer publicly belittle his professional staff without risking mass resignations. Knowing that we would not resign (because base-ball law does not permit us to seek another employer), Busch was using the occasion not only to revile us but to reassert the uniquely feudal privileges vested in him and other club owners by baseball's reserve system."

The Cardinals fell to fourth place that season (finishing thirteen games behind the "amazing Mets" of
New York). The players attributed their decline in part
to the devastating impact on team morale of their
owner's spring training speech. A few weeks following the end of this disappointing season, the Cardinals traded Curt Flood to the Philadelphia Phillies in
a "blockbuster" multiplayer deal. August Busch and
his front office managers claimed that the time had
arrived to "shake up" the team, but it seemed more
than a coincidence that the two players traded were
those who had held out for large salary increases that
spring—Flood and star catcher Tim McCarver. In return, coming to the Cardinals would be the talented
if often morose Phillie slugger Dick Allen, along with
infielder Cookie Rojas. Flood learned of the trade from
an assistant in the Cardinal front office early one
October morning; he was deeply hurt and angered
that General Manager Bing Divine, or owner Busch,
had not paid him the courtesy of a telephone call
before releasing the news to the press.

Flood did not look favorably on a trade in which
he had absolutely no say. After twelve years he had
become comfortable with life in St. Louis; he was deeply
involved in community service projects for underprivi-
leged youth, and his talent as a oil painter had led to
a lucrative art studio. He had also recently launched
a photography business. The prospects of playing for
the Phillies provided little consolation. His visits to Philadelphia over the past dozen seasons had given him an
unfavorable perception of the city as being the most
racist in the National League, what he referred to as "the
nation's northern most southern city." Adding to his misery
was an awareness that National League players considered Philadephia to be one of the league's least
desirable franchises when it came to the treatment of
their players: they traveled cheaply, and their salaries
ranked among the league's lowest. In addition, the
team frequently finished in the second division and the
penchant of Phillie fans for hurling verbal abuse at
their own team was legendary. Being subjected to the
critical barbs of Philadelphia sportswriters and the boos
and caustic comments from fans was considered the

special price an athlete had to pay as a member of the Phillies. Such unpleasant thoughts pressed in on Curt Flood as he contemplated moving from his adopted home. "I did not want to succeed Richie Allen in the affections of that organization, its press and its cat-calling, missile-hurling audience," he recalled.

The Phillies soon offered Flood a surprisingly lucrative contract for 1970 that would pay him $110,000, a sizable increase over his St. Louis salary. But the fact that he had no alternative other than to perform for the Phillies if he wanted to continue his baseball career rankled deeply in this proud and sensitive man. Yet Flood knew full well that under baseball's unique legal status, he had no control over his own destiny. If he chose not to play in Philadelphia, he could not play at all.

Like all major league players, Flood was subject to baseball management's special gift from the U.S. Supreme Court—the reserve clause. In 1922 Justice Oliver Wendell Holmes, in his majority opinion in *Federal Baseball League v. National League*, had specifically exempted organized baseball from federal antitrust laws. Following a curious line of legal reasoning, Holmes and his brethren ruled organized baseball was a local activity that did not participate in interstate commerce, although at that time the major leagues had teams located in seven states and the District of Columbia. The court had intimated, however, that Congress could change the special status accorded organized baseball, although in reality such a prospect seemed highly unlikely.

Within minutes after learning of his trade Flood told a friend, "There ain't no way I'm going to pack up and move twelve years of my life away from here. No way at all." The image of American slavery undoubtedly crossed the mind of this sensitive black man; he was also very much aware of the powerful social movements that had challenged many of America's repressive institutions and policies during the turbulent years of the late 1960s. As Flood contemplated his dilemma, he recalled a statement made by the ex-slave and antislavery leader Frederick Douglass: "If there is no struggle, there is no progress. Those who profess to favor freedom, and yet deprecate agitation, are men who want crops without plowing up the ground. . . . Power concedes nothing without a demand. It never did and never will."

From time to time Flood had spoken out against the reserve clause and other repressive baseball policies. "I was an expert on baseball's spurious paternalism," he later recalled. "I was a connoisseur of its grossness. I had known that I was out of phase with management. I therefore had known that I might be traded. Yet now, when the industry was merely doing its thing, I took it personally. I felt unjustly cast out."

A few weeks following the announcement of the trade, Flood took decisive action. He retained an attorney and consulted with Marvin Miller, executive director of the Players Association. Flood informed a stunned Miller that he wanted to sue baseball on constitutional grounds, contending that the reserve clause denied him freedom of contract as enjoyed by all American workers except professional athletes. An experienced labor negotiator, Miller understood Flood's anger and agreed fully with his interpretation of the situation. But he urged caution, noting that a suit would mean the thirty-one-year-old center fielder might not be able to play for any team during the several years it took the case to wend its way through the court system—to play would likely make the suit "moot" in the eyes of the courts—and there was no guarantee he would win. Miller warned that Flood was about to challenge a Supreme Court decision that had stood for nearly a half century. Not only would Flood be throwing away the $110,000 offered by the Phillies, but at the end of the litigation he might have difficulty finding employment. Would any team offer a malcontent player in his mid-thirties a contract? He could easily be the victim of a retaliatory blacklisting. Further, any hopes of becoming a coach or manager after his playing days ended would almost certainly be dashed.

Miller's cautionary comments notwithstanding, it took Flood only a short time to conclude the risk was worth taking. He was determined to proceed: "Win or lose, the baseball industry [will] never be the same." He asked for the support of the Major League Baseball Players Association, explaining to its executive

committee that he felt the reserve system gave baseball's owners "unreasonable powers" over the players.
"I spoke of the affronts to human dignity of a system
that indentured one man to another. I pointed out
that fair bargaining and real professionalism would
remain distant hopes in baseball until I fought my
fight." He assured the Players Association committee
that he would not settle out of court and would pursue
the issue to its conclusion. The committee voted unanimously to support Flood's courageous move.

Shortly thereafter Miller enticed Arthur Goldberg,
a former cabinet member under Presidents Kennedy
and Johnson and a former associate justice of the Supreme Court, to serve as Flood's counsel. As a first shot
in their legal stratagem, Flood sent a letter to baseball
commissioner Bowie Kuhn demanding the right to negotiate with other clubs. Kuhn's denial came forthwith,
and Goldberg filed in federal court. Kuhn's response of
December 30, 1969, was remarkable for its attempt to
tap dance around Flood's basic contention: "I certainly agree with you that you, as a human being, are not
a piece of property to be bought and sold. This is fundamental in our society and I think obvious. However,
I cannot see its applicability to the situation at hand."

Reactions to Flood's suit were varied. A few high-
salaried players—including such superstars as Willie
Mays, Carl Yazstremski, and the recently retired
Robin Roberts—denounced Flood's action as detrimental to the structure of baseball. Commissioner Bowie
Kuhn expressed shock and dismay. Baseball owners,
of course, universally condemned his suit. But Flood
was gratified by the support he received from most
players. Jackie Robinson, no stranger to pioneering
himself, and now firmly ensconced in the Hall of Fame
at Cooperstown, praised Flood's courage, drawing important parallels to the civil rights movement.

Flood received little support, however, from the
great preponderance of sportswriters and columnists,
who either failed to grasp the significance of the reserve clause or were chummy with management. Many
reporters apparently could not (or did not want to)
understand the legal issues at stake; they especially
could not comprehend why a talented player would

pass up $110,000 for the sake of upsetting the legal basis on which baseball's personnel system rested. Many writers unfairly charged him with being Marvin Miller's dupe or a radical black activist seeking headlines. Only a relatively small number of leading sports journalists—among them Howard Cosell of ABC, Red Smith of the *New York Times*, and Jim Murray of the *Los Angeles Times*—presented Flood's arguments in a fair and accurate manner. *Sports Illustrated* also weighed in with balanced articles that presented Flood's cause accurately and sympathetically. These favorable presentations were more than offset by vicious, and error-riddled, diatribes in the self-proclaimed Bible of baseball, the *Sporting News* (which, incidentally, had its offices in St. Louis).

The case of *Flood v. Kuhn* moved with surprising speed through the federal court system. In the first step, a New York federal district judge, Irving Ben Cooper, ruled against Flood on the grounds that baseball remained exempt from federal antitrust laws on the basis of the 1922 decision; like most federal district court judges, Cooper did not wish to rule in defiance of a prior Supreme Court decision. The following year a federal circuit court upheld Cooper's decision and in early 1972 the case came before the Supreme Court. On June 6 of that year Curt Flood lost his struggle in a 5–3 decision. Writing the majority opinion, Justice Harry A. Blackmun duly noted the "aberration" and "anomaly" of their decision that only organized baseball, of all professional sports and other forms of public entertainment, enjoyed exemption from federal antitrust laws. Blackmun wrote, "We continue to be loath, fifty years after *Federal Baseball* [the 1922 decision] . . . to overturn those cases judicially when Congress, by its positive inaction, has allowed their decision to stand for so long, and far beyond mere influence and implication, has clearly evidenced a desire not to disapprove them legislatively." In other words, the court's majority once more tossed the ball back to Congress. The Supreme Court simply did not want to tamper with the so-called national pastime.

The dissenting opinion of three liberal justices (William O. Douglas, William Brennan, and Thurgood

Marshall) provided little solace to Curt Flood. They held that baseball, like all other businesses engaged in interstate commerce, should be held to the same antitrust laws. The failure of Congress to redress the problem (as hinted at in the 1922 decision written by Justice Holmes), they claimed, "should not prevent us from correcting our own mistakes."

For all intents and purposes, Curt Flood's baseball career had ended. The Phillies sold his contract to the lowly Washington Senators, for whom he played in thirteen games in 1971 (having been assured that by so doing he would not impair his suit), but now at the age of thirty-three and having sat out a full season, Curt Flood found he no longer could compete at the high level he demanded of himself. He thereupon retired.

The Curious Case of Baseball

Although Curt Flood failed to overturn the reserve clause before the nation's highest court, his case proved to be a major turning point not only for major league baseball but for other professional sports as well. Although Flood's appeal had been rejected, the determined and principled manner in which he had pursued his cause had awakened professional athletes in all sports to the financial potential inherent in free agency: if they could negotiate with several teams, their salaries could be set by free market conditions and not by monopolistic ones. Who knew a player's real worth unless he was free to negotiate with all teams interested in his services? Within a few years the pendulum of power in personnel matters had swung away from the owners and professional leagues to the side of labor, the players. That Flood did not personally share in the enormous increase in salary levels that would result from these changes was indeed unfortunate, but he at least had the deep satisfaction of having been the man who precipitated the demise of baseball's infamous reserve system and, in the process, ushered in a new era that would see players' salaries increase dramatically.

A strange set of circumstances achieved what Curt Flood's legal battle failed to accomplish. That this occurred so soon after organized baseball had fought the Flood challenge so vigorously can be attributed only to the incredible stupidity, compounded by arrogance and stubbornness, of organized baseball's management. Central to this saga was Marvin Miller. In 1966 he had accepted the appointment to head the Major League Baseball Players Association, which for two decades had been a weak and ineffectual organization. He came to the position with little knowledge of baseball; indeed, a weekend tennis match constituted his major interest in sports. The association cared little about Miller's lack of experience in baseball. They wanted someone steeped in the process of labor negotiations, someone who understood pension plans and the legalities surrounding contracts and collective bargaining. Those skills Miller had in abundance. For sixteen years this native of Brooklyn had served as the chief economist and assistant to the president of the United Steel Workers. On his own playing field of high-level union politics and contract negotiations, he had demonstrated an ability to play hardball with several presidents of the United States as well as top management of the nation's powerful steel companies. Miller was stunned to discover the players' lack of control over their working conditions, and especially their low pay scale. He immediately plunged into his work, much of it directed to educating the executive committee members about the fundamentals of contracts and negotiations. He also learned that many players, including some of the most famous stars, were hostile to anything connected with unionism. They had been convinced by the owners that the reserve clause was essential to the health of baseball, and therefore to their own income.

Within a few years, however, Miller had gained the confidence of the players, their conservative inclinations notwithstanding. Essentially he educated them on their contractual rights and their potential for increased financial reward. Shortly after taking his position, he negotiated a lucrative contract with the Topps Chewing Gum Company, which included players' cards in its packages of bubble gum. Whereas the company had been paying a player just $125 a year for the rights to use his picture, Miller came away with a contract that included royalty rights based on gross sales. This agreement eventually put several million dollars into the players' pockets. Similarly he signed a licensing contract with Coca-Cola that poured substantial funds into the Players Association. Miller's ability to gain major concessions from the owners in 1968 solidified his support among the players. In that year he succeeded in negotiating the first basic agreement between the owners and the association that increased the minimum salary by 40 percent (to the then seemingly munificent sum of $10,000); the following year, after invoking the threat of a strike, Miller obtained major improvements in the players' pension and health benefits program.

While the Flood case went through the court system, Miller extracted a second basic agreement from management that elevated the minimum salary to $16,000 by 1975 and gave a player who had spent five years with the same team and a total of ten years in the major leagues the right to veto any trade. Perhaps most important, the owners also agreed to submit certain contractual disputes to impartial arbitration. The importance of that concession became apparent in 1974 when the leading (and future member of the Hall of Fame) pitcher of the Oakland Athletics, Catfish Hunter, became embroiled in a contentious dispute with team owner Charles O. Finley regarding a clause in his contract which stipulated that 50 percent of his $100,000 salary be paid in the form of the purchase of a tax-deferred annuity. When Finley discovered he could not deduct deferred payments from his taxes, he resolutely refused to honor Hunter's contract. Hunter had negotiated this contract to reduce his annual taxes and as an important part of his own retirement planning. When it became apparent that the penurious Finley would not budge, the Players Association filed a grievance on Hunter's behalf. Much to Finley's anger and the dismay of the owners, the attorney-arbiter Peter Seitz ruled in Hunter's favor. Not only did Finley have to make the $50,000 payment to the annuity company as specified in the contract, but because Finley had knowingly and willfully violated the contract, under the basic agreement Seitz declared Catfish Hunter to be a free agent.

For the first time in history, a major league baseball player was legally free of the reserve clause, and it had happened only because of the stubbornness of a team owner. Finley subsequently sued to overturn the arbitration decision in the California courts and lost. Catfish Hunter soon discovered what his contractual freedom meant for a pitcher who had won 161 games in just ten seasons. He signed a contract with the New York Yankees for $3.75 million over five years. The enormity of Hunter's contract electrified the baseball world. The free market meant that in 1975 Hunter would be paid $750,000 by the Yankees, a marked difference from the $100,000 Finley had paid him for his twenty-five victories the year before.

The following year, Marvin Miller adeptly orchestrated a sequence of events that dealt a death blow to the reserve clause. Early in his tenure as executive director of the Players Association, he had been surprised to read in the standard uniform player's contract that owners had the right to renew an unsigned player to a contract for one year. Although both players and management had assumed a player's contract could be extended forever even without his signature, that was not what the uniform player's contract said. Could it be that Miller had discovered a crucial weak link in organized baseball's legal armament?

In 1975 Miller, still smarting from the Supreme Court's ruling against Curt Flood, determined to find out, convincing two well-established pitchers, Andy Messersmith of the Los Angeles Dodgers and Dave McNally of the Montreal Expos, to play that season without signing a contract. As soon as the 1975 season ended, Miller filed grievances claiming free agency for Messersmith and McNally.

Although baseball commissioner Bowie Kuhn testified in the grievance hearings that a ruling on behalf of McNally and Messersmith would mean the financial bankruptcy of organized baseball, the arbitrator ruled simply that the uniform contract clearly stipulated a player could be renewed without his signature for no more than one season. He declared both pitchers free agents. For all intents and purposes, the reserve clause had been killed. A Kansas City federal district court upheld the arbitration decision, and the Supreme Court subsequently refused to consider an appeal of Judge John W. Oliver's ruling on behalf of the Players Association. Andy Messersmith, no longer constrained by the reserve clause, signed a $1.7 million multiyear contract with the Atlanta Braves. Having made his point, and his career already in peril because of an arm injury, Dave McNally retired, knowing he had struck a major blow for player freedom.

In the wake of these revolutionary developments the owners mounted a counteroffensive, deciding to lock out the players from spring training in 1976 pending the signing of a new basic agreement. Although many promanagement journalists mislabeled the decision of the owners to lock the gates on the training facilities as a "strike" by the players, Marvin Miller recognized the time had come for a reasonable compromise. After seventeen days the owners reopened spring training and negotiations commenced while the baseball season was played. The acrimonious negotiations finally concluded in July. Following Miller's advice the Players Association backed away from demanding complete free agency, agreeing in principle that a player could be bound contractually to a team for six years, after which time he could enter into a special "re-entry" draft. The owners also agreed to hike the minimum salary another 25 percent (to $21,000 a season), but the existence of what amounted to limited free agency brought market forces to bear on players' salaries. Within five years average salaries had increased to $100,000, a fact that grated heavily on management.

The result of management's unhappiness led to baseball's longest and most bitter strike in 1981. The owners clearly wanted to regain the upper hand in their labor relations; they especially wanted to restore the reserve clause or, failing that, somehow end the ability of the players to use free agency to obtain large salary increases by shopping their services around the two leagues. It is indeed ironic that the owners desperately wanted to protect themselves from each other! They wanted to establish policies that would prevent themselves from paying ever-increasing salaries for such top stars as Dave Winfield, who in 1980 left the San Diego Padres for a multimillion dollar ten-year contract with the New York Yankees. The bottom line issue was simple: who would control the levers of power in organized baseball, the owners or the players? Bowie Kuhn, whose judgment seemed to work at times to the detriment of those who employed him—the owners—put it succinctly in his 1987 autobiography, *Hardball:* "The players' association was growing so powerful, it threatened to take control of the game away from the clubs. It was an issue over which management was ready to hand-wrestle crocodiles." Believing a lengthy strike would destroy the solidarity of the Players Association—the owners assumed the players, now enjoying what seemed to be astronomical salaries, would not hold firm during a protracted strike—the owners took out a $50 million strike insurance policy with Lloyd's of London and quietly assembled an additional $15 million strike fund to protect against losses in income from ticket sales and television revenue. Marvin Miller learned from confidential sources that the owners believed the players would surrender within a week.

The owners designed their negotiating position so as to precipitate a strike. They wanted not only to win but to wound, even destroy, the Players Association. They also wanted to humiliate Marvin Miller, a man they had come to despise because of his successes in advancing the rights of the players. The owners' demands included the end to salary arbitration, the abolition of individual salary negotiations to be replaced by a salary schedule, and, most important, compensation to a team that lost a player to free agency. The owners believed if a team was forced to give up a top-notch player to the team from which it had lured another with a higher contract offer, it would effectively restrict, if not end, the free agency market.

The owners were sadly mistaken in their assumption that the players would not stand solidly behind the strike. Instead the strike lasted for fifty bitter days, starting on June 11, eventually ending in early August. The strike caused the cancellation of 713 games and made a mockery of the pennant races that year. The owners lost an estimated $72 million in revenue. It seemed no mere coincidence that the owners quickly settled once their strike insurance ran out. They abandoned their initial set of demands, agreeing almost completely to the terms advanced by Miller and the Players Association some six months earlier.

The owners had miscalculated badly, and the result was what they had feared the most—an orgy of free agency signings over the next few seasons that served to more than triple players' salaries. A few years later, in 1985, they would miscalculate again. For three years the free agency market virtually dried up as the owners piously professed no interest in signing available free agents. However, they were found guilty of collusion by an impartial arbitrator and ordered to pay those players who had been adversely affected a total of $280 million. Shortly thereafter the New York Yankees signed slugger Jack Clark away from the St. Louis Cardinals for $1.5 million a season and the free agency scramble was on once more.

The owners' worst fears about themselves had been realized. Recognizing that their fans demanded they make every effort to improve the quality of their teams, the owners found themselves in a bidding war with each other. Salaries jumped over the moon. In 1966 when Marvin Miller signed on with the Players Association the average major league salary was just $19,000, while many players toiled away an entire season for the minimum salary of $6,000. By 1975, the year before the Messersmith-McNally arbitration, the average salary had increased to $46,000. In 1991 the average major league salary had escalated to $891,000, with the minimum wage now $100,000. A few superstars earned enormous salaries—the San Francisco Giants paid their two leading hitters, Will Clark and Kevin Mitchell, $3.75 million each. Across the bay in Oakland, slugger Jose Canseco and pitcher Dave Stewart were drawing down $3.5 million each. But they were only two of more than twenty-five players earning at least $3 million that season. Daryl Strawberry temporarily led the salary derby, leaving the New York Mets for the Los Angeles Dodgers under a multiyear contract that paid him $3.8 million annually. In order to retain the services of pitcher Roger Clemens, the Boston Red Sox agreed to a four-year contract that would pay him a total of $21.5 million; the contract guaranteed the fastball pitcher $5 million in 1994.

At least the likes of Strawberry and Tim Raines of Montreal ($3.5 million) or Eric Davis of the Cincinnati Reds ($3.6 million) were considered to be among the leagues' elite players—recognized stars. As the 1992 season approached, the top free agency players available were scarcely of the superstar category, but the New York Mets, desperate to appease their fans for having lost the services of Strawberry, signed Bobby Bonilla for a cool $29 million over five years. How had Bonilla been able to command such a salary? Simply put, he was the best player available for free agency that year, but definitely not the best player in baseball. He had batted a respectable (but not awe-inspiring) .272 for the Pittsburgh Pirates in 1991; his abilities in the field were of less than Golden Glove potential—every ball hit toward him at third base or in right field (where manager Jim Leyland sometimes put him for his own protection) became an adventure. As the Mets prepared to embark for spring training in 1992, their player payroll exceeded $45 million. Shortly before spring training began, the Chicago Cubs, determined not to lose Ryne Sandberg to free agency, signed the star second baseman to a multiyear contract calling for an annual salary of $7.1 million.

The riches trickled down to others fortunate enough to become eligible for free agency at the right time, producing astounding results for truly pedestrian players. In 1991 the San Francisco Giants signed as a free agent pitcher Bud Black from the Cleveland Indians. This thirty-three-year-old left hander, who had a career 83–82 won-lost record, signed a four-year deal for $10 million. In 1991 he won ten games for the Giants; thus each of his victories set back the Giants a cool quarter of a million dollars. Or there was Dave Valle, a career .214 batter and lackluster catcher, who secured a three-year contract for $3.6 million from the cash-strapped Seattle Mariners. Just twenty years earlier, baseball's biggest stars, Hall of Famers Willie Mays and Hank Aaron, earned less than $200,000 each. Shortly after the 1992 season ended, the National League's most valuable player, Barry Bonds of the Pirates, stunned even the most seasoned observer of the money derby when he moved to the Giants for a six-year contract guaranteeing him $43.5 million. Reporters mercifully did not ask Curt Flood for his reaction.

The Sports Bonanza

Other professional sports also had to deal with the issue of free agency. In 1961 the NFL adopted a policy advanced by Commissioner Pete Rozelle that established free agency, but extracted such high compensation from the team signing a free agent, the practice was seldom used by teams seeking top talent. Rozelle interpreted the rule ruthlessly in the few cases that came to him for adjudication, awarding to those teams losing a free agent the compensation of first-round draft choices or players of established ability from the raiding team. The chilling effect of the so-called "Rozelle rule" convinced most teams to attempt to build their teams through the annual college draft rather than by seeking free agents. Similarly, the NBA shrewdly prevented free agency by imposing a "right of first refusal," which gave a team about to lose a free agent the right to match the new offer. The NBA later got the players to agree to a team salary cap that also curtailed widespread raiding of other teams.

When the federal courts found the Rozelle rule to be unconstitutional in 1975, subsequent negotiations between the league and the players resulted in management keeping the upper hand. In 1982 the players struck for nearly two months in an effort to gain increased compensation formulas and an expansion of their free agency rights. The basic concept of the Rozelle rule remained, which provided a team losing a free agent the right to compensation from much-valued draft choices. In 1987 the players once more went on strike to obtain the elimination of the fair compensation requirement, but union leaders handled their demands ineptly and found themselves confronted not only by a unified band of owners but by overwhelming fan hostility. The owners fielded replacement teams and the season went on, more or less; several leading players defected and the union surrendered. The impact of these complex machinations meant that football's management could keep professional football salaries much lower than those of baseball and basketball. In 1991 average NFL player salaries were $250,000, about 25 percent that of baseball and just 20 percent of basketball.

The suppression of player salaries in the NFL would have been even greater had it not been for the formation in 1960 of the rival American Football League, which created intense competition for players for a few years. Sonny Werblin, owner of the AFL's New York Jets, escalated the war between the competing leagues. He captured front-page headlines in 1965 when he signed quarterback Joe Namath out of the University of Alabama for the heretofore unheard of amount of $400,000. Namath's quarterbacking abilities and news-generating talents —both on and off the field—quickly repaid Werblin many times over. In response to his critics, Werblin declared he was simply following sound business principles; after all, the Jet's share of the league's lucrative $35 million contract with NBC made such salaries possible. Salaries in both leagues quickly jumped until the two leagues decided to merge into one league in 1967, thus putting a stop to such nonsense as operating in an open labor market. Competitive capitalism, after all, can be expensive if you are bidding for a commodity as scarce as an all-American quarterback.

Professional sports in America had indeed become a very big business. With the megabucks from television providing the major source of money, it is not surprising the nature of the ownership also changed. The early leaders of professional sports had often been men of relatively modest means; several operated their teams cautiously because they provided their primary source of income. Television changed all that, producing not only an incredible escalation in the value of a sports franchise but also the lure of vast public exposure. Thus there was drawn to professional sports a group of extremely wealthy businesspeople—mostly of the self-made variety—who found the opportunity to become public sports figures irresistible.

The archetype of the flamboyant owner was Cleveland shipping and manufacturing executive George Steinbrenner III, who acquired the New York Yankees in 1973. Almost overnight this arrogant and imperious business executive became a famous sports figure. He seemed to be in the headlines more often than his team, as he hired and fired managers on a whim, traded players with abandon, and offered enormous salaries to attract free agents. Operating out of the nation's media capital, Steinbrenner soon became one of the nation's most publicized men. Whether his goal was to improve his baseball team or simply to keep himself in the national spotlight was debatable; when he was forced to relinquish his control of the Yankees in mid-season 1990 following revelations of connections with underworld figures, Yankee fans cheered more loudly than they had in years. Those cheers turned to groans when baseball commissioner Fay Vincent announced Steinbrenner's reinstatement effective March 1, 1993.

When the leagues from time to time decided to expand they found they could demand enormous franchise fees and still find eager applicants. In 1991 the owners of the National League's newest expansion baseball teams, the Colorado Rockies and the Florida Marlins, forked over $95 million each just for the privilege of fielding teams in 1993. Among the more prominent new franchise owners who came on the national sports scene after having made huge fortunes in the business world were cable television mogul Ted Turner of the Atlanta Braves and the Atlanta Hawks, pharmaceutical executive Ewing Kauffman of the Kansas City Royals, McDonald's fast-food entrepreneur Ray Kroc of the San Diego Padres, California real estate developer Alex Spanos of the San Diego Chargers, oil executive Jerry Jones of the Dallas Cowboys, shopping center developer and operator Edward DeBartolo, Jr., of the San Francisco 49ers and the Pittsburgh Penguins, investment manager George Gund of the Minnesota North Stars and San Jose Sharks hockey teams, blue jeans manufacturer Robert Haas of the Oakland Athletics, pizza franchiser Donald Monaghan of the Detroit Tigers, media executive Gene Autry of the California (Anaheim) Angels, electric shaving company executive Victor Kiam of the New England Patriots, and automobile dealers Marge Schott of the Cincinnati Reds and Norman Braman of the Philadelphia Eagles. Prominent among those involved with the construction of a stadium for the Colorado Rockies was brewer Joseph Coors.

Although video rental entrepreneur Wayne Huizenga purchased the Marlins himself, the enormous cost of franchises has often made individual ownership difficult. This means that ownership of teams within a community sometimes falls to a company. The most glaring examples are the ownership of the New York Yankees during the 1960s by the Columbia Broadcasting System, the Chicago Cubs by the *Chicago Tribune*, and the New York Knicks by a corporate conglomerate so complicated in its structure that fans could not understand who actually owned their team. Often the finances of a team becomes deeply intertwined with the business interests of its owners, who make major decisions involving the team that are unrelated to sports issues. Consider the following episode: 1992 baseball commissioner Fay Vincent proposed moving the Chicago Cubs from the eastern to the western division of the National League. On the face of it this seemed to be a logical restructuring based on simple geography. But conditions in the modern business world of sports determined otherwise. This shift would have entailed the Cubs playing many more games on the West Coast, making for late-night games for East Coast television cable viewers. Because the Cubs' parent owner, the *Tribune* corporation, also owned the lucrative Chicago television superstation WGN, it not only blocked Vincent's realignment plan but played a major role in forcing Vincent's resignation as commissioner.

Although few teams report large profits in any season, the owners recognize a good business proposition. Lucrative tax benefits make franchise ownership quite desirable; among other things, owners can, incredible as it seems, actually depreciate the value of their players as they grow older. Although most teams report only small annual profits or losses, the value of the franchises grows rapidly. While the value of a professional baseball, football, hockey, or basketball franchise in the early 1960s seldom exceeded $5 million, thirty years later they are valued between $50 and $150 million. Those special few located in the largest media markets are estimated to be worth up to $200 million. In 1992 a consortium of local businessmen purchased the Seattle Mariners for $106 million; the Mariners, located in one of the smallest media markets, could boast of only one winning season in their fourteen-year history.

Although financial considerations figure in each owner's motivation, many demonstrate an obsession with winning championships. Because these highly competitive businesspeople have seldom encountered major setbacks in their business careers, some have great difficulty dealing with losing seasons. That only one team could win the World Series, the NBA championship, or the Super Bowl means they become frustrated—they are paying astronomically high payrolls and still not winning! That frustration often leads to continued turnover in coaches, managers, and players—a practice George Steinbrenner turned into a new art form with the Yankees. During his tenure as president of the Yankees he hired and fired eighteen managers, including the talented but explosive Billy Martin five separate times. Others, however, apparently care very little about the won-lost records of their teams, being content to reap the tax benefits and watch the value of their franchises grow.

The escalation in the value of professional sports franchises derives primarily from the enormous increase in the popularity of professional sports that television creates. Although franchises rely heavily on the sale of tickets and ancillary income derived from the sale of team paraphernalia, parking fees, food and beverage concessions, and the like, revenues generated from the sale of television rights fuel the economic boom in professional sports. Although astronomical players' salaries draw criticism, few fans really much care. Some critics raise the obvious questions about America's value system—how could a player who has barely graduated from high school command a multi-million-dollar contract when a dedicated public school teacher or a nurse seldom earns more than $30,000? Even the salary of the president of the United States is no more than that of a lowly utility infielder or a backup offensive lineman. Most sports fans, however, apparently care little about such issues as long as their teams continue to play and their games appear regularly on their television screens.

Ever since the escalation of salaries began in the 1960s sports executives have predicted the destruction of professional sports by high salaries. But they have cried wolf so often that no one takes them seriously. Thus when a good, but certainly not great, pitcher, David Cone of the Mets, won a salary arbitration in 1992 that granted him a contract of $4.25 million for the season, the news scarcely made the front pages of the sports pages; a few days later the Texas Rangers lost an arbitration hearing with outfielder Reuben Sierra, who had a most pedestrian five-year major league batting average of .273, but was awarded an annual salary of $5 million. Defenders of such pay levels contend that professional boxers earn much more—champions like Mike Tyson or Sugar Ray Leonard commanding $20 million or more for just one fight. Defenders argue that the salaries of sports' greatest performers pale in comparison with the incomes earned by movie stars or rock music performers. Others are quick to point out that the income of professional athletes lasts only a few years—the average career of a professional football player, for example, is less than four years. While some critics assail the high salaries, others contend they are merely the natural result of a free market.

Whether professional sports salaries can continue to climb remains uncertain. With television revenues providing the major source of rising salaries, many observers predict serious problems in the mid-1990s when existing television contracts expire. Flat or even declining television ratings have prompted many to predict that network and cable television bids will come in substantially below previous levels, thereby creating a financial bind for many franchises. Baseball, especially, seems vulnerable, with its television contracts with CBS and ESPN and its basic agreement with its players both scheduled to expire at the end of the 1993 season. One baseball executive predicted that "Armageddon" lurks just over the horizon. Does yet another lengthy and acrimonious strike loom in baseball's future?

Urban Rivalry and the Quest for Major League Status

Without much fanfare, professional sports has become an integral part of urban economic policy. Urban political and business leaders see an immediate economic benefit from the teams because they generate substantial tourist business. The Kansas City Royals, for example, routinely attract fans from the vast expanses of Kansas, Oklahoma, and Nebraska. The Cincinnati Reds boast that more than one-half of their 2.5 million spectators each year come substantial distances to visit the Queen City. Reds fans regularly journey from Tennessee, West Virginia, Kentucky, and distant parts of Ohio; during their visits they spend substantial sums in Cincinnati restaurants, hotels, and shopping malls, as well as at Riverfront Stadium. Economic development officials also view professional sports franchises as providing an important part of their arsenal in the serious job of attracting new business. It has become a matter of pride to boast of the number of "major league" teams a metropolitan area supports. Obtaining and keeping professional sports franchises has become an important part of the ongoing rivalry between major metropolitan areas.

Consequently, business executives and political leaders have become deeply involved in lobbying a league to obtain a franchise. It is not uncommon for mayors, governors, and congressional delegations to join with chambers of commerce in the quest for a major league team. In 1966 the NFL granted New Orleans a new franchise shortly after Louisiana senator Russell Long and congressman Hale Boggs played major roles in passing legislation excluding the NFL from antitrust laws in its merger with the American Football League (AFL). The *New York Times* reported that Commissioner Pete Rozelle "dangled an NFL expansion team for New Orleans" before these powerful politicians in return for the exemption. In the early 1980s Governor Bruce Babbitt led a determined group of Arizonans in pursuit of an NFL franchise, eventually luring the St. Louis Cardinals to Phoenix with an attractive package of financial incentives.

The boom in urban population unleashed by World War II created a fierce competition for professional franchises. Contrary to popular myth, the population of the older metropolitan centers of the upper Midwest and East Coast continued to grow during the postwar period. To be certain, many rust belt core cities stopped growing or even lost population, but increases in their suburbs produced impressive overall growth rates for the metropolitan areas. Such cities as Philadelphia, Pittsburgh, Chicago, Cincinnati, New York, Baltimore, and St. Louis suffered large population declines between 1950 and 1990, but growth in the suburbs more than offset the losses within the core city. The explosive growth of the sun belt cities, however, attracted the greatest attention. Warmer winter temperatures coupled with rapidly expanding economies lured millions of transients from the north, many of them relatively affluent retired citizens. Improved air conditioning technology made summers quite tolerable. By the 1960s such rapidly growing cities as Phoenix, New Orleans, Miami, Houston, Memphis, San Antonio, Tampa, St. Petersburg, San Diego, and Dallas had established themselves as important economic and political urban centers, and consequently became leading aspirants for major sports franchises as a symbol of their new "big league" urban status.

The various professional leagues responded by expanding into the south and west. The controversial relocation of two baseball teams from New York City to San Francisco and Los Angeles in 1958 set the process in motion. Over the ensuing three decades teams located in Kansas City, Oakland, Atlanta, San Diego, Seattle, Houston, Dallas-Ft. Worth, Denver, and Miami. During the 1960s Dallas, Atlanta, and New Orleans gained admission to the NFL, while the merger with the AFL added teams in several sun belt cities. St. Louis lost its NFL franchise to Phoenix in 1988. Similarly, the NBA either granted new franchises or absorbed teams from the disbanded American Basketball Association (ABA), leading to the location of teams in San Antonio, Seattle, Portland, Charlotte, San Francisco, Phoenix, Miami, and Orlando. Even hockey invaded the sun belt, with the expansion franchise Los Angeles Kings demonstrating the sport could attract a large fan base in a warm climate. In 1991 the nation's twelfth largest city, San Jose, having long chafed within the glamorous shadow of San Francisco, celebrated having surpassed it in population with the acquisition of a major league franchise, the Sharks of the National Hockey League. Defying traditional logic, subtropical Miami also welcomed a franchise in the NHL in 1993.

Not every city could acquire its own prime major league franchise, however, and consequently several new professional leagues made their appearance. The results were uneven. These new leagues invariably set off bidding wars for star players, thus intensifying upward pressure on players' salaries. Like the AFL in 1960, these new leagues were based on the assumption that television revenues would be forthcoming. The ABA, featuring such innovations as the three-point shot and a red, white, and blue basketball, and with the legendary George Mikan as commissioner, steadfastly persisted through a whirlwind of franchise changes for nine seasons before folding in 1976. While it lasted the league featured such outstanding performers as Julius ("Dr. J") Erving,

Moses Malone, Rick Barry, Billy Cunningham, and Dan Issel. The ABA also created headlines when it lured several of the NBA's top referees to jump to the new league for a bonus of $25,000 and substantial increases in salary (sometimes more than $15,000 a season); the presence of such well-known officials as John Vanak, Norm Drucker, Earl Strom, and Jack Madden on the floor gave the ABA instant credibility with serious basketball fans. Despite many valiant efforts, the ABA failed to secure an adequate television contract and was doomed to failure. In 1977 the NBA, having tired of salary wars for premier players with the upstart league, absorbed the league's strongest franchises (Denver, San Antonio, San Diego, and Indianapolis), while teams with such interesting nicknames as the Virginia Squires, St. Louis Spirits, Kentucky Colonels, New Orleans Buccaneers, and Pittsburgh Condors became the property of sports trivia buffs.

The founder of the innovative and interesting ABA was an intensely competitive young businessman from Los Angeles, Gary Davidson. Although his basketball league foundered, he himself made a small fortune. This financial success prompted him in 1974 to launch another new league, the World Football League; he quickly peddled a dozen franchises to willing investors. Although the league created a big publicity stir when it signed several established NFL players to large salaries, it failed to land the golden television contract and folded after two desultory seasons. Davidson had also founded the World Hockey League in 1971 with the dramatic signing of one of hockey's all-time greats, Bobby Hull, to a $2.75 million contract. The instant credibility that this dramatic move created enabled the new league to survive for several seasons; eventually the NHL absorbed four of its teams (Quebec, Winnipeg, Edmonton, and Hartford).

A similar fate befell yet another effort to found a new professional football league in the mid-1980s. The United States Football League (USFL) sought to attract television audiences by playing its games in the spring, but the ratings were so low that the league folded after just two seasons. It did stimulate salary increases within the NFL when such top college players as Herschel Walker signed with the new league. Walker received $4 million from the flamboyant financier Donald Trump to play for the New Jersey Stars. Walker's salary at the time was a blockbuster, but even more significant was the fact that he had signed a professional contract with one year's eligibility left at the University of Georgia. Having long used the colleges as a surrogate minor league system, the NFL had resolutely refused to raid colleges for their undergraduate talent. In the wake of Walker's shocking decision, the NFL recognized it had no legal basis on which to deny a college undergraduate the right to play professional football. Within a few years many of the league's top draft choices were underclassmen, much to the anger of college coaches and the NCAA. Eclipsing the shock of the signing of underclassman Herschel Walker was the incredible $40 million multiyear contract given to Brigham Young University's star quarterback Steve Young by the USFL's Los Angeles Express. Young's signing demonstrated to eager player agents new possibilities in packaging large salaries via the use of deferred payments, annuities, and other creative forms of financing.

Many other professional leagues made their appearance, some of them quite creative. For several years, two rival professional soccer teams languished on the fringes of the sports scene, never being able to attract an adequate fan base. A similar desultory fan response greeted an effort to launch a summer indoor "arena football" league. In the 1970s promoters sought to cash in on the current national tennis craze and established a team tennis league, featuring both male and female professional players. Teams with such exotic names as the Phoenix Racquets, the Boston Lobsters, and the Los Angeles Strings volleyed away in near oblivion for seven seasons before the league folded, unlamented and quickly forgotten.

The major impact of the surge in interest in sports was the expansion of the number of "major league" franchises. Baseball increased from sixteen teams in 1960 to twenty-eight in 1993. The NFL had only twelve teams in 1960, but grew to twenty-eight teams by 1976 when it granted franchises to Seattle and Tampa. The once eight-team NBA expanded to twenty-seven franchises by 1992. Three of its most recent additions were predictably located in the sun belt—Miami, Orlando, and Charlotte—with the other franchise given to Minneapolis-St. Paul, perhaps in compensation for the Twin Cities' loss of their beloved Lakers to Los Angeles in 1962.

Civic pride seems to be a fundamental factor in a city's desire to acquire a franchise. Cost seldom seems to be a major hurdle. Many city or county governments have to underwrite the cost of constructing an expensive arena or stadium as but one price of civic boosterism. With a few exceptions where private dollars pay most costs (e.g., Dodger Stadium and the Great Western Forum in Los Angeles, and Joe Robbie Stadium in suburban Miami), taxpayers in one way or another shoulder most of the expense. Some cities couple their plans to revitalize their inner cities with the building of modern athletic facilities. Oakland built a 15,000-seat basketball arena and a 45,000-seat baseball stadium in the 1960s as part of a slum clearance project. During that same decade Cincinnati, Atlanta, Philadelphia, and Pittsburgh constructed multipurpose stadiums in their inner cities to accommodate both their football and baseball teams. Houston, New Orleans, Minneapolis, and Seattle went one step further by building covered, or "domed," facilities big enough to accommodate both football and baseball indoors.

Indianapolis decided to forgo the large dimensions required by baseball when it constructed its Hoosier Dome as the centerpiece of a major downtown revitalization project. In 1984 following a bizarre series of secret deliberations, Indianapolis succeeded in luring the football Colts from Baltimore. After several years of confrontational negotiations with the political leadership of Baltimore and the state of Maryland regarding the construction of a new public stadium, Colts owner Robert Irsay surreptitiously loaded all of his team's equipment and records onto moving vans and departed for the Midwest in the dark of night. Only after the vans had cleared the Maryland state line did Indianapolis mayor William Hudnut proudly announce that the Hoosier Dome had secured an NFL tenant. The mayor of Baltimore, who had negotiated in good faith with the unpredictable Irsay, sadly condemned the move as "the final humiliation."

Determined not to lose its baseball team as well, the good citizens of Baltimore supported the construction of a new baseball park to replace antiquated Memorial Stadium. In 1992 the Baltimore Orioles opened the baseball season in its new Orioles Stadium at Camden Yards. City leaders viewed Camden Yards as a crucial part of their inner-city economic revitalization program. Unlike the drab, impersonal facilities built in the 1960s (classic examples are Cincinnati's Riverfront Stadium and New York's Shea Stadium), Baltimore's planners sought to recapture the nostalgia of an earlier baseball era by modeling their new ballpark on the venerable Wrigley Field in Chicago. The traditional ambience created at Camden Yards delighted baseball fans, although critics condemned the use of public funds to provide a facility for a privately owned team.

Baltimore officials also sought to avoid the planning mistakes made in many cities when new stadiums are built. They tried to make the architectural style of the stadium compatible with the surrounding neighborhood and to incorporate restaurants, hotels, and shopping areas within the overall plan. They also planned to utilize public transit systems. Because many of the facilities built during the 1960s and 1970s were located hard by major expressways, most spectators arrived by automobile and quickly retreated to the suburbs when the games were over. These facilities thus did little to stimulate the economic rebirth of the inner cities. Instead, critics angrily pointed to the neighborhoods and housing that were destroyed to make way for the new facilities. The anger of the Hispanic community, which saw thousands of people forcibly removed from their homes in Chavez Ravine in the late 1950s to make way for the construction of privately owned Dodger Stadium, remains a simmering point of contention in the City of Angels more than three decades later. Similarly, entire neighborhoods were destroyed in south central Atlanta when its stadium and associated urban renewal and freeway construction led to the removal of low-income black residents.

In other metropolitan centers, planners decided to abandon the inner city, capitulating to the powerful centrifugal pressures the expanding suburbs created. In Detroit, a city dedicated to the primacy of the automobile, planners opted to build the Silver Dome for the football Lions and the Palace for the basketball Pistons more than 30 miles from the metropolitan core along major freeways. The earlier failure of downtown Cobo Arena and the stylish Renaissance Center to reverse the decline of the central city made their decision to move to the affluent (and predominately white) suburbs an easy choice. This pattern was first established in 1959 when San Francisco's leaders located Candlestick Park on a landfill near San Francisco Bay several miles south of the city's core. Complex political considerations, compounded by poor planning, meant this 60,000-seat stadium would become legendary for its brutal chilling winds that move in off the water. In one memorable incident in the 1962 all-star game, a particularly sturdy gust blew Stu Miller off the pitcher's mound. With the construction of the Meadowlands complex across the Hudson River, the football New York Giants and Jets actually play in suburban New Jersey. In 1971 voters of Kansas City and Jackson County, euphoric over the Chiefs' upset victory in Super Bowl IV, voted to support the issuance of bonds to construct the Harry S. Truman Sports Complex in suburban Independence. The result is a 72,000-seat football stadium for the Chiefs and a separate 43,000-seat baseball park for the Royals, located at the confluence of two freeways some 15 miles east of downtown Kansas City.

Wherever they might be located, however, these facilities have become a source of community pride (with Candlestick Park perhaps a major exception) because they reflect the major league status of the metropolitan area. Few politicians dare openly oppose their construction for fear of incurring the wrath of the business elite that has its eye on the tourist dollar and the potential of luring new employers to a major league city. To be certain, in a few instances voters have rebelled, the most notable example being the defeat of four separate ballot measures to build a new park for the Giants. Much more typical and instructive of the use of sports as a means of urban promotion was the decision of the Florida community of St. Petersburg to construct a domed facility in the mid-1980s in hopes of attracting a major league football or baseball team. More than once it appeared that St. Petersburg's gamble would pay off. The Chicago White Sox, saddled with an antiquated stadium built in 1910, were sorely tempted, but a last-minute decision in 1989 by city and state governments to construct a new Comiskey Park prevented the departure of the team to Florida. Illinois business and political leaders, convinced the loss of a major league team would do severe damage, came to the rescue—with taxpayers' dollars—to save the franchise for the Windy City. In 1992 only desperate maneuvering led by grocery store magnate Peter Magowan of San Francisco prevented the move of the Giants to the Sun Dome. In response, the leaders of oft-spurned St. Petersburg contemplated taking their frustrations to federal court.

Conclusion

By now it seems that events in the boardrooms often overshadow those on the field. Sports has become big business in every sense of the word. The Boston Celtics' stock trades on national exchanges. The always dubious enterprise of city politics has become inextricably linked to the fate of local teams. Major corporations operate sports franchises as but one part of their conglomerate operations. The economic changes have come so fast and have been so pervasive, the casual fan often feels bewildered. It seems that hard-driving player-agents, skillful lawyers, labor negotiators, hard-nosed owners, and millionaire players now dominate the world of sport. Sportswriters find themselves writing less about the outcome of games and more about salary negotiations, player holdouts, arbitration disputes, season-threatening strikes, and stadium construction bond elections. Players salaries have become so high, many predict alienation of the traditional sports fan, a development that has never occurred but remains a distinct possibility. Sports in America has, indeed, become big business.

Billie Jean King is recognized as one of the greats of professional tennis, but her lasting legacy is that of a leader in the struggle against discrimination.

Chapter
6

Women and American Sports

It was one of the most bizarre moments in the history of American sports. A festive circuslike atmosphere pervaded the Houston Astrodome that September evening of 1973. Several midgets, dressed as teddy bears, skipped around the court and a bevy of cheerleaders shook their pompons to the rock music of "Jesus Christ Superstar." These distractions, however, could not mask that a great deal was at stake. A crowd of 35,000 had assembled to witness the much ballyhooed "battle of the sexes"—a tennis match between onetime U.S. Open men's champion Bobby Riggs and the current top-ranked woman player, Billie Jean King. Another 50 million people watched the match on television with Howard Cosell describing the action in grandiloquent fashion; Roone Arledge was not about to ignore the commercial potential of this unlikely but compelling drama.

Billie Jean King had wanted to avoid this match, but the irrepressible Bobby Riggs had given her no easy way out. Now fifty-five years old, with his skills declining, he continued to make a good living playing exhibition matches, often winning large side bets from his opponents and their supporters. A master of self-promotion and given to the outrageous, Riggs had shrewdly parlayed his few years as a top-ranked player at the onset of World War II into a continuing sideshow that enabled him to attract a following—and plenty of attendant publicity. No longer able to hit the ball with power, he relied on the considerable bag of tricks he had assembled over the years—back-spin drop shots, sharp angle returns of serves, well-placed lobs, tricky serves, and, especially, a canny ability to exploit any weakness in his opponent's game. When a large wager or a "winner take all" prize was on the line, he became a ferocious competitor. At such times he called on his most potent of weapons—his ability to distract his opponent and make him lose concentration. Riggs had essentially turned his ability to defeat younger, often more skilled opponents in pressurized matches into a high art form. He was the ultimate tennis hustler and he reveled in that reputation.

Never one to overlook a new angle, he had seized on the "women's liberation" movement as a new opportunity to be exploited. By the early 1970s the movement had hit full stride. Betty Friedan's myth-shattering book, *The Feminine Mystique* (1963), had touched a raw nerve among middle- and upper-middle-class women. Focusing on a widespread malaise among American women —"the problem that has no name"—Friedan described the frustrations that millions of women felt in lives devoted to the traditional roles of mother, wife, and homemaker. Just as racial minorities had mounted the civil rights movement to overthrow the bonds that tied them to a second-class citizenship, millions of American women had responded to the call for an assertion of the rights of women to pursue their dreams. In 1964 Congress amended the Civil Rights Act at the last minute to include provisions prohibiting sexual discrimination. When early efforts to implement this provision proved futile, women leaders banded together to create the National Organization of Women (NOW) and began to apply pressure at the local, state, and national levels. Among their major goals was adoption of the Equal Rights Amendment to the Constitution.

The women's movement, however, produced a substantial backlash, and within this context Riggs launched his most audacious hustle of all. He proudly proclaimed himself "the undisputed number-one male chauvinist in the world," and decreed that "a woman's place is in the bedroom and the kitchen, in that order." In the spring of 1973 he succeeded in luring one of the world's top-ranked women players, Margaret Court of Australia, to play him for a winner take all $10,000 put up by California promoters. Riggs envisioned the match as a means of spoofing women's tennis, of drawing considerable publicity to himself, and, of course, of making a cool ten grand in one afternoon . . . all of which he proceeded to do. If a fifty-five-year-old man could defeat one of the best women players, he and his supporters reasoned, it would indicate that demands by women professionals for more equitable treatment from the United States Tennis Association (USTA) lacked merit. When Court appeared for the match, the irrepressible Riggs presented her with a large bouquet of roses, a gesture that served its intended purpose of rattling his opponent. Riggs easily dispatched the nervous Australian in straight sets, much to the despair of women's rights advocates everywhere, especially Billie Jean King.

Having attracted considerable attention by his match with Margaret Court, Riggs proceeded to bait his trap for King. She had initially rejected his challenge, but in the wake of Court's humiliating defeat, King felt she had to respond. She made an ideal target for Riggs's chauvinistic showmanship. An aggressive, talented player, King had already won two U.S. Open singles titles and an amazing five Wimbledon singles championships. Equally tantalizing to Riggs, she had become a leading spokeswoman seeking equal treatment for women on the professional tour in terms of better locker room facilities, larger travel expenses, increased commercial endorsements, more opportunities to play key matches on center court, and equitable prize money. Her "women's lob" campaign had emphasized that the USTA was controlled by a group of "good old boys" who viewed and treated women's tennis as a second-rate bore, something to be tolerated but definitely not supported on a basis equal with the men.

Articulate and outspoken, Billie Jean King was described by *Time* magazine as "the personification of the professional female athlete that Riggs loves to taunt." The previous year King had achieved a major milestone in women's tennis when she won more than $100,000 in one season; because of low purses, she had to play in an unusually high number of tournaments (twenty-nine) to do so. That same year the men's top money winner, Australian Rod Laver, pocketed $290,000 while playing in only ten tournaments. Demonstrating that her feminist views extended beyond the lines of the tennis court, King shocked many by announcing she had undergone an abortion. Thus, at the time that Riggs issued his shrill challenge, women's tennis was just beginning to address long-existing discrimination. King feared if Riggs's challenge went unanswered, women's hard-earned gains might be lost. She also recognized that a loss to Riggs might set back the movement even more. And, of course, she saw a great opportunity to deflate a posturing windbag. When she agreed to play the match, Riggs chortled, "King doesn't stand a chance against me. Women's tennis is so far beneath men's tennis. That's what makes the contest with a fifty-five-year-old man the greatest contest of all time."

Newsweek correctly observed that the irrepressible Riggs had positioned himself as "the very model of male chauvinist self-confidence." Riggs told one news source, "Hell, we know there is no way she can beat me. She's a stronger athlete than me and she can execute various shots better than me. But when the pressure mounts and she thinks about fifty million people watching on TV, she'll fold. That's the way women are."

As prematch hype intensified, King refused to respond to Riggs's boorish taunting. While he made the rounds of the bars and parties in Houston, she put in hours of daily practice against male partners who sought to simulate the types of shots Riggs might attempt. The match aroused intense interest across the United States. Millions of dollars were bet on the outcome, much of it between men and women. Riggs's promotional genius had turned the match into a larger-than-life event that brought into sharp focus the many disparate emotions that the women's movement had unleashed.

The journalist Curry Kirkpatrick aptly described the atmosphere in the Astrodome on the evening of September 20, 1973, as having "all the conflicting tones of a political convention, championship prize fight, rock festival, tent revival, town meeting, Super Bowl and sick joke." Consistent with the garish atmosphere, the contestants arrived on the court in outlandish fashion, Riggs riding in a rickshaw with gold wheels pulled by several lovely, scantily clad women he called his "bosom buddies," King riding on an ornate litter borne by muscular bare-chested gladiators wearing costumes suggestive of ancient Egypt.

Much to the delight of women everywhere, King took control of the match early on. She smashed her opponent's tantalizing high lobs for winners, calmly put away his twisting drop shots with well-placed returns, and relentlessly ran her older opponent from one side of the court to another. Unlike most women players of that era, who preferred to play from the baseline, she aggressively attacked the net, cutting off Riggs's passing shots with crisp deep volleys he could not return. Playing with controlled ferocity, King dominated and then humiliated her crestfallen opponent. Midway through the first set it became apparent Riggs was a beaten man; he even demonstrated an uncharacteristic nervousness and appeared to be tired and uninspired. He glumly recognized he was facing a much superior player and his notorious efforts to "psych" her had failed completely. "Seldom has there been a more classic example of a skilled athlete performing at peak efficiency in the most important moment of her life," an admiring Kirkpatrick wrote. King decisively won the match in three straight sets and, much to Riggs's dismay, walked away with the purse of $100,000. Delighted feminist leader Gloria Steinem later recalled: "On college campuses women were hanging out of their dorm windows celebrating. The match had enormous symbolic importance." King herself perhaps summarized it best: "It helped women stand taller."

Indeed it did. But for Billy Jean King it amounted to merely one more step in her crusade to achieve equal treatment and greater opportunity for women athletes. Unlike many tennis players of her time, she did not come from the upper ranks of the American social order. Born in 1943 to working-class parents in Long Beach, California, her father a fireman, her mother a homemaker, Billie Jean Moffitt had always been a talented and determined athlete. When her father informed her at an early age that her passion for playing baseball would lead nowhere, she turned to tennis and soon became a leading player in southern California. At age fourteen, after receiving excellent coaching and encouragement from a local professional who taught at a public court, she told her disbelieving father she intended to become "the best tennis player in the world." Within a few years she proceeded to do exactly that. At age sixteen she became a nationally ranked juniors player.

After receiving intensive coaching from one of the great prewar women players, Alice Marble, Billie Jean won her first singles match at Wimbledon at age eighteen. By the time she enrolled at Los Angeles State University in 1961 she already ranked among the world's top ten women players—although that ranking did not entitle her to receive any scholarship assistance while playing for the school's women's tennis team. In contrast, her boyfriend (and soon to become husband) Larry King received a "full ride" as the seventh man on the six-member men's team. As she wrote in her autobiography in 1982, "We forget now, but it's only been in the last decade that women started getting athletic scholarships!" While husband Larry pursued a law degree in the mid-1960s, King underwent intensive work to improve her tennis game in order to make a run at the major championships. Armed with a new grip and more efficient strokes, coupled with her aggressive style, she quickly moved to the top of her profession. She lost in the Forest Hills (U.S. Open) finals in 1965, but the following year won the Wimbledon singles title, the first of an incredible twenty singles and doubles titles she would capture at the All-English Club before her retirement in 1983. Throughout the 1970s she continued to win her share of major tournaments, her intense matches with the superbly talented teenage prodigy Chris Evert doing much to stimulate interest in women's tennis. Despite severe knee injuries, which led to five major surgeries, she remained at or near the top of the tennis world until she reached her late thirties. By the time she retired she had won an incredible thirty-nine Grand Slam singles, doubles, and mixed-doubles crowns.

These achievements notwithstanding, Billie Jean King refused to be satisfied. As she compared the treatment of women tennis professionals with that of the men, her competitive fires blazed. The fact that women played for tournament prize money seldom approaching one-fourth that available to the men grated on her sense of fairness. She first publicly protested when she received just $1,500 for winning the Italian Open in 1970, while the male champion walked away with $12,500. In 1972 she received $10,000 for winning the U.S. Open while men's champion, Ilie Nastase, earned $25,000. She received just $4,800 for winning Wimbledon, but men's singles champ Stan Smith cashed a check for $12,500. Her stinging criticism of such blatant discrimination, however, startled the staid tennis establishment. She even had the temerity to suggest that a boycott might be in order.

Determined to end such disparities, King did not let rebuffs from the male-dominated tennis hierarchy curtail her campaign. Despite much opposition, including substantial resistance from fearful women on the tour, she succeeded in establishing the Women's Tennis Association in 1973 as a lobbying and negotiating organization. Her persistence and hard work contributed greatly to a separate women's professional tournament circuit; this new environment quickly helped produce better prize money and improved playing conditions. Neither shy nor unwilling to challenge the tennis establishment, King pushed forward the frontiers of professional tennis. Interestingly, one of the WTA's first advertisements referred to the women players as "ballbusters." The prize money gap soon closed, and in a symbolically important change, the USTA announced that it would offer equal prize money in the 1973 U.S. Open. In that same year King led a small group of women to secure funding for the Virginia Slims Tour (although she and other athletes had to overcome their qualms about receiving sponsorship from cigarette manufacturer Philip Morris Corporation). King and her lawyer-entrepreneur husband played key roles in establishing the World Team Tennis League, which featured men and women playing as equals on a team. Throughout her career she continued her crusade, founding *womenSports* magazine in 1974 to encourage females to participate in all sports.

King's pioneering efforts did not return to her the enormous financial rewards that would accrue to the top players who came after her. In 1973, the year of her watershed match with Riggs, the total prize money won by women players totaled $900,000. In 1992 it exceeded $25 million. She also received relatively small fees from endorsements. Whereas she earned an estimated $2 million throughout her tennis career, which spanned four decades, eighteen-year-old Monica Seles earned an estimated $7.5 millon in prize money and commercial endorsements in the single year of 1991.

Billie Jean King's career, both on and off the court, epitomized the emergence of women's athletics during the 1970s. By the end of the decade women had made great strides in such individual sports as tennis, golf, track and field, and swimming. And growing public awareness and political pressure regarding the discrimination against female athletes led to important advances in team sports—volleyball, basketball, and softball—as public schools and colleges and universities, however reluctantly, began to field teams.

King's unexpected announcement in May 1981 that she had had a seven-year lesbian relationship with her secretary and travel companion stunned the sports world. The issue of homosexuality had long lurked beneath the surface of the American sports world, reflecting attitudes prevalent in society. At this time homosexuals only rarely came out of the closet voluntarily; to do so would expose the individual to severe social and economic consequences. The reluctance to announce one's homosexuality was especially pronounced among athletes because of the strong biases that existed in traditionally conservative sports circles. Allegations that many women athletes were "masculine" and otherwise sexually aberrant had percolated in the rumor mills for decades; opponents of women's sports programs frequently exploited antihomosexual sentiment. Thus it is not surprising that when King's disaffected lover brought a "galimony" suit in a California state court seeking a substantial financial settlement, King initially denied the charges as "untrue and unfounded."

Two days later, however, she changed her story. Appearing before a hushed Los Angeles news conference, her supportive husband Larry at her side and her "stone-faced" parents in the front row, King acknowledged that she and Marilyn Barnett had had a long-term relationship that began in 1973 and had ended only in late 1979. She admitted she had permitted Barnett to live for six years in a $550,000 Malibu home owned by the Kings. A contrite Billie Jean King confessed, "I made a mistake and I will assume the responsibility for it. I only hope the fans will have compassion and understanding." King related that she had first met Barnett as a hairdresser, but she had invited her to become her personal secretary and to accompany her on the tour to take care of travel and living details. About six months later, Barnett alleged in her suit, she and the tennis star began "an intense relationship" that included "sexual intimacy." Her suit contended that she had about one hundred very personal letters from King in her possession, along with records of joint credit cards. Her suit demanded an income "commensurate with the lifestyle of King" based on verbal financial commitments she claimed were made to her.

Although King told the press conference, "The issue is not about money, it is about self-esteem," most observers disagreed. Barnett's civil suit asked for possession of the Malibu house and one-half of all King's earnings from 1973 through 1979, estimated to be well over a million dollars. Equally important, because of publicity surrounding the case, King faced the possible loss of what had become a substantial income from commercial product endorsements. Women sports leaders feared that the episode would confirm the persistent and widespread rumors about the sexual preference of female athletes, thereby irreparably damaging the advances in sports being made by women. But although the initial news made headlines everywhere, most sports fans continued their support of King. Prominent sportswriter

Pete Axthelm even suggested that because she had acted so forthrightly, the episode contributed to better understanding and greater tolerance of homosexuality. She did lose several sponsors within the next several months, including a lucrative contract with Avon Products to the tune of an estimated $1.5 million, but several other sponsors remained steadfast in her support; perhaps most significantly, NBC television did not remove her as a commentator on its high-profile broadcasts from Wimbledon. Most sports fans applauded King's courage and candor, and the issue soon subsided. In December 1981 King triumphed in a Los Angeles court when the judge denied Barnett's claims. In his decision Judge Julius M. Title denounced the plaintiff for "unconscionable conduct" in using the personal letters as "an express or implied threat of adverse publicity." He concluded with the harsh statement, "If that isn't an attempted extortion, it certainly comes close to it."

Ten years later, King enjoyed the status of an all-time great athlete and was engaged in a series of business ventures. The Marilyn Barnett affair had faded from memory. King had also made a major contribution to the popularity of the sport of tennis and to women's role in it: "Tennis had always been reserved for the rich, the white, the male—and I've always been pledged to change all that," she said. Although she had not planned it that way, she had also contributed to the demystification of homosexuality in America. She had served to reduce negative stereotypes to encourage a more complete understanding of the complexities of human relationships. In return the sports world demonstrated a new level of compassion and maturity. A decade later, when tennis star Martina Navratilova was hit with a similar lawsuit, it received only passing media attention.

Women Challenge Discrimination and Prejudice

About the same time Billie Jean King demolished Bobby Riggs and the myths on which his hustle rested, the third baseman for a woman's softball team in Connecticut told a reporter,

When I was growing up, I was better than all the boys in my neighborhood in any sport—baseball, basketball, even ice hockey. Oh, I could join their games in the park, but I couldn't play Little League baseball. Yes, I feel deprived. Lots of girls were deprived of sports as an outlet in those days. It's funny—a father would never think of telling his daughter to deliberately flunk a test in school, yet he'd discourage her from playing sports too seriously. People should never try to discourage you from something you're good at. If your body is something you can do things with on a sports field, then you should be allowed to.

Softball star Irene Shea's frustration aptly summarized the feelings of many American sportswomen at the beginning of the 1970s. The great majority of public schools and colleges and universities offered no competitive athletic programs for female students. Most did not even offer intramural sports. Conventional wisdom not only relegated women to the roles of mother, wife, and homemaker but also decreed an environment for young girls that would prepare them for their intended adult roles. This meant playing house, tending to dolls, and learning how to cook and sew. Girls who demonstrated athletic skills and the type of competitiveness encouraged in boys were judged by the negative stereotype of "tomboy." By the early 1970s, the women's rights movement began to intensify questioning of traditional stereotypes, building on the contributions of women, which began as early as the mid-1800s.

As the career of Billie Jean King demonstrates, it did not take long for the women's movement to affect the world of sports. The movement provided a new climate in which even the most reactionary of males felt compelled to respond to the demands for change. Those who controlled athletics at all levels grudgingly opened the doors for women's participation, under the very real threat of punitive action by the federal government. In particular, after many years of open sexist hostility and untold numbers of dire predictions about the bankruptcy of athletic budgets, they eventually had no choice but to fund women's programs. Title IX of the Education Act of 1972 stipulated that no individual "shall, on the basis of sex, be excluded from participation in, be denied the benefits of, or be subjected to discrimination under any educational programs or activities receiving federal financial assistance."

Passage of Title IX sparked an unusually quick and hostile response from the male-dominated athletic establishment. Father Edmund

Joyce of Notre Dame University, one of the leading power brokers in the inner political circles of intercollegiate athletics, denounced the new law as "asinine," and the longtime autocratic executive director of the National Collegiate Athletic Association, Walter Byers, angrily denounced Title IX as a vehicle of "impending doom." The NCAA lobbied Congress for exemptions for revenue-producing sports. Popular football coaches, Bear Bryant of Alabama and Barry Switzer of Oklahoma, traveled to the White House in 1975 to inform President Gerald Ford, himself a former gridiron star as a Michigan undergraduate, that the legislation would seriously damage their sport. When such efforts proved futile, the battle was joined at the level of the Department of Education, the federal agency charged with interpreting and enforcing the law.

Much of the ensuing debate revolved around how the Department of Education should interpret the law as it applied to high school and college athletic programs. No one disputed that the department had the ultimate power to withhold federal funding from an institution for noncompliance. Several conflicting viewpoints soon surfaced. A few sorry souls argued that compliance required women to compete on men's teams; jokes about women trying out for the Notre Dame football squad soon made the rounds, but a consensus calling for separate competition for men and women emerged out of the dialogue. Some spokespersons demanded that the total dollars budgeted for women had to equal that received by the men, which frightened the defenders of the high-cost sports of football and hockey. Others said the money should be dispersed based on total enrollment; if women constituted 60 percent of the student body, then 60 percent of the athletic budget should be assigned to women's sports. A more conservative position held that budgets should be determined on the basis of the percentage of participants—if 40 percent of a school's athletes were women, then they should receive 40 percent of the budget. Ultimately, after several years of study, the Department of Education in 1978 implemented a flexible position which held that women and men should have equal opportunity for participation and receive equitable funding, although controversy remained about how to include football within the equation. In the early 1990s the precise meaning of "gender equity" and how to achieve it in budgetary terms remained the most contentious issue in intercollegiate athletics.

The spate of conflict and controversy notwithstanding, passage and implementation of Title IX signaled a new era in American sports.

Despite setbacks and protracted delaying tactics by opponents, it represented a major victory for the advocates of equal rights and opportunities for females. At the time that Congress passed Title IX prevalent attitudes and value systems constituted an almost insurmountable set of obstacles to meaningful athletic competition for females. Although some meaningful girls' athletics programs continued to exist following draconian budget cuts during the Great Depression, they were very limited in size and scope. The notable exception to this rule existed in Iowa, where strong and popular girls' programs had existed since the 1950s. However, the overwhelming preponderance of American public schools did not offer competitive athletic programs for girls. Private schools did little better. Because most school systems ended compulsory physical education for girls at the eighth or ninth grades, they certainly could not be expected to fund interscholastic competition for girls. Most adults and educators apparently believed the place of girls at athletic events was on the sideline as cheerleader or drill team member, or as the cute homecoming queen presiding over the postgame dance. This same attitude also prevailed in the supposedly liberal climes of higher education.

These assigned roles grew out of the dominant perception of the role of girls and women in American society. Athletics were simply yet one more reflection of widely held sexual stereotypes long dominant in American life. "When I went to college in the 1930s," a woman physical education professor said, "we girls were taught that competition was dirty." Physical education experts also contended—erroneously to be certain—that regular physical exercise produced heavily muscled bodies. Popular myth held that if girls exercised too vigorously they would lose their femininity. But even the term *feminine*, used within this context, carried with it discriminatory overtones: "When we say 'feminine,'" psychologist David Auxter complained in 1972, "we mean submissive, a nonparticipant, an underachiever, a person who lacks a strong sense of identity, who has weak life goals and ambitions." That negative implication, which Auxter hoped to change, was perhaps most poignantly summarized by a Connecticut state judge in 1971, just one year before passage of Title IX. In dismissing a suit by a high school girl seeking the opportunity to try out for her high school's cross-country team, he intoned, "The present generation of our younger male population has not become so decadent that boys will experience a thrill in defeating girls in running contests, whether the girls be members of their own team or an adversary team. . . . Athletic competition builds character in our boys. We do not need that kind of character in our girls, the women of tomorrow."

Perhaps most damaging of all the negative attitudes surrounding women in sports was the malicious gossip that often dogged even the most attractive of female athletes—that rigorous physical exercise and training produced either an excessive heterosexual appetite or, conversely and much worse, homosexuality. A leading woman professional golfer of the 1970s, Jo Ann Prentice, complained that she and her fellow female athletes faced a catch-22 situation: "This is kind of how it is. If you get into town at the beginning of the week and you meet some guy whose company you enjoy and have dinner with him once or twice, the gossips start asking what kind of tramps are these babes on the tour. If you stay at a motel where everybody else on the tour has checked in, then the question is what are those girls doing back in those rooms alone?"

As a result of this mentality, most girls simply avoided sports and concentrated their energies on socially acceptable activities. They did not want to defy their nervous parents or the powerful influence of peer pressure. They did not want to seem unladylike. Their parents and teachers—and society at large—conveyed the strong message that girls who were athletic and competitive did not get asked to dances. Because so few girls made a serious commitment to competitive athletics in such a hostile environment, most parents and adult policymakers assumed that girls lacked any sustained interest in sports. As but one unfortunate consequence, a powerful myth held that girls lacked the physical coordination and strength to be successful in athletics.

Myths of this sort were nothing more than self-fulfilling prophecies. Owing to these pressures, girls did not spend much time perfecting their athletic abilities; because they received little, if any, encouragement from parents, teachers, and peers, they did not engage in the types of play that serves to develop athletes. Unlike their brothers, they did not receive the benefit of early coaching or the important psychological boost of parental encouragement. Few fathers ever thought about asking a daughter to toss a ball in the backyard or to shoot baskets, something they routinely did with their sons. Without the benefit of youth sports—however uneven the coaching might have been—by the time girls reached middle school age they had fallen woefully behind the boys in their athletic skills. Thus on those few occasions when they were called on to perform athletically, they appeared clumsy and awkward.

At its worse, popular mythology reinforced depressing perceptions of female athletes as sweaty, muscle-bound, man-hating women with hairy legs who flaunted their homosexuality. The venerable sports columnist Furman Bisher minced no words when confronted with demands for expanded sports programs for women: "What are we after, a race of Amazons? Do you want a companion or a broad that chews tobacco? What do you want for the darling daughter, a boudoir or a locker room full of cussing and bruises?"

In the wake of Title IX, however, such ridiculous, sexist images began to fall from public favor. Title IX stimulated a new sort of question: if sports do teach important values, such as dedication, the importance of practice and preparation, teamwork, goal setting, acceptance of authority, adherence to rules, sportsmanship, and performance under pressure—attributes generally believed to be conducive to successful adult lives and professional careers—then why should girls be denied such important opportunities? Such questions began to be asked more frequently by parents and educators. An educational psychologist at one of the nation's leading teacher training institutions, Slippery Rock State University, David Auxter placed the issue created by Title IX in a compelling context in a statement to *Time* magazine:

> We value athletics because they are competitive. That is, they teach that achievement and success are desirable, and that they are worth disciplining oneself for. By keeping girls out of sports, we have denied them this educational experience. Better athletic programs will develop more aggressive females, women with confidence, who value personal achievement and have a strong sense of identity. I think that would be a good thing for us all.

If sports provided young boys with lessons important to adulthood—teamwork, perseverance, preparation, competitiveness—then perhaps one of the reasons women had difficulty in establishing careers in business, critics contended, was their lack of athletic experience as youth.

The Federal Government Intervenes

Title IX came at a propitious time and the changes it wrought in the next two decades proved to be truly revolutionary. Although women athletic administrators of the 1990s can and do claim with justification that equality has yet to be achieved, the condition of women's athletics in the 1990s was truly a major improvement over what had existed two decades earlier. As they had for decades, public schools in 1972 virtually ignored girls when establishing athletic budgets, assigning facilities, and providing coaches. Most school districts throughout the United States simply offered no girls' sports programs at all; in an era when it was believed to be unfeminine to perspire, even the typical fifty-minute physical education classes were devoted primarily to dressing and showering. In those schools where limited interscholastic competition for girls did exist, the budgetary support lagged far behind that provided for boys. Even with the costly sport of football removed from the equation, allocation of funds remained hopelessly lopsided. Girls' coaches and game officials received far less than their male counterparts. In one example, the public schools of Syracuse, New York, in 1969 budgeted $90,000 for boys' programs, $2,000 for girls'; the following year budget problems forced a modest cut in the boys' sports programs of $3,000, but the girls' budget was completely eliminated. Discrimination extended beyond budgets; practice times on shared facilities—swimming pools, soccer fields, basketball courts—were skewed heavily in favor of the boys.

American colleges and universities at the time of the passage of Title IX provided a similarly depressing situation. At the University of Washington, for example, women's programs received a grand total of $18,000, less than 1 percent of the funding provided for the men. In five of the nation's most powerful conferences—the Big Ten, Southeastern, Big Eight, Southwest, and Pacific Athletic Conferences—less than fifty women received athletic scholarships; these same conferences provided five thousand "full ride" scholarships for football alone. At the college level the situation was no different; at Cortland State in New York, women's programs were budgeted for $18,000, the men for $84,000; Trenton State College in New Jersey provided its women just $15,000 of a total athletic budget of $85,000. Sexual discrimination even existed at Vassar, one of the nation's most prestigious traditional women's colleges. Just four years after it admitted its first male students in 1968, the men's athletic budget had grown to twice that provided for women.

With a few notable exceptions, the quality of coaching at all levels was also substandard. Most college women coaches were full-time physical education instructors, not professional coaches, and except for the handful of women's colleges, male athletic directors controlled the budgets. Only in 1971 did the leaders of women's athletics form a national body to direct their programs. Ironically, many of the myths and stereotypes that worked to the detriment of women's athletics found their way into the bylaws of the Association of Intercollegiate Athletics for Women (AIAW). This new organization reflected the thinking of its membership, primarily women's physical education instructors. The intent of AIAW did not seek to emulate the male model for intercollegiate athletics, but consciously sought to create a new model that would avoid some of the major flaws in men's athletics. It definitely did not create an organization to stimulate high-level intercollegiate competition. Its founders stressed their desire "to create an educationally sound and fiscally prudent model for women's intercollegiate athletic programs." Consistent with that philosophy, the AIAW prohibited the granting of athletic scholarships and tried to deemphasize competition and championships while encouraging good sportsmanship and participation. "We wanted to protect girls from the excesses of recruiting and exploitation. . . . When the AIAW was formed many men told us that scholarships were a bad influence on collegiate sports, that we should avoid making the mistakes they had made and stay out of the mess," the AIAW executive director explained. The initial AIAW handbook stipulated that any woman athlete receiving athletic-based financial aid would be declared ineligible. In 1975 the AIAW hierarchy concluded that the organization had been deceived by male athletic directors intent on preserving their own precious budgets; they thereupon changed the policy regarding scholarships. By 1981 64 percent of the AIAW membership granted athletic scholarships, but the scholarship budgets for women still remained far below those available to male athletes.

It took many years after the passage of Title IX before improvements became evident. In the early 1970s few women coaches had abilities comparable to men; they simply had not learned as young women how to coach the fundamentals of a sport, to develop team strategies, and to handle the pressures of directing a team during a game. Consequently, as public schools and colleges began to offer girls' and women's programs in the late 1970s, male coaches were hired to fill the void. For a time this pattern continued, although most men viewed such assignments with little enthusiasm. They preferred the more prestigious assignment of coaching boys' teams. As individual skills and team performances improved and budgets began to grow, however, the stigma for male coaches of coaching girls' teams declined appreciably. At the same time, the availability of qualified women coaches increased. Yet, in an extreme paradox, another form of sexual discrimination emerged. Men did not leave the coaching ranks to permit women to enter but instead retained their positions; as budgets improved and competition became more meaningful, many male coaches actually opted to coach females. Between 1972 and 1982 the number of women head coaches at the college level *declined* from 85 percent to less than 50 percent.

Ten years later the situation had not changed. Although women's athletic budgets slowly but surely grew, the common practice of maintaining separate men's and women's programs was phased out and the two programs were unified, almost always under a male athletic director. In 1992 only three universities competing at the Division I level had woman athletic directors.

The Case of Pamela Postema

The assignment of men officials to officiate contests provided another indicator of the male domination of women's athletic programs. Typically, in 1991–92 the Big Sky Conference certified as women's basketball officials only four women and forty men. Similar ratios existed in every other college conference in the nation. At the high school level, the story was much the same; less than 2 percent of all officials registered with the National Federation of High School Officials were women. In one typical high school officials' association that provided officials for half the schools in the state of Nevada, just three of ninety basketball referees were women, none of whom received prestigious postseason tournament assignments.

The futile thirteen-year effort by Pamela Postema to become a major league baseball umpire illuminates the issue of sex discrimination. Her goal of reaching the major leagues was a lofty one, because fewer than one of every hundred umpires who are assigned to a minor league ever make "The Show." In 1976 the twenty-two-year-old Ohio native began her quest on a disquieting note by having to threaten legal action just to be admitted to an umpiring school. Following her admission, the chief instructor, National League umpire Harry Wendlestedt, minced no words when she appeared on the field: "We're not making any concession, not changing our program for you. Do you understand the problems a young, single, attractive girl will face being in a class and on the field with some one hundred men of different backgrounds? Can you handle the pressure?"

Indeed she could, and after completing the school with a high rating, Postema received an assignment in the Class A Gulf Coast League. She resolutely moved up the ranks despite encountering many obstacles not faced by male umpires. Within five years she had progressed to the AA Texas League and in 1983 reached the AAA Pacific Coast League, a level that most aspiring major league umpires never make. Two years later she had the opportunity to be the home plate umpire at the Cooperstown Hall of Fame game between the New York Yankees and the Atlanta Braves, an assignment in which she acquitted herself very well. The following spring National League President Bartlett Giamatti invited her to work spring training, the final testing ground before appointment to the major leagues. She returned to AAA level that year but received another invitation to spring training the following year. Then came the devastating news: it had been determined she would not be promoted to the major leagues.

Although the supervisor of umpires followed policy by not releasing the basis for the decision, it was widely believed that although she had performed at a high level as a home plate umpire and had demonstrated knowledge of the rules and how to apply them, her performance as a base umpire was not up to major league standards. After spending 1990 as a crew chief in the American Association, she received her unconditional release; if a decision is made that an umpire will not be promoted to the major leagues, they are released to make room for younger aspiring umpires. Embittered and convinced that she was the victim of sexual discrimination, Postema filed a federal civil suit and vented her anger in a book while she assumed a position as a delivery truck driver for Federal Express. Her major mistake, she concluded, was seeking to avoid any relationship with feminism. Her frustration as expressed in her book aptly summarizes the problems faced by women attempting to succeed in the American sports world:

> When I started out, I figured that as long as you could do the job, it shouldn't matter what sex you were. . . . So I down played the whole thing . . . . I didn't want anyone to think that I was a charity case, to say, "The only reason she got promoted is because she is a woman." What I didn't realize was that baseball people were always going to put up new barriers. They said that I had to be twice

as good as a man to make it to the majors. . . . Nobody
in a power position in baseball right now is ever going to
say a woman is twice as good. I guarantee it.

After thirteen demanding minor league seasons and coming very
close to her goal, Postema could not contain her anger: "Let me be
blunt," she wrote. "Almost all the people in the baseball community
don't want anyone interrupting their little male-dominated way of life.
They want big, fat male umpires. They want those macho, tobacco-
chewing, sleazy sort of borderline alcoholics I worked with for 13
years." She complained that, "If somebody is a nonconformist like me,
we get shown the door. I'll never understand why it is easier for a
female to become an astronaut or cop or fire fighter or soldier or
Supreme Court justice than it is to become a major league umpire. For
Christ's sake, it is only baseball."

Whether Postema received fair treatment will probably never be
known. That she came so close but was not given the opportunity of
becoming one of the very small fraternity of some sixty major league
umpires was indeed a heartbreak; yet she had risen, in the face of
continued harassment by managers, players, and fans, to a level that
most aspiring umpires never achieve. The fate that befell her—to reach
the AAA level but not the big leagues—has happened to scores of male
umpires over the years. What Postema's story does clearly indicate,
however, is the continued difficulties faced by women in the male-
dominated circles of American sport in the 1990s.

Gaining Acceptance—Slowly

Although Title IX directly affected only those educational institutions
receiving federal assistance, it had a much wider impact. It created an
atmosphere in which barriers to girls and women began to be removed,
although seldom without conflict. Public recreation programs offered
more programs for women, and the number of women participating in
sports such as golf, tennis, cycling, running, and weight lifting increased steadily. By the late 1970s the number of women entrants in
distance races and jogging events nearly equaled those of males; twenty
years earlier most events were considered for men only. Of special
symbolic importance was the decision of Little League to permit girls
to participate. This decision came only in response to intense pressure

from parents and the courts. Confronted by seven federal lawsuits filed by the American Civil Liberties Union, Little League dropped its ban against girls, citing "the changing social climate." Support for programs for girls and women had grown so great that when the U.S. Supreme Court in its 1984 decision of *Grove City College v. Bell* placed severe restrictions on the application of Title IX, educational leaders did not attempt a general retreat. In this decision the court severely undercut the sports application of Title IX by declaring that discrimination practiced in one unit of a college did not require action against the entire institution, only the guilty department. And in 1988 no serious opposition appeared when Congress passed the Civil Rights Restoration Act of 1988 that restored the power of the Department of Education to withhold all federal funds from an educational institution in which one or more departments were engaged in sex discrimination, nor did many people complain when Congress decisively overrode President Ronald Reagan's veto of the legislation.

This change of attitude resulted from the rapid growth in popularity of sports programs for females. With the encouragement provided by Title IX, by the late 1970s most public school districts had implemented multisports programs for girls, with primary emphasis on basketball, softball, tennis, track and field, cross-country, and volleyball. More affluent schools added programs in swimming, skiing, and golf. By the early 1980s girls competed for conference and state championships. Most significantly, the quality of play and performance increased appreciably. Coaches demonstrated the same competitiveness as boys' coaches, and emphasized the importance of year-round training and practice programs. Specialized summer sports camps, long the exclusive province of boys, became a part of the summer regimen for high school girls.

With these important improvements came a fundamental change in attitude toward female athletes. Fears that excessive training would be harmful to girls were put aside; doctors and exercise physiologists now weighed in with expert testimony about the benefits of such regular and vigorous exercise for girls. Studies conducted by medical researchers dismissed traditional myths: sports do not harm female reproductive organs; women are no more fragile than men; the menstrual cycle does not impede athletic performance; women are capable of performing well in sports requiring endurance, agility, and speed. Fears that intensive training would produce a crop of ugly muscle-bound girls were discarded; if anything, it was discovered that such training actually enhances both the health and the physical appearance of female athletes. Serious female athletes in all sports undertook rigorous weight-lifting programs. Olympic gold medalist gymnast Mary Lou Retton, possessed of great strength and well-developed muscles, even graced a Wheaties cereal box and appeared in several television commercials. She became a new role model. Girls soon overcame the hesitancy of parents and peers as they channeled their energies into developing their bodies and their athletic skills. By the mid-1980s the cumulative effects of developmental youth programs, better coaching, and new public attitudes had their impact. Girls demonstrated that given the proper opportunity, they could be as competitive as boys. Attendance at games and matches increased with the quality of play; no longer were those cheering at the games only parents and boyfriends.

Similar changes occurred at the college level, although resistance by male-dominated departments seemed to be greater there than in public schools. The major reason for this was probably budgetary. Whereas high schools could mount comparable athletic programs for girls merely by hiring a few coaches and purchasing uniforms and equipment, colleges also had to provide full ride scholarship support. In 1980 this could amount to upward of $15,000 per athlete at a private college, $6,000 at a state-supported institution. Many athletic directors had once been football coaches, and they instinctively protected this most expensive of sports with a particular ferocity. Major battles erupted on some campuses, and guerrilla warfare persisted on many others. But over time the opposition diminished; however, it often required decisive intervention by a provost or president who feared adverse publicity and, especially, the loss of federal scholarship and research funding.

One of the early casualties of the growth of women's athletics was the AIAW. This small and politically vulnerable organization had carried the torch for women's athletics, however dimly, since its inception in 1971. But in 1980 the NCAA, having gone through its own awakening to new possibilities, announced it would inaugurate national women's championship tournaments in several sports for Division II and III member institutions; the following year it introduced national championships for Division I programs in eight sports and even expanded its executive committee to include women. Within a few months the AIAW began to lose members. Within two years the organization ceased operations after losing a federal lawsuit it had filed against the NCAA alleging monopolistic practices.

The ascendancy of the NCAA coincided with the growing re-
alization that womens' sports were here to stay. To what extent college
women's athletics have achieved parity remains a source of strong
disagreement. Budgets have continued to increase and the quality of
competition has improved markedly. Attendance and public interest,
however, has not necessarily followed. In only a few isolated instances have women's programs begun to generate substantial revenue
from ticket sales—basketball at Tennessee, Texas, Washington, Iowa,
and Stanford are major examples. In most instances, women's teams
have played in near-empty gyms and in near oblivion as the media
paid scant attention. National television coverage is one good indicator of the disparity that remains. Although CBS and ESPN began
telecasting a few women's events as early as 1979, coverage remained
skimpy. In 1992, for example, CBS provided extensive coverage of
the entire men's NCAA basketball tournament under its seven-year,
$1 billion contract; in contrast, CBS telecast only the women's final
three games. To obtain even this limited coverage, the women were
forced to play their games on successive days and at unconventional
times, to the detriment of championship-level play. Equality, as determined by the important indicator of prime-time television, remained
an elusive goal.

The debate over budgets and equity obscured an important fact.
Women's college athletics more closely approximated the ideal of the
"student-athlete" than did its male counterpart. It became a truism in
higher education that the cumulative grade-point average and graduation rates of women athletes far outstripped those of men. For one
thing, even the very best women athletes, unlike the men, could not
realistically aspire to professional careers. Women recognized that their
scholarships provided a once-in-a-lifetime opportunity to prepare for
careers and, with perhaps the very rare exception of a few tennis
players or golfers and a handful of basketball players willing to live in
Europe, the alternative of professional competition did not exist. Recruiting wars, however, did intensify. By the 1980s women's coaches
at Division I schools learned that winning was an important part of their
job description, as demanding athletic directors, expecting a return on
their increased financial investment, began to fire coaches with losing
records. Although no serious recruiting scandal hit the women's programs, rumors circulated widely in the coaching ranks about allegations
of illicit financial payments to top female athletes.

The Potential of the Female Athlete

Despite their new opportunities, women athletes still faced the persistent myth of female inferiority. Although Billie Jean King defeated an aging Bobby Riggs, no one seriously considered she could defeat Rod Laver or Stan Smith, two of the leading male tennis players of her time. All world records were held by men, with the performances of women lagging far behind. However, one of the most powerful testimonies to the success of women's athletics is the extent to which the gap between the performances of world-class men and women athletes has narrowed. The cumulative effect of improved opportunities, expert coaching, and modern equipment and facilities has produced a veritable revolution in the level of performance. Not only has the quality of play in such team sports as basketball, volleyball, and softball improved immeasurably, but so has the performance in individual sports. In such sports as distance running and swimming, women athletes are closing the gap between themselves and the men. In running events women have gained significantly on men. For example, in 1988 Florence Griffith Joyner's 100-meter world record was just .72 of a second slower than that of the world record held by Carl Lewis. In that same year teenage swimmer Janet Evans set world records in the 800- and 1500-meter freestyle events; her times excelled the world records held by men in 1972. Her American record time in the 400 meters of 4:04 was sixteen seconds slower than her male counterpart, but it was two seconds faster than the world's record set in 1968 by the legendary Mark Spitz. Evans might have been slower than her contemporary male champion, but she was faster than the world's best of a not-too-distant yesterday. In world-class competitions in such events as the triathalon and distance swimming, women have not infrequently equaled or bested the top male performances. By the early 1990s some performance analysts predicted that women would ultimately outperform men in selected events.

Only in sports that require the generation of physical strength, height, and power—for example, wrestling, football, basketball, weight lifting, rowing, and volleyball—are women unable to compete with men. However, in those sports that require dexterity, speed, agility, and endurance, women have demonstrated the capability of competing more or less on an even basis with men; these include softball, golf, gymnastics, riflery, horse racing, automobile racing, equestrian events, soccer, skating, field hockey, bowling, billiards, badminton, and archery. If sports were organized on the basis of weight and height, rather than on gender and testosterone-generated strength, then women and men would be on a reasonably level field of competition. As women athletes of all ages and at all skill levels demonstrated impressive levels of achievement and improvement, it became more and more accepted that such traits as persistence, self-confidence, intelligence, and desire are essential for success in sports and that they are not sex-based. Yet as women's programs have grown in stature and significance, many observers fear they are all too closely emulating the negative practices of men's programs that have rightfully attracted much deserved criticism.

Within two decades after the passage of Title IX and the pivotal tennis match between Billie Jean King and Bobby Riggs, women athletes have carved out a substantial niche for themselves in the American sports scene. Certainly women have not achieved parity with the men in terms of overall public interest; attendance at most women's events has lagged far behind comparable men's events. But there is evident a continuing and growing fan base in many sports, which translates into greater newspaper and television coverage. Many women athletes have become household words, comparable to their male counterparts. It was indeed unfortunate that the pioneering woman athlete Babe Didrikson Zaharias was not able to enjoy the increased popularity of women's sports. In 1932 at the age of eighteen she set world records at the Los Angeles Olympics in the javelin and 80-meter high hurdles. Extremely talented in several other sports, including swimming and tennis, she became a golf professional and dominated the sport until she was struck down by cancer in 1956. No woman athlete since has approached the diversity of the achievements of Babe Zaharias, but that is understandable in an age of increased specialization. Over the years since Zaharias's premature death extraordinarily talented women have provided sports fans with many memorable performances. Wilma Rudolph's multievent gold medal performance at the 1960 Olympics remains a standard of excellence. Ice skaters like Peggy Fleming (1968), Dorothy Hamill (1976), and Kristi Yamaguchi (1992) have inspired great public interest in a once largely overlooked sport with their gold medal victories at the Winter Olympics. During the 1970s Nancy Leiberman of Old Dominion University and Ann Myers of UCLA set a high standard of performance and dispelled many myths about the abilities of women to perform on the basketball floor, thereby helping ease the way for the sport's substantial growth in popularity during the ensuing years. The steely concentration and consistent performance over the years by such professional golfers as Nancy Lopez and Patty Sheehan have attracted many fans to the Ladies Professional Golf Tour. Similarly, the gold medal gymnastics performance of Mary Lou Retton at the 1984 Olympics or the blazing speed of such well-conditioned and finely trained sprinters as Florence Griffith Joyner and Jackie Joyner-Kersee at the 1988 and 1992 Olympics has done much to dispel any lingering doubts about the potential of women athletes.

Women tennis players, however, have received the greatest and most consistent public attention. Coming on the heels of the pioneering Billie Jean King have been such dominant players as the incredibly consistent Chris Evert and several challengers from around the world. Evert's matches over the years with the powerful Martina Navratilova have set a standard for competition that equals the intensity, skill, and excitement of the matches of the leading men players such as John McEnroe, Jimmy Connors, and Bjorn Borg. In the process they have helped create a much more positive attitude toward women's sports of all types.

Conclusion

During its early years the theme of the Virginia Slims women's tennis tour once echoed the dubious and perhaps demeaning sales slogan of its cigarette sponsor: "You've come a long way, baby!" During the two decades since passage of Title IX and the legendary King-Riggs tennis match, women athletes have indeed come a long way. Discriminatory attitudes and practices have been substantially changed; destructive myths have been shattered. Programs now exist at all levels of education, and treatment of women in the professional ranks is greatly improved. But as in other segments of society, the drive for equal opportunity and equal treatment continues. In 1992 only 2 of 100 U.S. senators were women, and just 29 women sat in the 435-member House of Representatives. Only two women served as governor of their states, and Sandra Day O'Connor remained the single woman ever to serve on the U.S. Supreme Court. Women made up less than 5 percent of the chief operating officers and senior vice presidents of the nation's major corporations, and on college and university campuses the hierarchy of department chairs, deans, vice presidents, and presidents remained largely a male bailiwick. Everywhere women professionals bemoaned the influence of the "good old boys' network" and the existence of a "glass ceiling" that denied them access to opportunity and power.

A cursory glance at the status of women's sports in the 1990s reveals the reality of American society. Television and newspaper coverage remains limited in comparison to that of men's sports, undoubtedly a reflection of the attitudes and interests of the general public. With the exception of tennis, television has been slow to provide widespread coverage of important women's events. The gap in budgets between men and women at the high school and college level has been greatly reduced, but obvious disparities remain. The new president of the NCAA told the 1993 convention that "gender equity" has become the most important issue before the organization and pledged decisive leadership to achieve that goal. Women coaches have encountered their own glass ceiling as they deal with male administrators who control the hiring process. A careful reading of the NCAA directory for women's sports indicates that males still hold more than half of all college coaching positions for women's teams; although no reliable statistics are available for the public schools, an examination of most school districts will indicate a similar pattern. In 1991 the NCAA demonstrated its growing awareness of the dawning of a new era when Judith Sweet of the University of San Diego was elected as the organization's first woman president; that she served with distinction served to advance acceptance of women's athletics within this traditionally male and highly conservative organization. However, the day when a talented woman is hired to coach a men's college team in a major sport has yet to arrive; in 1990 the University of Kentucky received considerable publicity when it announced the unprecedented appointment of a woman as an assistant basketball coach. Three seasons later no other school had emulated that example. In just two decades women have come a long way in the rough-and-tumble world of sport. Just as major obstacles to equal treatment exist in American society in general, so too do similar barriers remain in the world of sports.

Courtesy of UPI/Bettmann

The saga of basketball sensation Connie Hawkins illuminates the often corrupt and cruel world of major college athletics.

HARBRACE
BOOKS
ON AMERICA

SINCE 1945

Chapter 7

The Myths and Realities of College Athletics

The most discriminating experts agreed he was one of the best basketball players ever to have perfected his skills on the most demanding of testing grounds—the playgrounds of New York City. At 6 feet, 8 inches tall and 200 pounds, he was strong, agile, and lightning quick. Attached to his long arms were enormous hands that he used to dazzle his opponents with ball handling and passing wizardry. His fall-away jump shot, with the ball launched from behind his head, was impossible to guard and very accurate. During his senior year he led Brooklyn Boys High to an undefeated season and the city championship. He amazed onlookers with an incredible display of basketball talent—passing, shooting, rebounding, and defense. He topped off the season by starring in the national high school East-West all-star game, and was voted the outstanding player in the game. Not surprisingly, *Parade Magazine* named him to its high school all-America first team. He was unquestionably one of the very best high school players in the country. No knowledgeable basketball fan who had watched him perform his magic doubted he was destined to become a star in the NBA. The year was 1960 and his name was Connie Hawkins.

Not surprisingly the college recruiters came calling—in large numbers. Colleges and universities from across the land sought the services of this superbly talented seventeen-year-old; eventually some 250 institutions made a pitch. But life on a university campus was far removed from the world Connie knew. A sports reporter for the *New York Times* privately confided to a friend that the only thing Hawkins could not do at the college or NBA level was sign autographs, a caustic observation about his dubious level of academic achievement. That comment, although cruel, was not that great an exaggeration. Connie received a general diploma from Boys High, which merely attested to his having attended four years of high school but indicated he had not met the minimum standards for a regular diploma. His reading was judged no better than seventh grade level. A much publicized high school star, he had difficulty reading the many newspaper stories detailing his court heroics. He could not even read well enough to pass the written test to obtain a driver's license.

Hawkins's dismal academic record reflected the conditions in which he had grown up. Abandoned by his father when he was ten, Connie was raised by a near-blind mother whose total income came from the public welfare system. Connie had known nothing but a life of poverty. He often lacked shoes to wear to school, and never owned more than two pairs of pants at a time. He and a brother shared the same single bed in their dilapidated apartment in the heart of the Bedford-Stuyvesant section of Brooklyn; Bed-Sty held the dubious reputation of being one of the nation's most fearful slums. Because of basketball and his own intuitive sense of right and wrong, however, Connie had no problems with the law, avoiding the gang culture that thrived in his neighborhood. He was, in fact, a kind and gentle young man who was polite to everyone with whom he came in contact. But the street-wise Hawkins understood from many of his basketball pals that he could greatly improve his financial situation by playing basketball in college.

The recruiting letters began to arrive during his junior year, and after his sensational senior year the mailbox overflowed with correspondence from coaches across the country. He was spared the time-consuming task of talking to recruiters on the telephone because his mother could not afford one. Soon he was being deluged by assistant coaches and alumni making their recruiting rounds. The first few handshakes that ended with him unexpectedly holding a twenty-dollar bill surprised him, but after a time he came to expect this as part of the process. Little did Connie know that by accepting the money he was breaking the rules of the NCAA. But he had never even heard of the NCAA.

Nor did Hawkins comprehend what constituted a university. He had never been on a college campus until he began making recruiting visits in the spring of 1960. Naively, he later told his biographer, "I thought college must be kind of a big Boys High, but with girls and a better basketball team." Reflecting back on this period of his life, he later commented he could not recall a single recruiter ever mentioning academic requirements, asking about his intended major, or discussing career objectives: "When I think back on it, it was like they were all reciting a speech. Like they'd said every word over and over. They said they had a great school, the best coach in the country, and the dean was a nice guy. They talked about how they prepared you for the pros, or what a big field house they had. A lot of guys said how well they treated 'Negroes.'"

And recruiters let him know that if he came to their institution there would be plenty of new clothes and money, perhaps a private apartment and an automobile. Hawkins made innumerable recruiting visits— to Ohio, Indiana, Illinois, Colorado, Washington—fearfully flying in airplanes and eating robustly at fancy restaurants. It was heady stuff for a poor teenager from the streets of Bed-Sty. "I was traveling fast, maybe too fast," he recalled. "Every school bought me food and took me to night clubs and parties. They were offerin' me money and tellin' me to go downtown and pick out a few pairs of slacks. . . . I felt like I was in a fantasy. I had no money and no clothes and then suddenly people were givin' me things." His high school coach later told Hawkins's biographer of the instance when a recruiter for St. John's University, anxious to keep Hawkins in New York City for his college career, cut to the quick: "Look, Mickey," he said. "We want Hawkins badly. But I'm not going to bother you. You just collect the offers. When you get them all, pick out the best one and show it to me. Then we'll top it, no matter what it is." Hawkins was such a special talent that he was even recruited by professional teams. At the time the NBA had a "territorial rule" that permitted teams to select outside of the regular draft players who competed at colleges located within their territory. The New York Knicks tried to convince Hawkins to stay in New York City for college; the Boston Celtics proposed a deal that would have him attend Providence College.

Eventually, for reasons that seemed based on total confusion and exhaustion from the recruiting process, Hawkins decided to attend the University of Iowa. But he knew the bottom line: "They seemed like nice people, and they offered me the most money." At that time the Big Ten Conference still maintained the fiction that athletes had to meet academic standards to receive a scholarship; all of the scholarships given to athletes were for "academic" achievement. Although Hawkins's grades and test scores fell far below the university's requirements, he was admitted on probation without scholarship aid. On the face of it, he was expected to pay his own way until his grades reached a level where a scholarship could be awarded. However, a willing booster agreed to hire Hawkins at his service station at a salary that would cover all expenses with substantial spending money left over. His benefactor did not expect Connie to do any work, although he had to drop by the service station on payday to pick up his money.

Intelligent but woefully uneducated, Hawkins knew he was unprepared for college. During his senior year he spent several hours each week with the head of the Boys High English department, who put Connie through a rigorous reading program. When his tutor first consulted with the 6-foot, 8-inch senior he concluded that "There was no way on earth this boy could be ready for college. His academic record was pitiful."

This understanding teacher recognized that the universities recruiting him "hadn't the slightest interest in him as a student. They wanted a ballplayer." By the time Hawkins received his general diploma from Boys High his remedial study had elevated his reading to the eleventh- grade level, but his deficient scholastic preparation and underdeveloped study skills left him vulnerable to collegiate academic standards.

His life on the streets of New York could not have prepared him for life in the corn belt. Few black students attended this prominent state university, located in the middle of one of the nation's richest farming states with less than 4 percent minority population. Hawkins was welcomed for one thing—the promise that he brought to a basketball program which had big aspirations. A young and personable head coach, Sharm Scheuerman, himself an alumnus of the university, was in the process of building a program intended to compete for the national championship. At a time when a freshman could not participate in varsity sports, Hawkins generated enormous enthusiasm with his sparkling play at practice: crowds of ten thousand turned out for freshman intrasquad scrimmages just to watch Hawkins mystify the opposition with his amazing ball handling and shooting. Among his several crowd-pleasing tricks during warm-ups was simultaneously palming two balls in his enormous hands and dunking them both in one soaring move to the hoop. Excited fans talked expectantly about Hawkins teaming with junior forward Don Nelson, himself a future professional player and coach, and leading the Hawkeyes to a national championship in 1962.

Such was not to be. Except for his time on the basketball court, Connie's life in Iowa City was miserable. Overwhelmed by his classroom work and with few friends, he viewed Iowa City as a foreign land. The money from his "job," however, came regularly. After he had paid all his academic and living expenses, he still had $150 left each month. Although the coaches provided him with tutors for all of his courses, his academic performance was less than spectacular. Suffering from a background that made failure almost certain, Connie struggled mightily, encouraged by his coaches and plied with information by tutors. But as

he later recalled, "I honestly tried. I didn't want to flunk
out and have people laugh. I wanted to stay and play
ball. . . . But the readin' was killin' me."

Hawkins's academic problems soon paled in comparison with the unanticipated crisis that hit him in late
April of his freshman year. Any hopes that Hawkins
could pass academic muster and receive a regular
scholarship became moot when the press reported he
had been implicated in a new round of stunning revelations regarding the fixing of college basketball games
by New York City gamblers. Once more District Attorney Frank Hogan grabbed the headlines in his crusade
against the fixers. In the spring of 1961 his office charged
several well-known New York City area college players
and gamblers with shaving points. Central to the probe
was the shadowy figure of former Columbia University
star and onetime NBA player, Jack Molinas. A street-
smart product of upper Manhattan, the good-looking
and personable Molinas had been caught gambling
on his own team's games and barred from the NBA for
life. His banishment did not deter him, and he proceeded to take a law degree from Brooklyn Law School and
launch a successful practice, his prior record somehow
not preventing his admission to the New York bar. The
practice of the law, however, remained secondary to
his consuming interest in sports gambling. Although the
truth is difficult to discern from the many rumors surrounding his gambling activities, Molinas and bookmaker Joe Hacken combined their talents to build a
lucrative illegal betting operation, which the district
attorney alleged included trading inside information
and fixing contests. Molinas often "sold" games to gamblers who accepted his contention that he had a "fix"
on a college football or basketball contest; apparently
sometimes he did, sometimes he didn't. The journalist
David Wolf concludes Molinas and his associates operated a "nationwide gambling operation that . . . bribed
scores of college players to fix basketball games."

Connie Hawkins first met Jack Molinas the summer before he enrolled at Iowa. Always on the lookout
for future opportunities, Molinas made it a point to
introduce himself to Hawkins, obviously seeking to establish a relationship with the intent of enlisting this

prospective college all-American in his point-shaving operation sometime in the future. On several occasions Hawkins found himself in the presence of the ingratiating Molinas, accepting rides in his fancy Buick convertible, joining him for a sandwich or pizza, chatting casually after playing in a pick-up playground game. Unaware of the methods and intentions of sports gamblers, Hawkins never stopped to consider what interest this well-heeled lawyer might have in him. He knew nothing about Molinas's unsavory background and his ban from the NBA. He knew only that Molinas "seemed like a nice person," and that he was not particularly different from the many hangers-on who attached themselves to New York's basketball subculture. Hawkins later recalled, "One time he told me he knew how hard it was for poor kids their first year in school. He said if I needed help or money, just let him know. He said he liked me." By this time Hawkins had become accustomed to being approached by lots of individuals, many of them college recruiters or alleged "agents" who had connections with college programs; Molinas seemed no different, although unlike many of these figures, he did not slip Hawkins a $10 or $20 bill.

When Hogan made his first arrests in January of 1961 (he did not have enough evidence to collar the slippery Molinas until a year later), Hawkins was enduring his freshman year at Iowa City. He knew nothing about the unfolding scandal in his hometown. But one of Molinas's underlings named Hawkins along with several other players as involved in the gambling ring. Hogan dispatched a detective to Iowa City who returned Hawkins to New York City, where he was kept in custody and underwent an intensive interrogation that stretched over fourteen days. Hawkins was not given the benefit of legal counsel, nor was he informed of his constitutional rights. One of his interrogators made no apologies: "We were fighting an evil: organized fixing of college games . . . We got the big people like Molinas . . . If our methods got a kid to make a false confession, I'm sorry, but we had a job to do. And remember, everything we did was legal at the time."

Although Hawkins had never participated in shaving points—his interrogators were dumbfounded to learn he did not even know the meaning of a point spread—the experience naturally terrified the eighteen-year-old. Under intense pressure to produce indictments, the detectives used every trick available to break their suspect. Eventually Hawkins made several contradictory statements; investigators repeatedly warned him that unless he confessed he would face a jail sentence. Under this pressure and without legal counsel, the rattled youth confessed to a crime he had not committed. The major mistake he had made was accepting a loan of $200 from Molinas to pay for an airline ticket back to Iowa City after the Christmas holiday. He also freely acknowledged that he had mentioned some names of basketball players he knew to one of Molinas's associates, which the police interpreted as his having agreed to line up additional point shavers for Molinas.

In May District Attorney Hogan named Hawkins as one of fourteen players involved in a conspiracy to fix games; he had allegedly been an "intermediary" between known gamblers and college basketball players. The authorities never produced any evidence to link Hawkins to illegal activity—they had only the muddled confession they had extracted from him after two weeks of questioning. Eventually the district attorney recognized that Hawkins had not committed a crime and quietly dropped the charges. But the publicity prompted an embarrassed University of Iowa to sever all ties with Connie Hawkins.

But the story did not end there. Shortly after being informed he had been suspended from the University of Iowa, Connie told a newspaper reporter of his special financial arrangements at Iowa. The startling news that he had received nearly $300 a month from a prominent booster stunned basketball fans everywhere. Coach Scheuerman and athletic director Forest Evashevski denied any wrongdoing, but in 1963 the NCAA placed the university on one year's probation, considered by many to be a relatively minor penalty given the severity of the violations.

David Wolf quotes with approval an Iowa assistant coach's observations about Connie Hawkins's relationship with Jack Molinas and his henchmen:

I don't think Connie had the slightest idea what was going on with those gamblers. Here was a young fella, not worldly wise, and whatever his involvement it was strictly unintentional. This was a very naive eighteen year old.... He is a real fine young man. I feel sincerely that he has been the victim of circumstances—if not the circumstances of the ghetto, then the circumstances of people who are looking for someone like him to take advantage of.

What this coach failed to understand was that he and his fellow coaches at Iowa were also deeply implicated in the tragedy of Connie Hawkins. They had worked, however indirectly, with boosters to pay Hawkins to attend the University of Iowa, in a serious violation of Big Ten Conference and NCAA policies. They did so, not because they were evil men, but because they were also caught up in the compromising and competitive world of big-time college athletics. In the spring of 1961 they were merely among a cast of hundreds seeking to obtain the services of Connie Hawkins. Wolf succinctly states the dilemma facing the coaches: "The Iowa people were simply acting in the only manner it is possible to act—and still survive—in the big-time, profit-oriented college sports system. They had to win basketball games to keep their jobs, and to win they needed kids like Connie Hawkins. To get kids like Hawkins, they had to cheat."

The case of Connie Hawkins ultimately had a more or less happy ending. Barred from the NBA because of his alleged association with sports gamblers, Hawkins spent four years barnstorming the world with the Harlem Globetrotters for the munificent pay of $125 a week. He then played two more years in the relative oblivion of the fledgling American Basketball Association. During this time a lawsuit he had filed against the NBA wended its way through the nation's legal system; he eventually won a $1 million out-of-court settlement from the NBA, which also agreed to drop its permanent ban. He shortly thereafter signed a lucrative contract with the Phoenix Suns, beginning his "rookie" season in 1969. By this time he had married and was the father of two children. Embarrassed by the publicity surrounding his departure from the University of Iowa, he never publicly criticized the system that had nearly destroyed him. His talent intact despite a serious knee injury suffered playing for the Minnesota Pipers of the ABA, Hawkins made the NBA all-star team for four consecutive years. In 1992, at age fifty, he was inducted into the Basketball Hall of Fame in Springfield, Massachusetts.

College Athletics as Entertainment

Connie Hawkins's dreary story would surprise few knowledgeable observers of the complex world of big-time collegiate athletics. His experience is merely one of a long list of unhappy episodes involving young athletes caught up in a cynical system that has brought shame and humiliation to American higher education. The root cause is that college athletics in the United States has become a multimillion-dollar business. American colleges and universities, unlike their counterparts throughout the rest of the world, have assumed the role of providing sports entertainment for the public. The educational reformer and longtime president of the University of Chicago, Robert Hutchins, once dryly commented, "We Americans are the only people in human history who ever got sport mixed up with education. No other country looks to its universities as a prime source of athletic entertainment." In 1956 the veteran University of Michigan football coach and athletic director Fritz Crisler lamented that his profession had "discarded the principles on which football was established," because "we are applying professional tactics to educational ideals."

The comments of Hutchins and Crisler would be echoed frequently during the ensuing years as major college athletics developed into an enormous economic force. Because they managed to avoid the ethical and financial constraints under which academic programs had to operate, athletic departments succeeded in creating a system that served primarily the professional and financial interests of coaches and administrators. Unlike academic deans, athletic directors have been able to operate with only limited accountability to their institutional presidents, governing boards, state legislatures, and the public. This is because athletic departments established for themselves a special place within American society and its popular culture. The special status accorded intercollegiate athletics, however, encouraged massive corruption leading to widespread exploitation of athletes.

Sporadic reform efforts have failed conspicuously because athletic interests succeeded in building strong alliances with powerful local political and business leaders. These relationships helped thwart most reform efforts mounted by concerned faculty and presidents. It has long been overlooked by journalists that institutional presidents, even if motivated to impose proper accountability and ethical standards on athletic departments, are often constrained by their governing boards. Over the years many university presidents have learned to their frustration that members of their governing boards—which have the power to terminate presidents—have maintained considerably greater interest in a winning athletic program than in institutional integrity.

Several popular myths about the goals and benefits of intercollegiate sports have protected athletic departments from meaningful reform. That these myths do not hold up under careful scrutiny makes the mystique enjoyed by big-time college sports all the more intriguing. Included among these dominant myths are these: college athletes are first and foremost students; athletic competition provides an integral part of the education process; athletic departments are financially self-sufficient; athletic programs contribute greatly to academic fund-raising endeavors; and successful athletic programs are essential to the nurturing of alumni and public support.

The essential myth on which college athletic programs have thrived is that intercollegiate athletics are an integral part of the educational mission and program of American colleges and universities. Upon careful examination, however, it becomes clear that major college athletics have little to do with education and everything to do with the commercialization of athletics. It is often overlooked that those institutions which have declined to participate in major college programs have not suffered; if anything, their academic reputation has benefited as a result. The substantial academic reputation of the University of Chicago continued to grow after it dropped football during the 1930s, and no one has suggested that big-time athletics would in any way benefit Yale University or Cal Tech. Some institutions have even discovered, much to their dismay, that their academic reputation can be seriously besmirched by scandals in their athletic programs. Of course, some schools have been able to combine the two areas: the University of

Southern California, Notre Dame, and Michigan State University have all succeeded in developing national reputations first in athletics and then in academics. The president of Oklahoma University once joked—perhaps too candidly for his own good—that his job was "to build a university the football team can be proud of." Several leading academic institutions have also demonstrated over the years that an institution can compete nationally in athletics and still maintain its exceptional academic reputation: for example, Stanford University, Vanderbilt University, Duke University, UCLA, and the University of California, Berkeley. Several other universities, such as Rice and Northwestern, have resolutely stayed the course, but in the process found that remaining even reasonably competitive, especially in the revenue-generating sports, is extraordinarily difficult.

Although it is widely perceived that athletic success on the court or field readily translates into increased alumni contributions and legislative appropriations, university administrators know better. During the 1980s sports boosters at two major private schools, the University of San Francisco and Tulane University, vociferously warned administrators that if they dropped basketball programs in the wake of major scandals it would severely hurt fund-raising, but precisely the opposite happened. Donations to both institutions increased substantially after two courageous presidents summarily dropped their badly tainted programs. Development officers at major sports institutions report that they must continually combat resistance from potential donors who complain about the negative image of an "outlaw" athletic program. Several studies have indicated that winning teams, even national championships, do not lead to increased alumni giving; they do, however, stimulate increased donations to the athletic department. Experienced alumni and development officers know that wealthy individuals and foundation directors give primarily to specific academic programs, and such important donors are largely indifferent to sports. Most major gifts to universities come from foundations, trust funds, and wealthy individual donors and are often negotiated over a period of several months or even years, during which time the fortunes of athletic teams can fluctuate widely. Researchers have also found that no substantive relationship exists between winning athletic programs and legislative appropriations for public institutions. Governors and legislators, as individuals, might be rabid boosters of good old State U, but that enthusiasm has seldom translated into increased appropriations.

College Athletes

It is important to understand that the primary mission of major college athletic departments is to market a special form of public entertainment. Equally important is the fact that these programs receive only a small portion of their annual budget from institutional sources; they must raise the great bulk of their operating budgets themselves. This means they must secure booster donations, generate ticket sales, and attract television revenue. These financial imperatives inevitably translate into intense pressure on coaches and athletes to produce winning programs.

These financial pressures are ultimately transferred to the athletes. Those young adults who provide all-important victories have long been euphemistically called "student-athletes" by coaches and administrators; a close look at the experiences of athletes on campus, however, demonstrates that they often have little in common with the vast majority of nonathletes. This is especially true for those engaged in the preeminent revenue sports: men's basketball and football. These young men are skilled performers who produce enormous income for the athletic department. Their success or failure is measured in wins and losses, in championships and national rankings. Essentially the same expectations for victories also apply to those men and women athletes in the so-called nonrevenue sports. Instead of attracting large paying crowds, they are expected by their coaches—who are as intensely competitive as their football and basketball coaching peers—to dedicate themselves to their sport so as to enhance the overall athletic image of the institution.

It is beyond question that over the past half century many major college athletes have not belonged on a college campus. They lacked one or more of the necessary requisites: adequate high school education, basic academic skills, or the motivation to earn a college degree. For decades these types of student-athletes have endured the college environment because they had no alternative; it was the only way for them to perfect their special talents to qualify for a job in one of the professional leagues. For a much larger number of athletes who lack professional potential but thrive on athletic competition, college programs have provided their only realistic option to continue doing what they enjoy most. It is extremely doubtful that many students have elected to participate in athletics as the most efficient way to earn a college education. Considering the hours the average college athlete devotes to his or her sport over the calendar year in practice, conditioning, travel, and competition, they could have readily paid for the cost of a public university athletic scholarship by working at normal jobs that would most likely have entailed fewer hours per week.

College athletes receiving the so-called free ride are actually paid in kind for their labors. They receive "athletic scholarships" that cover tuition and registration fees, room and board, and required textbooks. Significantly, they are not paid cash. That is because they labor under the special designation of "amateur" athlete. During the late nineteenth century, as the modern world of sports took shape, most individuals who had the time and inclination to participate were well-to-do young men who played solely for the fun they derived from competition. Those athletes who came primarily from society's lower ranks and who took pay for their performances—boxers and baseball players—were looked down on. The concept of the amateur athlete was largely the product of a group of aristocratic Englishmen who played major roles in establishing the modern Olympic movement.

When American university administrators, having duly noted the revenue potential in athletic programs, took control away from student groups early in the twentieth century, they embraced with a special fervor the concept of the amateur athlete. It neatly meshed with the elitist views of the several private colleges that led the way in the formation of intercollegiate athletics. From the start college administrators made it clear that while it would be perfectly acceptable for the institution to make money from athletic programs, it would be morally wrong to pay the student for performing as an athlete. This concept became central to the philosophy of the NCAA.

On this questionable foundation, American collegiate athletics thus proceeded to build its gigantic money machine. All across America, students engaged in supposedly comparable extracurricular activities have long been paid for their efforts—journalists writing for the campus newspaper, officers serving in student government, secretaries typing faculty manuscripts, graduate assistants teaching discussion sections and grading papers, even those washing dishes in the dining hall. No administrator has dared suggest that student laboratory assistants should perform their duties for the sake of the educational experience to be derived from participation. But that is what they have succeeded in convincing athletes.

Athletic departments have recognized that the key to the effective functioning of their money machine has been the popular and widely accepted myth about the student athlete. However, former Indiana University and successful professional basketball player Isaiah Thomas got it right when he commented, "When you go to college, you're not a student-athlete, but an athlete-student. . . . Eight or ten hours a day are filled with basketball." Several independent studies conducted over successive decades have demonstrated that athletes in season have regularly devoted thirty to sixty hours per week to their athletic responsibilities—practice, games, travel, film study, meetings with coaches, weight training, and physical therapy. Even during the off-season, meetings, physical training, and informal workouts with teammates reduce the time commitment by no more than 25 percent. After a busy day of classes and practice, the tired, and perhaps injured, athlete has little time or energy left to study. Given this demanding regimen, it is not surprising that even regular class attendance becomes difficult. Assuming the athlete carries a normal load of fifteen academic credits and devotes the usual average of two hours of study per hour of class attended, then his or her work week quickly approaches seventy hours. In contrast, typical regulations governing on-campus part-time work for nonathletes prohibit more than twenty hours of work per week. For athletes whose academic preparation or skills are minimal, the academic burden becomes much greater.

Instead of attempting to reduce the time demands on these students, in their insatiable quest for additional revenue, athletic administrators have over the years actually increased the time required to fulfill the expectations of an athletic scholarship. Consider, for example, the length of seasons. During the 1950s the standard football season was nine, sometimes ten games. Only a small number of teams participated in postseason bowl games. By the 1980s the standard football season was eleven games and lasted for more than four months— virtually the entire fall semester—or even longer if the team was invited to participate in a postseason bowl game or the national playoffs. The number of football teams invited to bowl games approached forty. For those teams competing at levels below I-A (major college) and that reached the NCAA-sponsored national playoff finals, fifteen games were played; a season that began in mid-August lasted until the weekend before Christmas. Even worse, players often found themselves preparing for a national championship game during final examination week. In response to the lure of increased television revenues, selected teams participated in special season "kick-off" contests, or traveled overseas for games. As an incentive, the NCAA permitted these teams to play twelve "regular" season games. Until 1992 practice for the regular college basketball season traditionally began on October 15 with a schedule of twenty-eight games extending from Thanksgiving until March; responding to the lure of additional television revenues, the NCAA increased its postseason tournament from sixteen to twenty-four teams, then to thirty-two and eventually to sixty-four teams. Appropriately, the much ballyhooed Final Four games were often held near April Fools' Day. At the January 1993 meeting of the NCAA, executive director Dick Schultz recommended that the NCAA adopt a national playoff for Division 1-A football as a means of generating additional revenue.

In comparison to the college baseball player, however, the demands placed on football or basketball participants seems relatively small. In order to maintain their scholarships, baseball players have been required to practice throughout the autumn months, begin "spring" practice with the resumption of classes in January, play a schedule of more than sixty games that leads to possible national playoff tournaments concluding in mid-June. As the number of professional minor leagues declined, compliant major college baseball programs filled the void by providing de facto player developmental programs for grateful professional teams. Then there are the lonely and largely ignored distance runners: their scholarship commitment to the athletic department extends over the entire nine-month academic year, as the autumn months are consumed by cross-country practice and competition, the winter and spring months by the "indoor" and "outdoor" track and field seasons.

In 1991, following a major confrontation between a group of reform-minded presidents and their athletic departments, the NCAA ruling body established new restrictions of twenty hours per week that an athlete may devote to her or his sport. Coaches ominously predicted a "lesser product." Before the end of the first football season under this restriction one highly respected coach with nearly thirty years of collegiate coaching experience, Earle Bruce of Colorado State University, admitted to willfully violating the new regulation. Piously telling the press that he was "a rules guy," he also admitted he had found it impossible to change his ways and limit his time demands; perhaps most important, he intimated that he felt committed to exceed the limit because he suspected his opponents were also doing so.

The Student-Athlete: Fact or Fiction?

The issue of graduation rates has proved to be one area where the athletic establishment has found itself on the defensive. Embarrassingly low graduation rates give the lie to the myth that college athletes are primarily students and dedicated to securing a degree. During the mid-1980s Senator Bill Bradley and Congressman Tom McMillan, both all-American basketball players during their college careers at Princeton and Maryland respectively, held hearings regarding graduation rates of athletes, which eventually led to proposed legislation—lobbied against fiercely by the NCAA—requiring annual publication of graduation rates based on a federally mandated formula. For years institutions had cleverly massaged their graduation rates to disguise the fact that many of their student-athletes had majored primarily in maintaining athletic eligibility. The statistics that many institutions previously produced were often classic examples of dubious manipulation of data, master-pieces of statistical sleight of hand. McMillan and Bradley knew better and diligently pursued their quarry. They hoped to force the NCAA and its member institutions to produce data confirming what everyone already knew—that only a distinct minority of athletes competing at the major college level were graduating after *five years* of enrollment. Initial NCAA statistics released in 1992 covering the years of 1983–84 and 1984–85 indicated that less than one-third of those who completed their four years of eligibility ever graduated.

The furor over graduation rates, however, has tended to conceal ongoing abuses that have been endemic to some college athletic pro-grams. These include enrollment of academically unprepared athletes; fabrication or doctoring of transcripts; advisers recommending courses solely to maintain eligibility rather than meet degree requirements; tutors writing papers for athletes; enrollment in so-called Mickey Mouse courses; passing grades awarded to athletes who had not even attended a class. It is not surprising that independent sources have revealed that many athletes, even after completing four years of athletic eligibility, are not even remotely close to meeting degree requirements. They have taken a lengthy series of courses that meet conference and NCAA reg-ulations for athletic eligibility but do not conform to degree require-ments; popular among these ruses are physical education activity classes, extension and correspondence courses from institutions of questionable reputation, summer session workshop courses, and summer travel courses. As a consequence, many athletes find that after four years they are still at a freshman or sophomore level in terms of earning a degree.

At the extreme, there were the much publicized cases of professional football star Dexter Manley of Oklahoma State University and Creighton University basketball player Kevin Ross. After having exhausted four years of athletic eligibility and having been full-time students, both remained functionally illiterate. Manley told his tragic story to a congressional panel; Ross sued Creighton for educational malpractice.

Over strong objections by many coaches, and black college administrators in particular, the NCAA in 1986 passed new requirements for admission based on scores earned on standardized college admissions tests. To no one's surprise, what came to be known as Proposition 48 quickly produced serious allegations about substitutes taking the examination for unprepared high school recruits. Much to the NCAA's discomfort, black college officials roundly condemned the rule as racially biased because of its reliance on standardized examinations. One often overlooked consequence of "Prop 48" was that it forced many programs to rely heavily on the dubious practice of recruiting junior college transfers.

The Continuing Dilemma of Recruiting

Maintaining the eligibility of athletes with questionable academic skills or motivation, however, has often been much easier than recruiting them in the first place. The folklore surrounding college recruiting abuses is replete with an endless array of stories, which if they were not so tragic would be humorous. At the height of the Watergate investigations, Indiana University basketball coach Bob Knight wryly commented, "When they get to the bottom of Watergate, they'll find a basketball coach." The acerbic Knight—an outspoken critic of the cheating that occurs in the recruiting process—missed his target in this case (the major culprit actually proved to be a former third-string lineman from Whittier College), but his assessment was based on a sound understanding of the ugly morass of college recruiting.

At any given time during the 1970s and 1980s, more than 20 percent of the major college programs were either undergoing an investigation by the enforcement division of the NCAA or were on probation for serious recruiting-related violations. Only a minority of major college programs were immune to the epidemic of recruiting violations—because the stakes were so high. Coaches who consistently lost, no matter how high their graduation rates or how clean a program they conducted, seldom retained their positions for long. Athletic directors, their eyes glued to the bottom line of their budgets, knew that winning programs generate increased ticket sales and greater booster donations. Winning meant that television revenues would pour into the athletic department coffers and the team would be invited to lucrative postseason tournaments or bowl games. Instead of facing termination, the coach could expect a multiyear contract, complete with substantial raises and bonuses. But everyone knew that all of these desired outcomes hinge on a successful recruiting program.

Perhaps Forrest "Peahead" Walker, head football coach at Wake Forest in the early 1950s, best described the crucial importance of recruiting for a college coach: "You don't go bear hunting with a switch." Nothing about that laconic statement has changed in the ensuing years. When they are given to total candor, college coaches unequivocally state that games are seldom won by dedicated work on the practice field or by superior coaching or brilliant game-day strategies—they are won primarily in the rough-and-tumble world of recruiting. Because a successful recruiting program holds the key to winning, the temptations for breaking the NCAA rules are great. An embarrassing record of transgressions has been the result.

Forest Evashevski, a winning coach and later director of athletics at the University of Iowa, told a journalist in 1957 that the only goal of college athletics is "to go out and win." He confessed, "At most colleges the pressure is on the coach from the president on down. The coach enters into a tacit understanding with the president that he will recruit good ball players by any means short of larceny. And if the coach doesn't come through with good recruiting, out he goes."

The budget of any organization reflects its priorities. It is not surprising to learn that a hefty slice of athletic department budgets are devoted to recruiting. Successful (i.e., winning) programs devote a high priority throughout the year to recruiting; teams have a designated recruiting coordinator. Many prospects are identified through subscription to national and regional high school athlete evaluation services, who sell their information. Coaches also rely on their personal networks of friends in the high school and junior college ranks for recommendations.

So-called bird dogs assist in identifying prospects for a fee. Newspapers and magazines are constantly scanned for information. After a prospect is identified, usually in her or his junior year, coaches carefully evaluate the individual's abilities by watching games, both in person and on film. Assistant basketball coaches with major recruiting responsibilities often attend more than a hundred high school games a season, in the process missing some of their own team's games. The number of coaches sitting in the stands at summer basketball camps often exceeds the number of the players enrolled. Top blue-chip players, especially, are deluged with letters and telephone calls from coaches, some highly desired players receiving a letter almost daily for more than a year from recruiters. Even university presidents have been called on to call or write a hot prospect.

From start to finish, the entire process is degrading both to the coaches and the players, but it is a game that has to be played. Every possible angle is considered in wooing a prospect; streetwise recruits quickly learn how to bargain for the best deal, often discovering their talents are worth considerable sums. That frequently results in the simple payment of cash to recruits. In 1988 the University of Kentucky found itself in very hot water when twenty $50 bills fell out of a package in the Emery Express office; the monies had allegedly been sent by an assistant coach to a recruit in Los Angeles. One coach from a marginally competitive Division I program during the 1970s, in hot pursuit of a blue-chip basketball player from the inner city of Los Angeles, later admitted he arranged for an annual supplement of $10,000 to the legitimate scholarship. When the coach made that offer, this future all-American and professional star derisively dismissed it with the statement, "Coach, you aren't even close." Although many coaches manage to rise above such shenanigans—especially those at well-established programs with national reputations for winning—recruiting provides the lifeblood of all programs. Unfortunately, many coaches, under intense pressure to win and fearful that their rivals are engaged in cheating, feel compelled to do likewise.

The sordid practice of recruiting has helped produce a substantial body of revealing literature. These books and articles indicate that although coaches and enthusiastic boosters have seldom reached the level of criminal behavior, they have bent, twisted, and outright broken the rules governing recruiting established by the NCAA. Illicit payment of cash to players has been commonplace, often approaching the six-figure level for a four-year stint of eligibility. Other enticements include special considerations for parents, including cash, even jobs; transportation for the player; special housing arrangements; keys to new automobiles. The list of universities and colleges that have been punished for recruiting violations reads like a "who's who" of American higher education—the number of those never receiving severe NCAA sanctions is considerably smaller than those who have. Coach Jerry Tarkanian, whose twenty-two-year college coaching career at Long Beach State and Nevada Las Vegas (UNLV) was plagued by a continued feud with the NCAA's enforcement branch, once joked that he preferred recruiting junior college players because "their cars are already paid for." Possessor of one of the highest winning percentages in college basketball history, Tarkanian departed UNLV in 1992 amidst a storm of controversy for a short-lived career as head coach in the NBA. He left behind one national championship trophy as well as a cluster of worried university administrators pondering allegations about an ongoing NCAA probe into possible of major rules violations.

The NCAA discovered that no matter how aggressive its enforcement efforts, coaches still cheated. Coaches obviously preferred to risk the possibility of being caught and having to suffer the typical sanctions associated with probation: loss of television revenues, banishment for one or two years from postseason play, a reduction in the number of assistant coaches, restrictions on recruiting, the loss of a handful of scholarships. Such punishments seemed to deter the wholesale cheating not even slightly. A substantial increase in the number of NCAA investigators and their budget likewise had no discernible impact. Because they lacked the power to require individuals to divulge information, the investigations often ran into stone walls of silence. Investigations into specific allegations often dragged on for several years, thereby greatly reducing the impact of the eventual sanctions; the guilty parties oftentimes had long since moved on by the time penalties were announced, leaving their innocent successors to suffer the consequences of their actions. However, because the number of institutions hit by various penalties for major violations grew so large, offending institutions suffered only temporary damage and, apparently, little embarrassment.

It was out of a sense of near desperation that in 1985 the NCAA adopted the so-called death penalty. This provided for the curtailment of play for two or more seasons as penalty for a consistent pattern of major transgressions indicating a lack of "institutional control" over the athletic program. In 1987 the NCAA assessed such a penalty for the first (and as of the writing of this book the only) time. The culprit was longtime Southwest Conference powerhouse Southern Methodist University. Not only had the football program been found guilty of five major violations in prior years, but a new three-year investigation indicated that a group of boosters had made monthly payments to more than a dozen top Mustang football players—reaching an annual "payroll" in excess of $60,000. A subsequent book-length investigative report by the journalist David Whitford indicated that a consistent pattern of rampant rules violations had occurred in the SMU football program for more than a decade. Aggressive and wealthy boosters put up the illegal payments as well as providing automobiles and apartments for players. The NCAA's investigation concluded that a continuation of illicit payments to thirteen players was approved by the chairman of the SMU governing board, William Clements, even after the institution learned of a renewed NCAA probe. Apparently, Clements and other officials feared that to shut down the operation would lead to several players spilling the facts to the NCAA. The fact that Clements had served as a former deputy secretary of defense under Presidents Nixon and Ford and governor of the state of Texas only underlined the extent to which the "win at any cost" fever had infected collegiate athletics and society's top leaders— individuals who should have known better.

The shame that SMU suffered was great. The United Methodist Church's southwest jurisdiction council of bishops voted to abolish the SMU board of governors. SMU president Donald Shields resigned, citing health reasons; Coach Bobby Collins was fired but later resurfaced as an athletic fund-raiser for the University of Southern Mississippi. However, the coach under whom the illicit activity allegedly had originated, Ron Meyer, moved with impunity to professional head coaching positions with the New England Patriots and the Indianapolis Colts. He categorically denied any knowledge of wrongdoing during his six-year tenure at SMU. Perhaps the most bitter punishment that SMU's football boosters suffered was that when SMU resumed its football program after a two-year hiatus, it endured several humiliating losing seasons. By 1992 the losses had piled up to the point where ticket sales sagged and a $4 million deficit plagued in the athletic budget. Rumors flew around Dallas that the board of governors was considering the impossible: dropping football.

It is widely believed that many other programs have committed as great, or greater, excesses than those which surfaced at SMU. Basketball coach Gary Colson, long respected for his strong adherence to NCAA rules, has condemned the pressure to win that he and other coaches feel. He was fired by the University of New Mexico in 1988 despite winning an average of eighteen games for each of his eight seasons at the Lobo helm and running a "clean" program that graduated a majority of his players. That he had resurrected a "renegade" program that had been severely hit by NCAA sanctions when former coach Norm Ellenberger had been caught submitting counterfeit transcripts for academically deficient recruits also counted for little. Although Colson came very close, he was not able to get his team into the lucrative NCAA tournament, or as the current sports cliché went, he was incapable of taking the Lobos "to the next level." Following his termination, Colson could still laugh at one ironic twist: when he took the position a local sports reporter had told him that the only way he could win at New Mexico was by cheating, but if he did the writer would report it in his column. In the months leading up to Colson's termination, that same journalist wrote several columns demanding Colson's firing. Colson's plaintive cry could have been uttered by many a college coach: "It's the administration, the athletic director, the president, the board of regents—they want wins, money, prestige, and TV time. They get the coach backed up against the wall. What's he gonna do?"

College Athletics as Big Business

Gary Colson's lament strikes at the heart of the dilemma of major college athletics. Modern intercollegiate athletics has become very big business. Not only did athletic budgets at some institutions reach the incredible level of $20 million annually by the early 1990s, but they have also become, in the special jargon of economic development specialists, generators of an enormous multiplier effect on local economies. The licensing and sale of "official" athletic wear is but one of the more visible examples; motels and restaurants in such college towns as Lawrence, Kansas; Chapel Hill, North Carolina; College Station, Texas; and Knoxville, Tennessee, rely heavily on big game days to generate substantial chunks of their annual revenue. Booster club membership— which can run to five figures—is considered a prerequisite in many communities for acceptance in social and business circles.

On college campuses, the relatively high salaries of coaches and athletic directors have long been a source of faculty discontent. By the early 1990s salaries for "revenue sports" coaches routinely exceeded $100,000; in extreme cases total compensation packages often reached

$500,000 or more. When he left UNLV's beleaguered basketball program in 1992, Jerry "Tark the Shark" Tarkanian was the highest paid employee in the state of Nevada, his university salary of $216,379 far exceeding that of his university president, athletic director, or even the governor of the state! That substantial figure did not include his several other sources of income (rumored to include an athletic shoe contract, sports camp, a hefty incentive bonus for making the NCAA tournament, and commercial endorsements) which were estimated to more than triple his base income. Although Stanford University refused to reveal the compensation package paid for famed football coach Bill Walsh when he was hired in 1992, no university official protested published estimates that placed it above the half-million dollar level. The total "package" for University of Kentucky basketball coach Rick Pitino was estimated that same year to approach $700,000.

What is often not known is that the great preponderance of college athletic departments seldom show a profit at year's end; many departments routinely run deficits, only to be bailed out by generous transfers from the general university budget. If academic deans administered their budgets like many directors of athletics, the full fury of legislative committees and governing boards would result. But athletic administrators and coaches have largely been shielded from accountability by the popular mythology in which big-time college athletics has shrewdly enshrouded itself.

The real beneficiaries of college athletics are those in charge. As their power and income have increased, they have carefully protected themselves from outside scrutiny and control. On many campuses the athletic department is placed outside the budgeting process of the rest of the institution; some are even protected from institutional interference by separate incorporation. A close look at their operations often reveals a lack of control over their expenditures. Although they operate major business enterprises, many athletic directors lack basic business experience or expertise. For the most part they are former coaches, not trained in budgeting or business decision making; they are not trained to have an acute eye for the bottom line. They have been conditioned by the not-for-profit tradition of higher education. During the 1980s the athletic directors at the universities of Illinois and New Mexico were forced to resign because audits turned up major problems with the expenditure of funds. Vice presidents of finance and budgeting at universities across the land have continually confronted the lack of institutional control in athletic departments. Murray Sperber, author of the incisive *College*

Sports, Inc., concludes from a mountain of evidence he has assembled that one of the major untold scandals of college athletics is that many athletic departments lack basic budgetary control because athletic directors "can play with their programs' revenues and not worry too much about the red ink on the floor."

Central to an understanding of college athletics is an appreciation of the powerful role played by the NCAA. Many observers from outside higher education understandably have long been mystified about its philosophy and methods. At times it has appeared to be weak and vacillating, at other times excessively overbearing, even outrageous in its policies and decisions. It has long been criticized, perhaps unfairly, for alleged inconsistency in applying the rules. It has been charged repeatedly with treating established powerful institutions with favoritism, and newcomers in quest of national titles, such as Tarkanian's UNLV, with a special vengeance. There can be no question, however, that it has been woefully slow in responding to issues relating to principle and has tended to resist much needed reform. The NCAA took an indifferent position relative to racial discrimination during the 1950s and 1960s; it adamantly opposed demands for equal treatment of women's athletic programs during the 1970s. It has treated legitimate concerns of athletes with disdain, especially the demands for reasonable payment in return for services rendered. These many criticisms led to the publication in 1993 of a penetrating study of the policies and practices of the NCAA by economists Arthur A. Fleisher III, Brian L. Goff, and Robert D. Tollison. They present a critical academic analysis of an organization riddled with inconsistencies in policy application. But they conclude one major constant exists: the organization has operated as an economic cartel, preventing open market competition in intercollegiate athletics by encouraging collusion among its members to maintain its monopolistic power. In particular, they conclude, the NCAA has created its policies related to student athletic eligibility with an eye to keeping labor costs at a minimum.

The ruling body of college athletics has protected with special vigor the financial interests of its member institutions. All of this stems from one essential fact. Throughout its history the NCAA has been controlled by coaches and athletic directors (most of whom were former coaches themselves) and they have operated the organization with their own special interests in mind. If the organization had become in fact what it proclaimed itself to be in principle —an organization controlled by institutional presidents and faculties — the history of intercollegiate athletics may have more closely approached the lofty ideals so often proclaimed by the public relations machine of the NCAA. But that has not been the case.

Throughout its history the NCAA has operated on a simple, if unwritten, objective: to enhance the power and independence of athletic departments within their institutional setting. This has often resulted in policies designed to protect financial interests, frequently in willful disregard of the educational mission and institutional integrity of its members. Its slick television commercials notwithstanding, the NCAA never championed in a consistent and purposeful manner the educational needs of the students who fell under its wing. The econometric analysis of Professor Fleisher and his associates concludes that the effect of NCAA policy is to treat athletes as an economic cost to be controlled. The creation and implementation of the complex and convoluted body of rules and regulations governing recruitment and eligibility serve the interests of the powerful cartel of the NCAA.

With the arrival of television, the size of the economic pot grew rapidly. The NCAA quickly established complete control of the televising of football, and during the 1960s its basketball tournament became a bonanza, ultimately leading to a billion-dollar contract in the 1990s. All of these factors contributed to the organization's monopoly. As Fleisher and associates write,

> The reality of its [NCAA] actions reduced output, increased prices, and increased profits in intercollegiate athletics. Although some, including spokespersons for the NCAA, have suggested that the input restrictions merely maintain amateurism and competitive balance, the output restrictions are clear signs of rent-enhancing collusion. The only rationale, for example, behind the NCAA's study of television's impact on attendance is that of a profit-maximizing cartel. The monopolized television contract, the expansion of the basketball tournament, and similar actions fall squarely into the cartel explanation of NCAA behavior.

The ultimate irony of intercollegiate athletics is that over the years scores of major universities and colleges have been found to be in serious violation of the rules they themselves had established. In the years immediately following World War II, the NCAA moved from its minimal role of establishing the game rules for various sports and conducting national tournaments to becoming a regulatory and rules enforcement body. It was not until after the war that the NCAA acquired authority to police the behavior of its members; previously, academic leaders held to the naive premise that each institution was morally bound to police its own ranks. Widespread media reports of recruiting violations, coupled with the shocking revelations of academic cheating at West Point and the basketball gambling scandal, eventually gave the lie to this myth, producing intense pressure for reform.

The first attempt at gaining control over member institutions fizzled badly. In 1948 the NCAA convention adopted the so-called Sanity Code, which decreed that any financial aid given to an athlete had to come through regular financial aid channels and that any aid must "be awarded on the basis of qualifications of which athletic ability is not one." This blatant attempt to reduce the cost of athletic programs at the expense of athletes drew criticism primarily from southern institutions that, at the time, lacked the athletic traditions of more established eastern and midwestern universities. Immediately several member institutions openly and flagrantly violated the code. An attempt to suspend seven of those institutions barely failed to receive the necessary two-thirds vote of the membership at the 1950 convention. Consequently, and in near desperation, the annual convention of members established the authority of the association to investigate and punish member institutions for violations of the association's policies. The intent was to assure that all member institutions competed on "a level playing field." These compliance concerns coalesced with the obvious need for management of a coherent policy on television rights for college football games and for the regulation of post-season bowl games. During the 1950s the NCAA thus became a powerful force in intercollegiate athletics, having the power to establish and enforce policies governing the entire scope of intercollegiate athletics. And with its control over television rights, it also now sat on a potentially enormous pot of new money.

The record of the organization in providing the desired level playing field has been a dismal one. Over the years the great majority of its Division I membership suffered the embarrassment of being punished for rules violations. If the ultimate goal of sports is to teach good sportsmanship and adherence to established rules, then higher education has failed dismally in setting a good example. During the 1980s, for example, 111 colleges and universities received various sanctions for violations. And many institutions were punished for multiple violations in more than one of their sports programs.

Conclusion

In 1929 a specially funded commission by the Carnegie Foundation concluded that sports at the collegiate level was riddled with corruption and hypocrisy, commenting that "the ethical bearing of intercollegiate football contests and their scholastic aspects are of secondary importance to the winning of victories and financial success." More than half a century later, a blue-ribbon panel commissioned by the Knight Foundation issued a much heralded report which essentially concluded that nothing much had changed since 1929, only the size of the scandal had grown to much greater proportions. The distinguished panel of educators and public leaders on the Knight Commission felt compelled to focus on fundamental principles: only individuals capable of meeting an institution's academic requirements should be permitted to compete on its athletic teams; recruiting policies and practices need a complete overhaul; booster involvement needs to be eliminated, or at least strictly controlled; and coaches and administrators must be held accountable for their behavior. When the report was released in 1991, former Notre Dame president and co-chair of the commission Father Theodore M. Hesburgh expressed his hope that the report would be implemented: "We would love to put the sleaziness of college sports to rest."

The Knight report proposed a model for reform that placed primary responsibility for academic integrity, financial honesty, and public accountability on the campus president. Significantly, the commission chose not to place responsibility on athletic directors, coaches, or faculty athletic committees. It emphasized that only a strong and committed president could assure institutional compliance. In a public statement directed to all institutional heads, the commission stated: "You are the linchpin of the reform movement. At your own institution your efforts are critical to a sound athletic program, one that honors the integrity of both your institution and the students who wear your colors. Together with your colleagues across the nation you can assure that college athletics serve the best ideals of higher education."

Indicative of the growing sentiment that only strong presidential leadership could save the sinking ship of college athletics was the election in 1993 of only the second university president to head the NCAA, all but one of the organization's previous leaders having come from the ranks of coaches and athletic directors. The selection of Joseph N. Crowley, the president of the University of Nevada, Reno, perhaps signaled that a fundamental change was about to occur in college sports. Crowley had for years played a leadership role among a small coterie of campus presidents who wanted to assert their dominance over their own athletic departments as well as the NCAA. To this end he had chaired a committee that proposed a radical new approach to rules compliance—five-year certification based on institutional self-studies and external peer review, similar to the academic accreditation process which had served higher education well for decades.

Crowley's election was not the result of a quirk, but the result of the President's Council within the NCAA finally asserting its influence. Led by such reformers as Charles Young of UCLA, Thomas Hearn of Wake Forest, John DiBiaggio of Michigan State, and Gregory O'Brien of Tulane, institutional presidents indicated their intention of controlling the organization. Crowley's election sent a strong message indicating that a group of concerned presidents had decided the time had come to address important issues, including gender equity, academic progress of athletes, recruitment policies, and fiscal control. Those who wanted these issues addressed in a meaningful fashion interpreted Crowley's election as a signal that the long period of dominance by coaches and athletic directors had ended. The increased interest of the presidents came not just from sudden awareness of responsibility. Rather it stemmed from a healthy dose of enlightened self-interest. They now recognized that if the NCAA could not put its house in order, intervention by the federal government loomed large. The haunting possibility that higher education might lose control of its athletic programs to the federal government created a rush for internal reform.

"In recent times," one university president commented in an article in *Sports Illustrated* shortly before Crowley's election, "several universities—indeed entire conferences—have seemed willing to sacrifice even minimal academic standards in exchange for producing winning teams. . . . Now that the presidents have discovered how to reform intercollegiate athletics, we have no further excuses for scandal and failure." That these words were written by the recently installed president of the University of Iowa, Hunter Rawlings III, provides an appropriately ironic twist. It was, after all, the University of Iowa that had provided Connie Hawkins with his only collegiate experience as a so-called student-athlete.

Muhammad Ali rocks defending champion George Foreman with a hard right during their heavyweight title fight in Zaire on October 30, 1974. Ali will be remembered as one of boxing's all-time greats, a man whose courage in challenging public opinion during the turbulent 1960s equalled his bravery in the ring.

HARBRACE
BOOKS
ON AMERICA

SINCE 1945

Chapter
8

Bigger
Than Life:
Sports and
American
Society

From the time he was a young child no one ever accused Cassius Marcellus Clay, Jr., of being modest. Even *before* he captured the world heavyweight championship he boastfully proclaimed to anyone within earshot that he was "The Greatest." Many students of boxing ultimately came to the conclusion that in his prime, he was indeed one of the best of all heavyweight champions, with more speed than Rocky Marciano, more cunning than Gene Tunney, greater stamina and ability to take a punch than Rocky Marciano, a more complete repertoire of punches than Joe Louis, and charisma greater than Jack Dempsey. Perhaps he *was* the greatest; arguments on that topic will rage forever in the taverns of America. There can be no question, however, that he excelled in generating controversy. Even the first black heavyweight champion, flamboyant Jack Johnson, seems almost modest in comparison. No sports figure in American history has so polarized a nation by taking unpopular positions on explosive issues. That he did so to his own detriment out of deep personal conviction is beyond question. In the process he demonstrated far greater personal courage than he ever did by entering the ring against the likes of Sonny Liston or Joe Frazier.

He created a succession of public outcries by resolutely refusing to follow the expectations of a public accustomed to black champions, like Joe Louis, Floyd Patterson, and Jersey Joe Walcott, who conducted themselves in a circumspect manner. He defiantly followed his conscience by embracing the Black Muslim faith, by insisting on being called by his Muslim name of Muhammad Ali, even to the point of intentionally inflaming racial passions in his prefight comments. By rejecting induction into the U.S. military in 1967, he underscored the growing national opposition to the war in Vietnam. These actions exacerbated resentment among those who felt he did not demonstrate the proper sense of patriotism or even the personal modesty expected of athletic greats; by continually proclaiming himself "The Greatest" and by predicting the round (sometimes correctly) in which he would dispatch his next opponent, Ali seemed to many fans to be an insufferable braggart. To a wide spectrum of Americans he became the worst of all possible public persons; he was a "bad nigger."

Muhammad Ali burst on the American scene during the midst of the tumultuous 1960s, and his actions reflected the polarized values of a society suffering embittered social conflict. His announcement the day after capturing the heavyweight championship that he had converted to the Black Muslim faith produced an avalanche of unfavorable responses. "I believe in the religion of Islam," he said, "which means I believe there is no God but Allah, and Elijah Muhammad is His Apostle. This is the same religion that is believed in by over seven hundred million dark-skinned peoples throughout Africa and Asia." Defiance sparkling in his eyes that February day in 1964, the freshly crowned twenty-two-year-old world heavyweight champion told stunned reporters, "I don't have to be what you want me to be. I am free to be who I want."

Although black response was divided, his announcement produced an overwhelmingly negative response from white America. His insistence on being called by his newly adopted Muslim name, Cassius X, and a few months later Muhammad Ali, added to the public outcry. Even the generally tolerant *New York Times* refused to use the new name for several years, not until he completed the necessary legal paperwork to that effect. A small religious group that had its roots in the depressed northern ghettoes of the 1930s, the Black Muslims adhered to such central tenets as belief in the moral superiority of blacks and a flat rejection of the central objective of the civil rights movement: racial integration.

The growing influence of Black Muslims among younger, often poor urban blacks greatly concerned the leaders of such establishment civil rights organizations as the National Association for the Advancement of Colored People (NAACP), the Congress of Racial Equality, and the Southern Christian Leadership Conference. Rejecting the goal of racial integration, Muslims advocated racial separation to preserve the integrity of blacks from being despoiled by "white devils." Malcolm X and other leaders had inspired considerable fear with a strident rhetoric that went to the extent of endorsing violence as a means of self-protection; they denounced Dr. Martin Luther King, Jr.'s, prescription of nonviolence as extreme folly. Their advocacy of black nationalism and racial separation thus constituted a direct challenge to the long-accepted goals of racial harmony and social integration. In essence they had the temerity to challenge one of the central precepts of American liberalism. That Malcolm X and the Black Muslims also emphasized the importance of sexual fidelity, education, the rule of law, and the work ethic and condemned the use of alcohol and illegal drugs was lost on their legions of critics.

When the news media learned that the feared Malcolm X himself had helped convert the new heavyweight champion away from his Baptist faith, the public reacted swiftly and with hostility. The prominent sportswriter Joe Cannon said that Ali's new faith was "more pernicious [a] hate symbol than . . . Nazism." The revered Joe Louis expressed dismay: "Clay will earn the public's hatred because of his connections with the Black Muslims. The things they preach are just the opposite of what we believe. The heavyweight champion should be the champion of all the people. He has responsibilities to all the people." Dr. King also expressed his concern: "When Cassius Clay joined the Black Muslims and started calling himself Cassius X, he became a champion of racial segregation and that is what we are fighting against."

The criticism that greeted Ali's announcement about his religious conversion was mild in comparison to what erupted when he refused induction into the U.S. Army for religious reasons. In 1966 he had expressed his antiwar sentiments with the oft-quoted line from one of his poems: "I ain't got nothing against them Viet Cong." By the time of his dramatic decision the following year his impressive array of boxing skills had been amply demonstrated by demolishing eight challengers; thus his refusal to join the armed services took on immense symbolic significance. The American people had come to expect their heavyweight champion to personify traditional patriotic values. Joe Louis had served in World War II and Rocky Marciano in the Korean War. By the time Ali refused to take the symbolic step forward at a Houston induction center in February of 1967, the American people had become sharply divided over the war. His announcement coincided with an outbreak of antiwar protests that engulfed many college campuses and urban centers. Angry black spokesmen, pointing to the high number of young blacks in Vietnam, charged that draft laws protected middle-class whites while young black men were serving and dying in disproportionate numbers. Ali told a cluster of dubious reporters that American policy in Vietnam conflicted with the teachings of the Koran. "We don't take part in Christian wars or wars of any unbelievers." Outside the induction center national television showed a group of black youth demonstrating their support for Ali's stand, reading aloud from the writings of the martyred Malcolm X, chanting "Black power!" and "Stop whitey's war!" One protester shouted into a microphone, "America is a house on fire. Let it burn, let it burn." Such defiance frightened and angered middle America, and Ali suffered the heavy consequences.

Ali immediately felt the sting of institutional retaliation. The New York Boxing Association moved with amazing speed, stripping Ali of his heavyweight championship and suspending his boxing license just one hour after he refused to enter the military. The World Boxing Association quickly followed suit, as did several state commissions. The State Department, under court order, lifted his passport, making it impossible for him to travel outside the United States to pursue his boxing career on more friendly terrain. Suddenly bereft of both his title and means of livelihood, Ali lamented, "I want to do what is right, what'll look good in history." He asked, "Am I a fool to give up my wealth and my title and go lay in prison? . . . Do you think I'm serious? If I am, then why can't I worship as I want to in America? All I want is justice." He confessed his puzzlement: "Blacks and whites are dying in Vietnam so those people over there will have the freedom to worship as they want. So how come I can't do it here?" In the rush to vilify the ex-champion, an angry public, including most members of the media, missed an important subtlety. Ali did not necessarily oppose the American war effort, just his own participation. Learning that Joe Louis had criticized his actions, Ali responded in a characteristic fashion that only exacerbated the delicate situation: "Louis, he doesn't know what the words mean. He's a sucker."

After an all-white jury in Houston found Ali guilty of refusing induction into the military, federal judge Joseph Ingraham gave him the maximum sentence of five years' imprisonment. During the course of the trial the judge ruled that a member of the Black Muslims did not qualify for exemption from the draft for religious purposes. The ex-champion remained free while his lawyers pursued appeals through the federal court system, but the specter of serious jail time loomed. "I'm not scared about going to jail," Ali said. "Somebody's got to stand up. If I went to jail for robbing a bank or beating somebody up, I'd be going for nothing. But I don't mind going for what I believe in." Actually, Ali did spend ten days in jail in December of 1968, his offense being driving an automobile without a valid driver's license. His irate attorney contended that this unusually severe sentence in a Miami court was based on Ali's religious affiliation and his stand against the draft. "He got sentenced for being Cassius Clay. Everyone is caught up in the hate Clay hysteria."

The maelstrom of controversy that surrounded Ali underscored the importance Americans attach to their sports figures. It also demonstrated that the world of sports is inextricably linked to the broader issues of American society. Ali's immense athletic talent and his unique personality only served to intensify the public scrutiny under which he operated. Born to working-class parents in Louisville, Kentucky, on January 17, 1942, he grew up in the Baptist faith. Although he and his father, a talented sign painter by trade, had their difficult moments, Ali grew up in a warm and nurturing family. "At one time our people were poor financially, but we was rich with health, rich with friends," he recalled. The youngster never demonstrated interest in school, and eventually received a certificate of attendance upon completing high school. From an early age, however, he demonstrated an acute awareness that he was a black person in a society controlled by whites; being refused admission as a child to a Louisville movie theater while in the company of white friends proved to be an important turning point. Although his lack of formal education often revealed itself, he possessed an inquisitive and perceptive mind.

By the time he finished elementary school, young Cassius Clay had recognized that many opportunities available to whites were denied him. When he concluded that boxing offered his main chance, he pursued his dream with a fierce determination, becoming a dedicated boxing pupil in a local gymnasium. He soon began to attract local attention as a boxer, winning a bout on local television at the age of thirteen. His coach told his parents, "This kid has tremendous reflexes, a natural ability, a good mind for a great boxer." During his high school years he won national Golden Gloves and Amateur Athletic Union light heavyweight championships.

From early childhood he regularly engaged in seemingly erratic behavior designed to attract attention. "I've been an attraction ever since I've been able to walk and talk," he later recalled. "When I was a little boy in school, I caught on to how nearly everybody likes to watch somebody that acts different. . . . I always liked to draw crowds." Early in his development as an amateur boxer he learned that outrageous conduct—demeaning his opponents, predicting the round in which he would score a knockout, loudly proclaiming his superiority—served a real purpose by intimidating opponents; in candid moments he confided to his close friends that this behavior also helped him overcome any self-doubts he might have. His penchant for making himself the center of attention intensified after he won the light heavyweight gold medal at the 1960 Olympics in Rome. He entered the professional ranks with the sponsorship of a consortium of prominent Louisville businessmen. He benefited enormously from the astute guidance of trainer Angelo Dundee, struggling with his inexperience in several close bouts. After winning a series of bouts against increasingly skilled opponents, he brashly predicted that he would be the next heavyweight champion. Promoters came to appreciate his prefight comments because they created public interest and increased ticket sales. He attracted media interest by reciting primitive poetry that predicted the round in which he would knock out his upcoming opponent. Before his first New York City fight in 1962 against the seemingly formidable Sonny Banks, he told a disbelieving cluster of sportswriters, "The man must fall in the round I call. Banks must fall in four." Banks did, and Cassius Clay was on his way.

After nineteen consecutive professional victories, fourteen by knockout, Cassius Clay met the vaunted Sonny Liston for the world heavyweight championship. He was just twenty-two years old, and in the minds of nearly every boxing expert woefully inexperienced and unprepared for Liston. A convicted felon (armed robbery) whose sullen demeanor and efficient fighting style presented an aura of invincibility and ruthlessness, Liston had won the championship by demolishing Floyd Patterson in just one round. Rocky Marciano, among others, urged that the fight be cancelled, fearing Clay's career, if not his health, would be ruined. The boxing commissioner in California announced he would not sanction the

fight in his state because it was "a dangerous mis-
match" that could result in "grave injury to the young
challenger." During the weigh-in the morning of the
fight, Clay seemingly went berserk, shouting epithets
at the impassive Liston as his face quivered with emo-
tion. "You're a bear. I'm going to whup you so baaad!
You're a chump, a chump!" he screamed hysterically.
The "Louisville Lip" had lived up to his name. Witnesses
to this event were stunned, many concluding that Clay
had become consumed by fear. His outburst, however,
was simply a more elaborate and calculated version
of a ploy he had used many times before.

With nearly a million viewers watching on closed
circuit television and 8,300 fans in the Miami Convention Hall, Clay quickly dispelled any doubts about his
ability. Using his quickness, the prohibitive 7–1 underdog immediately negated Liston's powerful punches,
even mockingly dropping his hands to his sides and
daring "the ugly bear" to hit him. As Liston futilely
flailed away, Clay repeatedly punished him with sharp
left jabs. "Float like a butterfly, sting like a bee," he and
one of his handlers had repeatedly chanted during
training. By round four he was stinging his demoralized
opponent with impunity. In less than twelve minutes,
Sonny Liston had been transformed from a fearsome,
seemingly omnipotent fighter into a frustrated, beaten
man, his face a bloody mess. He lasted only two more
rounds as the increasingly aggressive and confident
challenger pounded away with both hands in a devastating display of power and speed. A soundly beaten
Sonny Liston refused to come out when the bell sounded
for round seven. While Liston slumped in his corner an
exuberant Clay danced around the ring, shouting wildly
at the press row: "I told you! I told you! I'm the greatest!"

The next day the new champion stunned the
world with his announcement that he had become a
Black Muslim. Soon thereafter he denounced his "slave
name" and demanded to be called Cassius X, the X
being symbolic of his lost African heritage. A few months
later he changed his name again to Muhammad Ali
at the request of the leader of the Black Muslims, Elijah
Muhammad. Contrary to widespread disbelief, Ali's
religious conversion was sincere; he never wavered

in his dedication to the teaching of Islam. He let it be known that contrary to popular convention and public expectations, he was going to be his own man. He understood that his decision would be at an enormous personal sacrifice, but he could not have fully appreciated the extent of that cost. Potential sponsors shunned him, costing him millions of dollars in advertisement endorsements.

Race had always provided an important aspect of boxing's symbolism, but Ali seemed intent on accentuating its importance. After easily defeating Liston in a return match, Ali turned to his next challenger, former champion Floyd Patterson. A quiet and dignified man, Patterson had demonstrated a safe traditionalism during his relatively brief reign as champion, assiduously avoiding controversy. In the days before their November 1965 fight, this dedicated Roman Catholic criticized Ali's embrace of the Black Muslims. He questioned not only the champion's judgment but also his patriotism. He refused to use Ali's Muslim name, pointedly referring to him as "Cassius Clay." At a press conference Patterson equated the Muslims with the Ku Klux Klan: "I have nothing but contempt for the Black Muslims and that for which they stand. The image of a Black Muslim as the world heavyweight champion disgraces the sport and the nation. Cassius Clay must be beaten and the Black Muslim's scourge removed from boxing." Patterson had long lent his support to the civil rights movement, and when he signed to fight Ali he announced he intended to "take back" the title for America. Referring to the Muslims as "a menace" to America, Patterson's electric comments intensified the clash of values symbolized by the impending championship fight: "I believe the Muslim preaching of segregation, hatred, rebellion, and violence is wrong." His opponent, he charged, "is disgracing himself and the Negro race." The November 1965 championship fight in Las Vegas took on intense racial overtones at the very time when America was contemplating the meaning of the recent rioting in Watts, the growing chorus of discordant cries demanding "black power," and the bloodbath surrounding civil rights demonstrations in the South.

The controversy did not end with the fight; sharply different versions of it still vie with each other today. From the first round it became apparent that Patterson was hopelessly outclassed. A recurrence of a serious back injury compounded his problems. Round after round, Ali pounded him with an amazing assortment of blows while using his quickness to avoid Patterson's seemingly lethargic punches. Patterson gamely hung on, refusing to quit while absorbing brutal punishment. The referee later said, "It was hurting me to watch. . . . He lobbed his punches like a feeble old woman." To Patterson's supporters, Ali seemed to be convulsed with hatred, even taking pleasure in torturing his opponent. Following the twelfth round TKO, they condemned Ali for bad sportsmanship, even cruelty. Convinced that Ali purposely prolonged the fight after Patterson had been rendered helpless merely to humiliate him, *Life* magazine called the fight a "sickening spectacle." Ali's defenders, and they were relatively few, contended that Ali merely pursued a sound ring strategy, and reminded fans that boxing is a blood sport. Howard Cosell, a prominent defender of Ali, even contended that Ali had been kind to Patterson by not ending the fight with an embarrassing early knockout.

The Patterson fight set the stage for Ali's frequent exploitation of the racial issue in later fights. In 1966 challenger Ernie Terrell pointedly referred to his opponent by the name of Cassius Clay and questioned Ali's patriotism by referring to his opposition to the war in Vietnam. Ali responded by humiliating Terrell in a ferocious beating. Beginning with Terrell, Clay fell into the habit of characterizing his black opponents as "Uncle Toms" and later drew on savage racial imagery by calling Joe Frazier "an ape." Ali thus stimulated the ancient ghost of antiblack sentiment among white fans and focused attention on the growing divisions within the black community as well.

The issue of racism, however, assumed a secondary level in the public eye after Ali refused to join the army. Following his conviction on April 28, 1967, and his swift forced exit from boxing, Ali spent three and a half years speaking on the college lecture circuit, articulating his views on his newly found faith, the role of blacks in American society, and his refusal to serve in Vietnam. He appeared on more than two hundred campuses, and although his audiences were overwhelmingly friendly, it was not unusual for a heckler to interrupt him with cries of "nigger draft dodger" or variations on that theme.

In his opposition to the war, Ali was ahead of public opinion. His thinking anticipated future trends in public opinion. Following the Tet offensive in February of 1968, the American people began to turn against the war. President Lyndon Johnson carefully examined the polls following his near defeat to an antiwar candidate in the New Hampshire primary and shocked the nation by announcing he would not seek reelection. As antiwar protests increased in size and ferocity, one of Ali's strongest defenders among the political establishment, Senator Robert F. Kennedy, moved toward capturing the Democratic nomination while making opposition to the war the centerpiece of his campaign. Ali also had a strong supporter in Howard Cosell, whose trenchant television and radio commentaries presented Ali's position in a compelling fashion. Cosell condemned the action of the athletic commissions in withdrawing Ali's boxing license as "an outrage, an absolute disgrace." Cosell dismissed the commissioners as "political hacks" and "men of such meager talent" who not only refused to grant Ali due process but bowed to political pressure because the former champion "failed the test of political and social conformity." Slowly but inexorably, however, public admiration and support for Ali began to grow as enthusiasm for the war waned and Americans began to view racial issues with a greater degree of sensitivity.

By 1970 public opinion made a decisive swing in his direction. He became increasingly recognized as a brave and honest man who had the courage to stand up for his convictions in the face of intense public pressure. In that year a changed public opinion—and a court order by the New York district judge—led to his reinstatement by the New York boxing commission. The district court judge was startled to learn that the boxing commission had previously granted licenses to some ninety convicted felons, including rapists, murderers, armed robbers, child molesters, and military deserters; in light of such comparisons, not surprisingly, Judge Walter Mansfield found the boxing commission's action in stripping Ali of his license "arbitrary and unreasonable discrimination" and a severe violation of his constitutional rights under the Fourteenth Amendment.

Ultimately, the U.S. Supreme Court unanimously overturned Ali's conviction on June 21, 1971. During its early deliberations the justices had originally voted 5-3 to uphold, thereby sending Ali to jail. But the mood of the country had changed, and the justices apparently sought an out. They seized on a minor discrepancy in the government's case to overturn the conviction. In so doing, however, the Court delicately sidestepped ruling on whether Ali's religious faith merited a military exemption as a conscientious objector.

Shortly before the Supreme Court handed down its decision, Ali returned to the heights of the boxing world in one of the most memorable matches in the history of boxing. It was the first of three slugfests with Joe Frazier. Few fights in boxing history have had such an enormous buildup or produced such interest as the one on March 8, 1971. It certainly was the biggest purse ever offered by a promoter up to that time: $2.5 million to each man. Both Ali and Frazier entered the fight undefeated in their professional careers. Ali's legacy now was on the line: those who hated him cheered for Frazier; those who supported him cursed Frazier. Bryant Gumbel recalls his emotions as a young black as the fight approached: "It's very difficult to imagine being young and black in the sixties and not gravitating towards Ali. . . . He was a heroic figure, plain and simple."

Following his lengthy layoff, Ali had difficulty regaining his previous fighting form. In late 1970 he had defeated Jerry Quarry and Oscar Bonevena, but astute observers recognized that the four-year hiatus had reduced his physical skills. Ali conducted his usual prefight psychological warfare—including caustic references to Frazier as "an ape" and "a gorilla"—but the defending champion refused to join in the debate. The fight lasted for fifteen brutal rounds; for ten rounds they fought to a standoff, but then Frazier's youth prevailed

as Ali's legs lost their resilience. In the last round, Frazier
floored the ex-champion with a monstrous left hook;
only instinct and courage enabled Ali to finish the bout
on his feet. Frazier won a unanimous decision and Ali's
enemies were delighted. But Ali came back to win a
rematch in January of 1974 and the following October
reclaimed the championship by knocking out George
Foreman in Zaire. In 1975 in Manila he once more
defeated Frazier in a dramatic championship fight—
which poet Ali dubbed "the thrilla in Manila"—that
saw both men push the outer edges of courage in
taking, and administering, incredible punishment.

Ali ultimately paid a heavy price for his courage.
Like many athletes, he refused to concede that his
physical abilities had diminished with the passage of
time. In his forty rounds in the ring with Frazier he
absorbed devastating blows to the head. Subsequent
encounters with such younger fighters as George Foreman, Leon Spinks, Ken Norton, and Larry Holmes also
exacted a heavy toll. Despite his loss of speed, Ali
continued his career—against the advice of his physician, Ferdie Pacheco. After Holmes administered an
unmerciful ten-round beating in Las Vegas in 1980,
Ali reluctantly retired at the age of thirty-eight. Shortly
thereafter he began to demonstrate the physical
symptoms of what fight fans call "punch-drunk"—
slurring words, memory loss, nervous tics, and quak-
ing hands. Subsequent physical examination indicated that the thousands of blows Ali had absorbed over
nearly three decades as an amateur and professional
boxer had produced permanent neurological damage. In 1984 doctors at UCLA Medical Center diagnosed his affliction as Parkinson's disease, a serious
debilitating disorder of the central nervous system that
affects speaking, walking, and memory.

By age fifty he was a mere shadow of his former
self, living on a small farm in Michigan, devoting
much of his time to study of Islam, living off modest
reserves saved from his glory years. Civil rights and
political leader Andrew Young admiringly assessed
Ali's impact on American society: "Muhammad was
probably the first black man in America to successfully break with the white establishment and survive. He

set his own course religiously, politically, and cultur-
ally. And in that sense, he was very important because he established a new concept of equality."

The Enduring
Question of Race

Muhammad Ali streaked across the American sports world like
a blazing comet. In his prime he was a sparkling boxer, his
talent glorious to behold. He also inspired a spectrum of reactions ranging from anger to exhilaration to confusion. Like no other
American sports figure, Ali first divided a nation and then provided a
mechanism for healing. By sticking to his convictions, he forced the
American people to examine their innermost values and to confront
important public issues.

Ali also inspired others to speak out on social issues. Prominent
among these was a young sports sociologist from the University of
California, Harry Edwards. This former track star at San Jose State
University attempted to organize a boycott of the 1968 Olympics by
black track and field athletes because of the early inclination of the
International Olympic Committee (IOC) to permit the participation of
South Africa and Rhodesia at Mexico City, despite their apartheid
policies. Edwards's protest also incorporated other grievances, including insufficient representation of blacks on the U.S. Olympic Committee (USOC) and a dearth of black coaches. By 1968 boycotts and
demonstrations by black activists had become almost commonplace in
the United States. On several college campuses black athletes had
threatened strikes to achieve their demands for more black athletic
administrators, coaches, and trainers. Several schools in the Western
Athletic Conference had to deal with a refusal by blacks to compete
against Brigham Young University because of the policies of the Mormon
Church preventing blacks from entering the priesthood.

Encouraged by moderate success in staging a boycott against a
major track meet in Madison Square Garden in February of 1968,
Edwards turned his attention to the Mexico City games. However, a
subsequent ruling by the Mexican government forbidding Rhodesian
athletes to enter the country and an IOC announcement suspending
South Africa took the steam out of his movement. Edwards nonetheless
persisted in pushing for a boycott, increasing the scope of his demands.
The assassination of Martin Luther King, Jr., in Memphis on April 4,

1968, added an emotional dimension to his effort; but despite great publicity, the boycott eventually fizzled. In no small measure, this resulted from the personal campaign waged by track star Jesse Owens, himself a member of the USOC, who traveled the nation to counter Edwards's campaign. Owens invoked traditional patriotic arguments while arguing, in an ironic twist, that the Olympics should be kept out of politics. The efforts of this soft-spoken black man from Cleveland, who had greatly embarrassed Adolf Hitler at the 1936 Berlin Olympics by winning four gold medals in track and field, met with considerable success. Many black athletes agonized over their individual decisions, but for personal and policy reasons ultimately decided to compete. All that remained would be a few symbolic "black power" gestures by sprinters Tommie Smith and John Carlos on the victory stand during the playing of the nation anthem. Images of their bowed heads and raised clenched fists, vividly captured by ABC television and newspaper photographers, infuriated the American people and members of the USOC. Summarily reprimanded and expelled by both the IOC and the USOC, Carlos and Smith received little public sympathy and considerable grief from an irate American public.

The furor over black power at Mexico City soon faded from the public dialogue as a new era of healing and conciliation ensued. The new respect and genuine affection showered on Muhammad Ali became symptomatic of a more accepting national mood. Violent civil rights demonstrations gave way to serious discussions about the best way to accelerate racial understanding and to enable minorities to gain greater access to the opportunities of American life. A stagnating economy and an energy crisis created new public agendas; a decade characterized by protest and violence gave way to concern over economic growth and energy policies. By ending the military draft and eventually bringing closure to the war in Vietnam, President Richard Nixon helped create an atmosphere in which issues could be addressed in a calmer, more deliberative fashion. Nixon's dramatic trip to China in 1973 also helped create a climate conducive to greater acceptance of racial and cultural differences.

During the 1970s black athletes took a decided step forward as they received greater recognition for their skills and less for their political or social beliefs. As racial stereotypes became less pronounced, blacks also received greater acceptance as individuals. Kareem Abdul-Jabbar (formerly Lew Alcindor) became one of the nation's most popular college and professional basketball stars, and Henry Aaron surpassed Babe Ruth's record, receiving more cheers than racial jeers. Overt racism certainly did not disappear from American sports, as Aaron's melancholy memoir suggests, but it definitely was in a period of slow decline. The quiet and dedicated Arthur Ashe, a native of Richmond, Virginia, received public acclaim after he became the first black to win the Wimbledon men's singles tennis championship in 1975, having earlier made history by winning the U.S. Open in 1968. Affluent whites continued to flock to NBA games, even though the teams had become predominantly black. Widespread fears that this would drive white customers away proved incorrect. With regularity blacks received Heisman trophies and most valuable player awards; they even appeared with increasing frequency in commercial endorsements. In 1975 and 1976, baseball fans everywhere thrilled to the play of the "Big Red Machine" from Cincinnati, generally recognized as one of the best teams in history. This powerful and exciting team provided vivid testimony to the ideal of racial and cultural diversity, featuring such stars as Hispanics Davey Concepcion and Tony Perez, blacks Joe Morgan and George Foster, and the feisty homegrown white dynamo from a Cincinnati working-class neighborhood, Pete Rose.

In the final analysis, sports helped the American people to focus on the important and complex issue of racism. During the 1980s Michael Jordan and Earvin "Magic" Johnson became two of the most popular men in America; the appearance of black quarterbacks no longer stirred controversy. Traditional racial stereotypes faded before the reality of a new and vibrant generation of black athletes. People thrilled to the incredible acrobatics of "Air" Jordan on the basketball court and laughed at the antics of oversized lineman-turned-ball-carrier William "The Refrigerator" Perry of the Chicago Bears, just as they had earlier cheered the dedication and determination of Olympic decathlon champion Rafer Johnson in 1960, and contributed to the fund to assist professional basketballer Maurice Stokes bravely fight the crippling disease of encephalopathy, which left him completely paralyzed and unable to speak. Americans of all backgrounds and races learned from their association with sports that remarkable human beings come in all sizes and shapes and colors, possessing different talents, personalities, and temperaments.

Sports and Real-Life Concerns

As in the case of Stokes, the public also learned athletes are subject to the tragedies that beset the human race. With increased television and other media coverage, the seasoned fan came to understand that even the greatest athletes, no matter their skill level, are human. This in part has come from a much expanded scope of responsibilities assumed by sports journalists, who no longer feel a responsibility to protect star athletes engaged in antisocial or other destructive behavior. The impact of the Watergate scandals during the early 1970s glamorized investigative reporting, and the best of sports journalists took heed. Following the example of Howard Cosell, journalists now report sports news within a much broader and more meaningful social context. One can only hazard a guess as to how the nation's most famous baseball hero, Babe Ruth, would have fared with the media had he played during the 1990s instead of at a time when the media do not routinely describe the private lives of athletes. At the very least, the Babe's notorious womanizing, alcohol abuse, gluttony, and general penchant for destructive behavior would not have been kept from the public view. More than likely, he would never have achieved his mythical stature in American life, his achievements on the baseball diamond notwithstanding.

Athletes in the post-Cosell, post-Watergate era know their personal behavior can eclipse their performance on the field. Most athletes, but certainly not all, thus use a greater degree of discretion in conducting their private lives. Unfortunately, depressing stories about drug abuse, alcoholism, tax evasion, womanizing, even violent criminal behavior frequently command headlines on the sports pages of American newspapers.

Even though the American people had become somewhat inured to learning about off-field tragedies involving sports figures, the announcement in October of 1991 that Magic Johnson had tested HIV positive stunned the nation. For a decade the issue of how to combat the deadly new disease of acquired immune deficiency syndrome (AIDS) had been before the American public. Although the numbers afflicted were minuscule when compared with victims of cancer and cardiac disease, the fatal disease had assumed a high political profile because the two major groups initially most susceptible to the disease were male homosexuals and drug abusers. The intense questions revolving around the rights of homosexuals made AIDS a major issue in American politics. Presidents Ronald Reagan and George Bush had responded less than enthusiastically to demands for increased federal funding for research and preventive educational programs because they feared losing support from powerful single-interest groups within the Republican camp. Fundamentalist evangelical Christians strongly opposed AIDS education programs, especially in the public schools, because of their strong condemnation of homosexuality, their opposition to sex education programs in public schools, a strong moral aversion to substance abuse, and their insistence on sexual abstinence until marriage.

Magic Johnson's announcement that he had tested positive for the first stage of the incurable disease—human immunodeficiency virus, HIV—helped produce a more enlightened public understanding of the nature of the disease, hopefully leading to better public policy. On the basketball court, this backcourt star of the Los Angeles Lakers could indeed perform magic with his breathtaking ball handling and shooting skills; only Larry Bird of the Boston Celtics and Michael Jordan of the Chicago Bulls enjoyed comparable popularity among professional basketball fans. Johnson's popularity, however, transcended his athletic skills. His smile and good nature were infectious. Manufacturers had discovered that he could sell products ranging from soft drinks to athletic shoes. At the time of his announcement, Johnson earned an estimated $15 million annually in endorsement fees alone.

His announcement that he had contracted HIV from one or more of innumerable heterosexual contacts carried with it a powerful message: Even the nation's most famous are not immune to the deadly disease. After Magic's revelation, no longer could a somewhat blasé general public continue to contend AIDS was a special disease somehow reserved for homosexual men and drug abusers. In 1992 retired tennis star Arthur Ashe announced he had contracted AIDS from tainted blood transfusions during heart surgery in 1984. Less than a year later the nation mourned Ashe's death at age forty-nine from AIDS-complicated pneumonia.

Following Johnson's agonizing announcement, his life went on an emotional roller coaster, demonstrating the extraordinarily complex emotions the disease can provoke. On the advice of his physicians, he immediately retired from the Lakers, thereby condemning this perennial premier team to a mediocre season. He was welcomed, however, the following summer as a member of the 1992 U.S. Olympic basketball squad, serving as captain of the "Dream Team." For the first time, professionals were permitted to compete for the Olympic basketball championship. His physical skills still not markedly affected by his disease, Johnson played at a high level and helped the United States easily win the gold medal. His performance in the Olympics prompted him to announce he would rejoin the Lakers for the 1992–93 season; his doctors estimated he could play in at least sixty of the team's eighty-two regular season games if certain precautions were taken. But several NBA players privately expressed fears they might contract the virus from Johnson through open cuts; these fears intensified when he was removed immediately from a preseason exhibition game after shedding a few drops of blood from a scratch. Although medical experts said the danger of contracting the disease in such a fashion was extraordinarily small, the danger nonetheless did exist, at least theoretically. In the face of rumors about certain star players expressing reluctance to be on the court with him, a somber Magic Johnson announced his re-retirement before the season began. He planned to devote himself to national educational programs about the disease and to pursue, perhaps, opportunities to own or manage a professional sports franchise. By this time some of the corporations that had proudly displayed his endorsements had quietly decided not to extend his contracts. Magic Johnson's life expectancy was estimated at between six to ten years.

Comparable tragedies had tested the mettle of the American sports world during the 1980s. Many of these were related to the epidemic of drug abuse that had swept the country. Drug usage, of course, was nothing new in the grand scheme of things. During the nineteenth century the growth of cities contributed to a rapid increase in the use of cocaine, heroin, and morphine. Interestingly, for a time cocaine enjoyed considerable popularity; physicians even prescribed it to treat a wide variety of ailments. Some early cigarettes contained traces of cocaine, and it was one of several secret ingredients originally used by the makers of the popular soft drink Coca-Cola. By the turn of the century, however, the deleterious side effects of cocaine were recognized, and local and state governments instituted efforts to control its use. The federal government joined the effort in 1914 with the passage of the Harrison Anti-Narcotic Act, but illegal drug usage nonetheless continued to grow, especially in the cities.

The motion picture *Blackboard Jungle* stunned the nation in 1954 with its vivid depiction of drug use in the inner cities of America. That extremely negative image of drugs was modified during the heyday of the counterculture in the 1960s; the incredible growth in popularity of hallucinogenic substances, especially marijuana, stimulated interest in other, more powerful mind-altering drugs such as LSD. During the 1970s cocaine became the drug of choice. Although the counterculture faded from prominence early in the 1970s, one of its lasting legacies seemed to have been to make drug use acceptable behavior among certain segments of society. Marijuana and cocaine, for example, were popular among some members of the American middle and upper classes, but they extracted a staggering toll among vulnerable groups, especially the young and the poor. An intensive "war on drugs" waged by governments and private organizations had no perceptible effect in stemming either growing addiction or recreational use; by the 1980s the drug culture had inflicted severe damage on American society.

From the beginning, drugs made their way into locker rooms and the homes of America's athletes. The door had already been partially opened by many coaches who either openly condoned or winked at the use of painkillers and performance enhancers such as amphetamines. Policies against drug usage were dutifully and soberly announced by athletic organizations at all levels, but actual enforcement was given relatively low priority. Widespread use of amphetamines (popularly called uppers) to increase player intensity, anabolic steroids to improve body mass and strength, and powerful painkillers to make it possible for athletes to perform despite injuries had spread by the end of the 1960s, although public awareness remained minimal. The usage of such drugs grew during subsequent decades.

Not until June of 1986, however, when two well-known athletes died within three days of each other from cocaine overdoses, did the sports world begin to take the dangers of drugs seriously. The shocking death of University of Maryland basketball star Len Bias received intense publicity; network television news programs used his death as their lead story, and newspapers gave it front-page coverage. The popular and talented all-American had been the top draft pick of the Boston Celtics, and upon his signing a lucrative multiyear contract the Celtics' astute president, Red Auerbach, euphorically stated that with this one stroke of the pen the Celtics had assured continued success. Upon his return to Maryland after signing with the Celtics, Bias suffered a heart seizure and died while at an all-night party at his campus dormitory. An autopsy revealed that his heart seizure was induced by cocaine. A subsequent investigation revealed that Bias was not the victim of a onetime lark, as his friends and coach intimated; he had in fact been living with a drug problem for some time. While a stunned nation mourned his death and contemplated its implications, Cleveland Browns' defensive back Donald Rogers died under similar circumstances in his hometown of Sacramento.

These two unnecessary deaths helped underscore to the American people the tragedy being wrought by the nation's drug epidemic. While many sports figures gave speeches and appeared on television urging youth to "Just say no to drugs," many of their fellow athletes were fighting serious drug problems. Revelations of widespread drug usage among the nation's elite professional athletes became so commonplace during the 1980s that it no longer made headlines, even on the sports pages. Many stellar performers had their careers ruined and their lives shattered by their inability to "say no." Among the most notable of a large and growing group was the very talented, left-handed pitcher Steve Howe. Seven times arrested for violating drug laws, he was suspended four times from the game, twice given "life" suspensions that lasted for little more than a year. Americans both cheered and decried the leniency shown by organized baseball to Howe, but the ambivalence that surrounded his much publicized addiction only reflected the nation's confusion about how to deal with drugs. Such outstanding professionals as defensive lineman Dexter Manley of the Washington Redskins and New York Knicks' basketball star Michael Richardson received permanent suspensions from their leagues, which, unlike Howe's, were not summarily waived. One NBA star playmaker, John Lucas, bravely fought his addiction, winning many friends with his courage and ultimately with his operation of a drug treatment and rehabilitation center for other athletes. In 1992 his personal triumph over cocaine was rewarded when he was named head coach of the San Antonio Spurs.

Although the revelation of drug use by some of the nation's top athletes seemed to become almost commonplace, it continued to draw the attention of the public. However, the use of another type of drug, also dangerous and also potentially lethal, had the curious effect of producing little in the way of condemnation or criticism. Since at least the 1940s athletes in sports that placed a high premium on size and strength had been taking muscle mass–enhancing drugs, commonly known as anabolic steroids. These synthetic male hormones produce rapid muscle growth, with the potential of turning a good shot putter or weight lifter into a superior performer. During the 1950s it was widely suspected that athletes from behind the Iron Curtain were using such drugs to build their speed and power; the strength and prowess of the East German women Olympians and Soviet weight lifters and discus throwers became legendary. By the 1960s it was virtually a given that nearly all world-class weight lifters used steroids.

During the 1960s college and professional football players discovered that they too could become stronger and faster if they took the most popular of a wide range of anabolic steroids, Dianabol. By the mid-1970s it was estimated that 50 percent of professional football players had at least experimented with steroids, and that up to 75 percent of linemen and linebackers were dedicated users. Among these was two-time all-pro Lyle Alzado. After his retirement, this ferocious defensive end admitted that without the magical powers of Dianabol he would never have been capable of performing at the professional level. Alzado began to use the drug in 1969 while an undergraduate player at obscure Yankton College in South Dakota. Within two years his weight had increased from 190 to nearly 300 pounds; even more impressive, his speed and strength improved as well. When the league began testing for steroids, Alzado successfully devised means of masking his usage. During his long career, which included stints with the Cleveland Browns, Denver Broncos, and Los Angeles Raiders, he became famous for his intensity and fearlessness. Many suspected, but only he knew, that it resulted from his use of steroids. He had long since graduated from Dianabol to other more exotic forms of synthetic testosterone—drugs with such exotic names as Cypioate, Bolasterone, Quinolone, Anavar, and Equipose.

Did his trainers and coaches know, or even encourage, his use of steroids? They did, he told a journalist in 1991, although they avoided saying anything specific. But he knew his coaches liked the results. Their silent approbation was clear: "I think the coaches knew guys couldn't look the way they did without taking stuff. But the coaches just coached and looked the other way."

For more than fifteen years, Lyle Alzado lived a giant self-deception. He knew these drugs were dangerous, placing the user at risk from a wide range of possible side effects, including hypertension, edema, diabetes, testicular shrinkage, sterilization, jaundice, high cholesterol, hardening of the arteries, and liver and kidney disease. Steroids also had the propensity of further compounding potentially lethal physical ailments by producing serious mood alterations, such as depression, moodiness, and a propensity toward violence and other antisocial behavior. At age forty-one Alzado's steroid usage apparently caught up with him. He suffered from extreme dizziness and fainting spells, debilitating headaches, weight loss, and severe fatigue. He developed an ominous limp, and shortly thereafter doctors informed him that he suffered from an inoperable brain lymphoma. His physicians were unwilling to state that the tumor resulted from steroids, but Alzado himself had no doubt. He died in 1992.

The ultimate dilemma that confronted Lyle Alzado—and an unknown number of other athletes—was that without steroids he could not have had a successful career in football. To these individuals the rewards apparently outweighed the risks. Alzado estimated that 90 percent of those he knew in professional football used muscle-enhancing drugs—almost certainly an exaggerated figure—but many knowledgeable observers set the number more realistically at about 50 percent.

For nine years Steve Courson toiled on the offensive lines of the Pittsburgh Steelers and Tampa Bay Buccaneers. He did so only by opting to use steroids, having been introduced to them, he claims, by an assistant coach at the University of South Carolina. Courson became one of a very few football players to speak out against the intense pressures placed on them to bulk up. He estimates that at least 50 percent of players in power positions, primarily linemen and linebackers, he knew during his NFL career used steroids. Although he refused to give names, he did say about locker room conversations with his fellow Pittsburgh linemen: "We talked like a bunch of pharmacists talking shop." At age thirty-six the glory (and substantial income) of a professional football player ended for Steve Courson; he had been diagnosed with a very serious heart condition, among other major ailments. Asked if he would do it over again, he says no, but adds, "If I had to do it all over again, I wouldn't have been a professional football player."

Steroid use quickly moved from the professional to the college level, and then into the high schools. One expert in the mid-1980s estimated that more than a million youngsters of high school age use steroids, many of whom do not even have a significant athletic interest—they simply want to look powerful. These young people mirror a growing national obsession with body image and appearance. The popularity of sexually attractive male "hunks" and physically strong women have contributed to increased use of body developmental supplements. Health food stores offer a wide variety of supplements, primarily high-density protein supplements, all packaged with pictures of incredibly muscular men and women on the labels. The late 1980s saw the appearance of human growth hormones (hGH), which like steroids are associated with possible serious side effects. But hGHs offer athletes seeking quick muscle growth new options because they are not susceptible to detection in established tests.

The Fitness Phenomenon

Increased interest in physical appearance and body strength coincided with the incredible growth of the popularity of health fads, dieting, and exercise that swept the nation. It took hold during the pivotal 1960s. The image of vitality and vigor projected by the nation's most youthful and apparently most athletically inclined president since Theodore Roosevelt contributed greatly to this phenomenon. John F. Kennedy's highly publicized interest in physical activity, symbolized by his family's particular attraction to a very physical version of touch football, contrasted vividly with the staid pictures of his predecessor, Dwight Eisenhower, riding in a golf cart or recovering from heart attacks and major surgeries. Kennedy's heavy emphasis on physical fitness masked the fact that he had been sickly most of his life, and that as president he suffered from severe physical ailments. His acute back problems were well known, but he and his close associates concealed his serious adrenal gland deficiency. Although it was widely suspected, only after his death did the nation learn that he required large doses of cortisone to treat a severe case of Addison's disease. Ironically, these treatments gave him the appearance of good health by helping him maintain a proper body weight; until he began cortisone treatments in the mid-1950s Kennedy appeared gaunt, even malnourished.

President Kennedy's heavy emphasis on the physical condition of the American people resulted from no mere whim. In part it grew out of a series of studies indicating the American people were becoming increasingly overweight and sedentary; the president made 50-mile hikes a temporary national rage and urged schoolchildren to meet the challenge of a national fitness test. But it also meshed conveniently with his desire to project an image of national strength and vitality to the world, in particular to the Soviet Union. A consummate cold warrior, Kennedy realized that by promoting fitness he also underscored the high stakes of the Cold War.

In addition to the quadrennial Olympics, one of the most pronounced forms of competition between the United States and the Soviet Union was the space race. The success of the Soviets in putting the first satellite into orbit in 1957 set off a frenzied American response, resulting in Kennedy's pledge that the United States would put a man on the moon by the end of the 1960s. In 1961 test pilot-turned-astronaut John

Glenn became the first American to orbit the earth; he became an instant hero as a grateful and proud public showered its adulation on the Ohio native.

The admiration with which the American people viewed its new space age heroes stemmed from a special fascination with individual bravery and high technology. It also played a key role in stimulating the physical fitness phenomenon. Air Force physician Kenneth Cooper, a former high school track star, had long enjoyed his regular long-distance runs. He found they not only contributed greatly to maintaining his healthy body but also helped release the tension and stress that plagued his profession. The results of his intensive research helped Cooper convince the Air Force that regular aerobic exercise could provide the physical and mental fitness required of jet pilots. He found that thirty minutes or more of exercise that increases the heart rate to 130 beats a minute three times a week provides impressive cardiovascular benefits. America's first group of seven astronauts all came under the influence of this dedicated guru of fitness.

When the media reported that the astronauts regularly took long-distance runs, millions of American people joined in the fun. Cooper's brief book *Aerobics* became a bestseller in 1968 and went through several editions. For many decades, the American people had generally looked with skepticism on the sanity of those few hardy souls who voluntarily dedicated themselves to serious distance running. No longer. Running and jogging became the new national rage; its adherents claimed a wide range of benefits: weight control, lowered blood pressure, stress reduction, better sleeping patterns, even enhanced sexual performance. Cooper, however, did not insist on running. He wrote that aerobic dancing, racquetball, swimming, or even fast-paced distance walking provide the same benefits. But under the powerful example of the astronauts, running or jogging became the aerobic exercise of choice. Americans flocked to sporting goods stores to buy special running shoes and clothing, learned to check their heart rate, invested in digital wristwatches with stopwatch timing mechanisms (just like the astronauts wore in space), took to the streets and parks to huff and puff, religiously kept their "runner's diary" to plot their progress, and on the weekends entered 10,000-meter "fun runs." Casual conversations at the office or on the commuter train now included knowing discussions about endorphin release, "hitting the wall," interval training, the benefits of "carbohydrate loading," "cross training," and the comparative advantages of aerobic and anaerobic effects.

Races and "runs" became a new form of mass participation—sort of Woodstocks on the fly, with "highs" being generated by the release of endorphins rather than from smoking pot. In Phoenix ten thousand runners of all sizes, shapes, and ages appeared for the annual 10,000-meter race along irrigation canal banks, and 25,000 Coloradans each Memorial Day entered the "Bolder Boulder" race at the foot of the Rocky Mountains. Ever since the early 1900s a few hundred distance runners in San Francisco had participated in the annual Bay to Breakers race over a 7-mile route beginning at the foot of the Bay Bridge and ending at the oceanfront beyond Golden Gate Park, but during the 1960s the race began to grow in size and popularity. It became, in the San Francisco tradition, a special event, with many runners running in wild costumes; others, joined together by a rope or other means, entered a unique "centipede" competition. By the late 1970s the Bay to Breakers annually drew more than 100,000 runners and had become one of the biggest community events in the city—part rock concert, sometimes part social protest, and definitely a most unusual race. On a much more serious level, the New York City Marathon attracted more than twenty thousand serious runners in the 1980s; less than two hundred had entered the race the year John Kennedy won the presidency.

Kenneth Cooper could not have anticipated he would help create a movement that would literally transform attitudes toward physical fitness in American society. It became increasingly fashionable for people of all ages and both sexes to be physically fit. Thin definitely became "in." Affluent Americans did not hesitate to spend substantial sums of money to achieve the desired effect. Much to their delight, fashion merchandisers discovered that fitness devotees wanted to be stylish while exercising. No longer did traditional gray cotton exercise garb suffice; colorful fabrics soon filled the stores. Through clever advertising many companies created an acceptance of sports gear as appropriate clothing in nonathletic social settings. The pioneering Nike Corporation created a new model for corporate development. The company began as a manufacturer of scientifically designed shoes for joggers and distance runners. Recognizing that this market, although profitable, had inherent limits, Nike's management soon expanded its line of sports shoes to include all sports. It also neatly complemented its primary line of footwear with new types of stylish athletic clothing. The result was phenomenal growth and the emergence of a new Fortune 500 company, for a time the darling of Wall Street investors. From the beginning Nike had many determined competitors, and the plethora of running shoes on the market has produced so much confusion that *Runner's World* magazine regularly publishes articles comparing the merits and defects of running shoes; these articles read like technical reports in an engineering journal.

Within this environment, the health club business has boomed. These often luxurious facilities charge their clientele hefty fees for access to modern exercise equipment and facilities—stair step machines, electric treadmills, computerized stationary exercise bicycles, sophisticated weight lifting equipment, indoor running tracks, squash, tennis, and racquetball courts, and swimming pools. After a strenuous workout, saunas, steam baths, whirlpools, and even masseurs await to soothe tired and aching muscles. One firm aimed only at one market segment, the dedicated weight lifter—the popular Gold's Gyms spread across the nation, locating in cities large and small to meet the demand of serious body builders. This firm, too, inspired many competitors seeking to cash in on the muscle trade. As a manifestation of the sexual revolution, these businesses appeal to both men and women; it has become fashionable for both sexes to have the "buffed" look.

During the early days of television, the seemingly indefatigable Jack Lalane had instructed housewives about the virtues of exercise, but he labored in semioblivion to a small and largely indifferent morning audience. By the 1970s television was awash with exercise programs. Videotapes marketed by actress Jane Fonda and the effervescent Richard Simmons, among others, helped popularize exercise performed to rock music. Aerobics classes became the craze for millions of women (and increasing numbers of men), and no profit-minded health club operator could succeed without offering a wide variety of aerobics classes.

A century after the American people had first discovered the joys of bicycling, the sport returned to popularity with a special high-tech emphasis. Inspired in part by the spectacular success of Greg Lemond, who became the first American to win the Tour de France in 1986, Americans of all ages and abilities turned to distance cycling and racing as a means of achieving the desired aerobic effect without having to endure the leg injuries endemic to runners. Just as specialty stores for runners (pioneered by Boston Marathon winner Bill Rodgers) had previously sprung up across the nation, now a new breed of bicycle stores appeared in shopping centers everywhere, offering the latest in engineering and metallurgical advances for the serious cyclist.

In the wake of the popularity of such charismatic players as Jimmy Connors, Billie Jean King, Chris Evert, and John McEnroe, a tennis boom took off in the 1970s; it would not reach its crest until the mid-1980s. At its high point, an estimated 10 million Americans took up the game in a more or less serious fashion. Tennis is a demanding sport that requires good eye-hand coordination, emotional control, physical agility and endurance, and a competitive nature. Many tried the game, found it too frustrating, and moved on to racquetball. Played indoors, primarily at fitness clubs, racquetball has provided millions with a fast-paced aerobic option.

The fitness movement naturally stimulated interest in nutrition and diet, generating even greater emphasis on physical appearance and style. Many women had long been sensitive to expectations that they maintain their "girlish" figures and an increasing number of men became more conscious of their appearance—the traditional "beer gut" no longer seemed humorous but became an embarrassing symbol of lack of self-control. Medical research established beyond question the relationship between obesity and the silent killer of hypertension. During the 1960s Americans learned from their physicians about the importance of cholesterol levels; high levels were often traced to a diet high in saturated fats. Diet and weight loss, linked to preventing killer diseases, became a national obsession. Jean Nidetch demonstrated the important relationship between mental outlook, proper food selection, and personal discipline with her successful Weight Watchers program. Weight Watchers has enjoyed enormous popularity and for two decades led the so-called weight loss industry in revenue. In the 1980s California entrepreneurs Jenny Craig and her husband developed a similar but much more expensive program with more than a thousand Diet Centres located in upper-middle-class shopping malls.

Food and beverage companies have responded with alacrity to these trends in public attitude. Soft drink companies have gained market share with noncaloric diet versions of their traditional sugar-laced drinks, and food companies have found that the word *light* (however defined or spelled) can generate new sales. One national company, touting its reduced-calorie variety of beer, produced a series of popular humorous television advertisements featuring rival cries of "less filling" and "tastes great" offered by former (and often overweight) professional athletes.

Inevitably the health craze focused on cigarette smoking. The federal government bowed to public pressure and banned television and radio cigarette advertisements, and the American Cancer Society launched an aggressive, sustained attack on the cigarette industry with many studies connecting smoking to cancer and heart disease. Although the industry has defended itself successfully in several highly publicized court cases alleging wrongful death, such corporate giants as Philip Morris and R. J. Reynolds have found themselves on the defensive. Restaurants have created no smoking sections, and state and local governments have banned smoking in public places to prevent secondary exposure. After a period of sustained controversy, the FAA banned smoking on all domestic flights; public schools now include antismoking components as part of their health education curricula. No longer a glamorous habit, smoking has declined in popularity. By 1990 less than 30 percent of American adults smoked, nearly a 50 percent decline since the high tide of smoking popularity in the two decades following World War II.

Although the fitness movement has produced many positive benefits, a small minority have gone to unusual, even dangerous, extremes. Dieting in some has led to the life-threatening eating disorders of anorexia nervosa and bulimia. Women, especially, are vulnerable to eating disorders, which seem connected to an obsessive fear of weight gain. Self-induced vomiting, dangerous use of laxatives, and excessive use of diet pills are all manifestations of these disorders. Often associated with teenage girls, excessive weight loss provides a dramatic example of taking a good idea—proper diet and weight control—to excess. This dramatic problem, however, obscures a far greater danger related to the American obsession with dieting—the inability of many dieters to keep their weight off after a successful weight loss program, leading to a yo-yo effect of periodic losses followed by weight gains, a pattern that places the body under serious strain and may contribute to internal organ damage.

Obsessive distance runners, although few in number, have attracted an undue amount of publicity. Driven to improve their times, to win races, or merely to demonstrate to themselves that they possess complete self-control and discipline, they engage in training programs that often produce serious injury. Of course, one person's destructive behavior is another person's dedication. Whatever the distinction, many distance runners demonstrate a level of dedication to their training that borders on obsession. They boast of training regimens that exceed 100 miles a week. The human body often cannot cope with such demands. Stress fractures have become a commonplace affliction, although the steely disciplined individual sometimes refuses to halt his or her training to enable them to heal.

The triathalon has added a popular new twist to fitness competition. Combining distance races of bicycling, running, and swimming into one demanding competition, the triathalon attracts only the most committed. Athletes repeatedly push the outer limits of human endurance. For most runners the completion of a marathon is a major achievement, but some runners are not satisfied with running several marathons a year; 26 miles becomes merely a warm-up for the ultramarathon of 50 miles. Others have pushed the limits of endurance even further; one such example is the several hundred hardy souls who each year enter a 100 mile race that crosses the Sierra Nevada in eastern California, the route rising upward to 8,000 feet above sea level and requiring competitors to run on treacherous terrain for up to twenty-four consecutive hours. The sudden death of Jim Fixx in 1984, whose *The Complete Book of Running* had enjoyed a long stay on the bestseller lists, helped to restore a modicum of sanity to the fitness movement. That Fixx, who regularly ran more than 300 miles a month and whose appearance at age forty-three constituted the apparent picture of perfect health, died of a massive heart attack resulting from serious but undetected heart disease along a lonely Vermont road while in the early stages of one of his daily runs brought a heavy dose of reality to the movement.

Betting the Line

Although the quest for physical fitness undoubtedly has produced some excesses, its overall impact has been all to the good. It has also reaffirmed the powerful influence of sports on American life. Americans have not only become superspectators but also superparticipants; at least in theory participation has replaced spectating as the preferable behavior. But even while watching a sports contest, millions of Americans also want to participate. This they have, in increasingly large numbers, by placing bets on sports events. Sports and gambling, of course, have long maintained a close relationship. During their formative years in the late nineteenth century, baseball and boxing grew in popularity in part because of the interest they received from gamblers. The 1919 White Sox scandal that rocked professional baseball occurred after years of speculation about fixed games; rumors about fights thrown by boxers were also commonplace. Bettors on horse races have long fretted about jockeys on the take and doped horses. Revelations that seven members of the Chicago White Sox had accepted bribes from gamblers to throw the World Series merely confirmed widespread suspicions. The scandal led to the creation of a near-despotic office of commissioner under former federal judge Kenesaw Landis, who created strong antigambling policies and enforcement procedures. Although baseball has freed itself from the influence of gambling, periodic scandals hit the American sports world, none more traumatic than the ones involving college basketball. Such revelations have convinced many Americans that gambling poses a serious threat to the legitimacy of sports. This readily translates into a very negative public image of those who operate illegal bookie operations and those who place wagers with them.

The image of sports betting and those who participate, however, has improved markedly in the three decades following the conviction of superfixer Jack Molinas and his associates in 1963. Encouraged by the growing popularity of sports in general, and galvanized by the influence of television, sports betting grew rapidly, and in the process gained widespread public acceptance. Instead of being regarded as a sinister influence, sports gambling became more and more socially acceptable. State governments gave gambling an increased sense of legitimacy by establishing lotteries. In 1964 the first state lottery opened in New Hampshire; New York and New Jersey soon followed suit. By 1990 twenty-nine states and the District of Columbia offered lotteries; in that year state treasuries (*after* payouts to winners) benefited in excess of $10 billion.

The lotteries eroded the high ground long held by antigaming forces. By the 1970s most sports pages not only published betting odds on major games but even carried columns that featured betting advice from expert handicappers. In 1976 CBS Sports signaled the new status of gambling by including Jimmy "the Greek" Snyder as one of its regular Sunday NFL commentators. For thirteen years, the Greek's weekly commentaries on the pregame show analyzed betting lines, discussed the nuances of point spreads, and touted his picks. Snyder's appearance on television provided sports gambling with a legitimacy shocking in its totality. Only his highly publicized, blatant racial comments in 1988 led to his departure from the television screens, not a public uprising against gambling.

The son of Greek immigrants, Demetris Snyodinos grew up in the drab, economically depressed river town of Steubenville in eastern Ohio during the Great Depression. As a youth he earned money running errands for local bookies, spending much of his time in smoky pool halls, learning the subtleties of his future profession by studying the racing forms and sports pages before placing his own bets. By the time he finished high school, Snyder had mastered the art of running craps games in a local gambling hall, handled complex odds on horse races, and learned the laws of probability governing the distribution of playing cards. He possessed one of the most important tools for a successful professional gambler—an uncanny ability to retain and manipulate numbers in his head. Recognizing the importance of getting the best betting advantage, Snyder concentrated his efforts on sports events because his numbers indicated they gave the intelligent gambler the best chance for success. After he moved to Florida so he could closely monitor its several racetracks, Snyder's reputation grew rapidly among gambling circles on the East Coast. During the 1950s his reputation and questionable associations led to intensive scrutiny by the Senate committee on organized crime headed by Senator Estes Kefauver. It also led the FBI to charge him with illegal transmission of betting information across state lines, a charge to which he pleaded nolo contendere. In 1974 he received a full pardon from President Gerald Ford.

In 1963 Snyder moved to the rapidly growing gaming mecca of Las Vegas, becoming one of the city's premier sports odds makers. He had a special knack for setting the point spread at precisely the right number to stimulate equal monies being wagered on each side. The bookmaker makes his profit from the "vigorish," his commission; in a typical legal bet in a Nevada sports book, a winning bettor would wager eleven dollars to win ten, the difference providing the sports book's profit margin. Snyder quickly became an influential Las Vegas personage, writing a column for the *Las Vegas Sun*, working as a public relations manager for Caesar's Palace Hotel-Casino, and even joining forces for a time with Las Vegas billionaire developer, casino owner, entrepreneur, and resident eccentric Howard Hughes. Snyder's sports service company provided the rapidly increasing number of Nevada sports books with point spreads and odds.

Snyder's rapid ascent in Las Vegas coincided with the expanded popularity of sports betting in the United States. During the 1930s the state of Nevada had licensed sports and race books, but their number remained quite small. In 1976, however, the powerful Nevada Gaming Commission decided to permit them to operate within the confines of its casinos. This important decision reflected the growing interest in sports wagering, as well as a desire by Nevada's decision makers to cash in on a new opportunity. It also indicated a growing public toleration of so-called victimless crimes and activities once considered vice.

The nature of the typical sports bettor also changed significantly; no longer was he some shady Damon Runyan character living on the edge of society such as a youthful Jimmy the Greek had encountered in the grimy bars and pool halls of Steubenville. Now the sports bettor would likely be a well-educated professional who enjoyed the competitive challenge of matching wits with odds makers and other gamblers. Some of the most enthusiastic sports bettors were businesspeople, physicians, professors, accountants, attorneys, and government managers. Sports wagering not only afforded them the possibility of making money but also provided an exciting environment—what gamblers fondly refer to as "the action." Psychological profiles of the new breed of sports bettors included prominent characteristics long admired in American society: independence, decisiveness, courage, self-confidence, risk taking, and clarity of judgment. Compared with other forms of gambling, sports betting holds out a much greater potential for winning because it rewards skill. One of the most famous of the new breed of sports bettor, the legendary Lester "Lem" Banker of Las Vegas, says that the major traits that helped make him a wealthy individual are his abilities to assemble and analyze enormous amounts of information and to act decisively on his empirical decisions.

Because sports betting is legal only in Nevada, it is impossible to determine with precision its size and scope in the United States. However, conclusions of many researchers are staggering. Nevada gaming figures are themselves impressive: $1.8 billion was wagered in 1990 through the state's seventy-four licensed sports books, more than a 300 percent increase since casinos began opening their sports books in 1976. That year gamblers legally bet $20 billion in the thirty-nine states that permit betting on horses, dogs, and jai alai. In the first two years of its operation, 1989–90, the sports lottery in Oregon generated $14 million in profits. Estimates of total monies bet on sports through illegal channels fluctuate greatly, but gaming experts place the figure in the range of $60 billion annually. As but one form of comparison, in 1990 Americans spent a total of just $8 billion to purchase tickets to all of the nation's movie theaters.

With such large sums in play, the business of operating a sports betting operation has become quite sophisticated. Gone are the days when a bookie kept track of his plays in his head or on the back of an envelope; now he uses a computer. Michael Roxbury, whose Las Vegas Sports Consultants firm provides the "spread" for most Nevada sports books and the Oregon lottery, operates out of a large penthouse office suite filled with computers and high-tech communications equipment. His is a most precise business; the setting of a betting line only a point or two off can mean multimillion-dollar losses for his clients.

It is widely understood, but never admitted, that the illegal bookies outside of Nevada remain in close contact with the legal gaming businesspeople in Nevada. Both know their enterprises rest on the confidence of their customers that they are running a completely honest operation. Bookies outside of Nevada, in fact, serve an important function in preventing the fixing of a contest because they are ever alert to the flow of monies into all contests. Any unusual pattern quickly sets off an alarm that will resonate across the land. It is now widely accepted that the type of point-shaving scandals of the 1950s engineered by New York City gamblers would be virtually impossible to execute in today's sports gaming environment. Too many sophisticated people, too many eyes and ears, too many dollars are now involved. Professor Garry Smith makes the point very well: "Rigged or fixed sporting events are anathema to bookmakers. . . . In order to protect themselves . . . bookmakers carefully monitor betting patterns. If an unusual pattern emerges, they will stop taking wagers on the contest." Smith makes an intriguing, if not ironic point: "While it may seem oxymoronic, illegal bookmakers actually help keep sports on the up and up."

Professional sports leagues have long taken a position adamantly opposed to any form of sports betting. The growth in popularity of the NFL, for example, has occurred simultaneously with the popularity of television and sports betting. Much to the dismay of NFL officials, professional football is by far the most popular sports betting venue, other than horses. For example, in January 1993 Nevada sports books handled slightly in excess of $50 million on the Super Bowl game. The point spreads can be set with greater precision, and gamblers have available to them enormous bodies of information from which to make their betting decisions. And, courtesy of satellite television, bettors can watch the game on which their money is riding. League opposition to gambling is viewed as hypocritical by many sports authorities because betting has contributed greatly to increased interest and attendance. Various professional leagues have routinely required athletes to attend lectures on antigambling policies and have employed detectives to maintain continued vigilance against gambling influences. The NFL expended great sums of money in a futile effort to prevent the state of Oregon from offering its sports lottery, and provided crucial support for federal legislation in 1992 that made sports betting illegal in all states except Nevada (with an option for New Jersey to be determined by 1994). Organized baseball, having suffered through the scandal of 1919, has an inflexible rule forbidding any player from betting on baseball, and for decades has waged a relentless war against any hint of gambling influence.

Baseball's crusade against gambling, however, did not save one of the sport's most famous players. In 1989 Cincinnati Reds manager and certain future Hall of Fame inductee Pete Rose severely disappointed his millions of fans when he accepted a lifetime ban for allegedly betting on major league baseball games; some feared he might have even bet on some Cincinnati games for which he was manager. A living national legend, widely acclaimed for his dedication to the game, Rose had done the seemingly impossible in 1985 by breaking Ty Cobb's career total hits record of 4,191. Pete Rose's fall from a high pedestal was indeed a shock.

Organized baseball began its investigation of Rose in 1986, having picked up several indications that he might be violating its no-gambling policy. Despite his great popularity among baseball fans, Rose had long lived on the edge. For some time it was widely known that Rose bet heavily on the horses and frequently associated with a group of unsavory individuals well known to Cincinnati's police department for their coziness with drug dealers and bookies. When reports of the investigation were leaked to the press in March of 1989, the good burghers of Cincinnati rallied to their homegrown star's defense. Their support turned into incredulity when, after months of stoutly maintaining his innocence, Rose suddenly agreed to accept a lifetime ban from Commissioner A. Bartlett Giamatti. Although the final agreement drafted by lawyers contained a statement to the effect that there was no "official" finding Rose had bet on baseball, the punishment he accepted was that reserved only for those who did. In announcing Rose's lifetime ban, Giamatti, in response to a reporter's question, stated that it was his belief Rose had indeed bet on baseball. As the details of the story unfolded, only the most biased of Rose defenders could dispute Giamatti's contention. Journalist Michael Sokolove's subsequent book revealed a life that for years had been obsessed with gambling; Rose even had a bank of five television screens connected to a satellite dish in his home so he could simultaneously monitor his many bets. Sokolove states that Rose placed several bets by telephone on almost a daily basis. His minimum bet usually ran $1,000 and he made many larger ones, often dealing with five bookies in different cities.

Despite his betting zeal, Rose apparently was an extremely inept gambler, losing large sums, that forced him to borrow money and even to sell some of his most prized baseball memorabilia to pay off his debts.

Pete Rose, baseball's all-time leading hitter and a competitor without peer, had lived a life of self-deception. Shortly after he left baseball, Rose's life turned even more sour when he pleaded guilty to income tax evasion. Between 1984 and 1987 he had failed to report income of $348,720 from the sale of baseball memorabilia and appearance fees at baseball card shows. Rose was sentenced to five months in a federal minimum security prison in 1990. On a "Phil Donahue" television show in November of 1989, Rose finally admitted what he had so long refused to recognize: he was a compulsive gambler: "After I was suspended from baseball on August 24, I decided to see a psychiatrist. . . . Since then I have come to learn and accept the fact that I do have a problem related to gambling . . . and I am getting help."

As the sensational story of Rose's fall unfolded, many commentators focused on the "disease" of compulsive gambling. Five percent of the American people, experts contended, suffer an uncontrollable urge to gamble. Despite widespread acceptance of the belief that gambling can become a disease, no clinical evidence supports such a contention. Could it not be, argued a minority, that by recognizing compulsive gambling as a disease, individuals are excused from accepting responsibility for their own destructive behavior? Others preferred to draw a moral judgment, such as U.S. Senator Dennis DeConcini. "Gambling is a significant threat to American youth, who may grow to view sports gambling as acceptable behavior." The senator from Arizona, who led the successful drive in Congress to prohibit states from extending sports betting beyond the confines of Nevada and Oregon, believes, "Sports in our country are not, and never should be, about winning and losing money." The director of the National Center for Pathological Gambling concurred: "Compulsive gambling has become the national addiction of the 1990s. It is time to enjoy the game for the sake of the game, not for the sake of the bet riding on it." Others view the issue differently. Pointing to the fact that a substantial segment of sports bettors come from the ranks of professional men and women, the head of the North American Association of State and Provincial Lotteries said, "The indisputable fact is millions of Americans wager billions of dollars annually on sports events." Bill Bergman argued, "This hasn't resulted in the demise of professional sports. Indeed, attendance and TV revenues are at an all-time high."

Conclusion

Perhaps the most telling conclusion to emerge from the continued debate over the morality of sports betting resulted from the case of Pete Rose. Although it was the worst scandal to hit baseball since 1919, it did not damage professional baseball in the slightest. Nor was there any negative fallout on other sports. Although opponents of sports gambling used the Rose episode to support their position, the American public, while regretting Rose's personal situation, overwhelmingly concluded that they saw nothing about which to become overly concerned. Fully 60 percent of the American people, according to national polls, felt Rose had been too severely punished, with only 30 percent agreeing with Giamatti's lifetime ban. Overwhelmingly, they condemned a decision to deny Rose eligibility for election to the Hall of Fame; a majority, in fact, felt that he deserved only a one- to two-year suspension. Ironically, the Pete Rose affair indicated just how great public acceptance of sports betting has become.

The evidence is clear that gambling had become an obsession for Pete Rose. Sports fans recognized his personal failing for what it was, an individual tragedy, and extended to their fallen hero a message of compassion and understanding. Perhaps they also perceive that they too have succumbed to an obsession—with sports itself.

Epilogue

Sports came of age as a major social force during the half century following victory in the Second World War. Although they had played a significant role in the lives of American communities ever since the late nineteenth century, sports assumed a much greater role in the new era of electronic communication. From the earliest days of commercial television sports received considerable attention, but during the 1960s they achieved maturity under the creative genius of Roone Arledge. The powerful influence of television not only greatly stimulated interest in sports, but also produced major changes. The commercial imperatives of television demanded changes in traditional schedules and game times, and eventually even produced modifications in the rules of the games themselves. As television spawned the age of the superspectator, such new phenomena as Monday night football, Super Bowl Sunday, and the Final Four became integral parts of the rhythm of American life. Professional leagues and franchises increased rapidly in number, intensifying rivalry between cities that wanted to achieve "major league" status. Responding to the powerful lure of television revenues, major college programs became even more powerful economic and political forces on campuses. Their tepid response to criticisms regarding the distortion of academic values and institutional integrity remains one of higher education's more complex unsolved problems.

The great upsurge in popularity made sports a very big business. This is attested to by the escalation in value of professional franchises. The most lucrative baseball and football franchises now are estimated in value at above $150 million. No one has benefited more than the superstar athletes, whose salaries have increased at a staggering rate. Angry critics have denounced these multimillion-dollar salaries as a perversion of the nation's value system, often drawing comparisons of athletes' contributions to society with those of teachers and nurses. The salaries of Charles Barkley or Jose Canseco, however, have nothing to do with social value and everything to do with the workings of a free labor market. Although skeptics have long predicted that the economic bonanza of professional and collegiate sports will eventually collapse, it has not yet done so. Continued increases in sporting goods sales, game attendance, and television ratings and revenues suggest that predictions of a major downturn are unwarranted.

The powerful postwar economic expansion underpinned the spectacular growth of sports. Economic growth produced not only substantially higher levels of discretionary income, but also more leisure time. America's postwar affluence contributed heavily to the boom in bowling, tennis, golf, and slow-pitch softball. It also intensified the importance attached to youth sports. Little League baseball became a rite of passage for young boys, and communities everywhere placed considerable importance on their high school sports programs.

Sports often reflect major national issues. When the women's rights movement gained momentum during the 1960s, reformers turned immediately to sports as one of the first areas in which equality was sought; one result of this effort, Title IX, demonstrated the positive impact that federal legislation could produce. Billie Jean King is unquestionably one of the great female athletes of the century, but will be remembered by future generations primarily as a leader in the crusade against sexual discrimination. King's career is but one good illustration of how powerful social, economic, or political forces can quickly come into focus via the world of sports. Jackie Robinson contributed much more to the overturning of racial segregation than most civil rights attorneys, and the intensity of how the American people approached the Cold War could not be seen more vividly than in their determination to mount powerful Olympic teams to compete against the communist bloc nations every four years.

Sports thus has become a national obsession. By 1980 the first fulltime twenty-four-hour sports channel became a regular part of television fare. Sports bars, with their satellite dishes and large-screen television sets, have become much more than a passing fad. In New York City radio station WFAN, a twenty-four-hour radio sports station, enjoys continued high ratings in the nation's largest media market, spawning a host of imitators across the nation. Sports gambling has grown rapidly, producing ambivalent public responses while intensifying interest in sports. In 1990 investors even attempted to publish a national sports newspaper designed along the lines of the Gannett Corporation's *USA Today*. It failed as a commercial enterprise because of undercapitalization, not for a lack of public interest.

Sports in modern America thus has taken on a significance much greater than the wins and losses reported in the daily newspapers, becoming a powerful metaphor for life in the United States. Recalling his teenage years during the late 1940s, David Halberstam writes, "The world of baseball seemed infinitely more real and appealing than the world around me. . . . Encouraged by Mel Allen and countless sportswriters, I believed that I knew the Yankees not only as players but as people—they were part of my extended family." Halberstam captures one of the essential qualities of sports. They provide Americans with a safe and comfortable haven in an often confusing, unstable, and disturbing world. For spectators and participants alike, sports entails a release from the pressures of modern life. Millions of Americans have found special pleasure in their identification with teams, in defeat as well as in victory. Lifelong participant sports such as golf, tennis, swimming, cycling, and bowling have helped individuals find meaning and continuity in their lives. Within the past quarter century the boom in physical fitness and diet awareness has expanded the scope and influence of sports. Some academics argue that a discussion of sports, properly defined, should be confined to the arena of competition between teams or individuals. However convenient that definition might be, it fails to take into consideration the close relationship between the physical fitness boom and the growth of traditional participant and spectator sports in modern America.

The half century that has passed since World War II has been marked by far-reaching change. The rate of scientific and technological advances has been mind-boggling. Nuclear power, space travel, bio-medical science, computers, and satellite communications have reshaped the world's economy and politics. Fundamental changes have occurred apace in family life, social organization, and the workplace. The America of the 1990s is a much different and seemingly a much less secure place than it was in 1945. Caught up in this era of turbulent change and vast uncertainty, many Americans have found a refuge in sports. The void often left unfilled by politics, work, family, or religion has been at least partially filled by an increased involvement in the world of sports. Critics of America's obsession with sports abound, and any knowledgeable citizen can readily produce a lengthy list of serious problems that deserve attention. These problems notwithstanding, sports continue to maintain a special place in the lives of the American people. Englishman Roger Bannister—the sportsman who first broke the once seemingly impenetrable barrier by running a mile in less than four minutes—effectively explained this phenomenon when he wrote that he viewed involvement in sports as essential for both individuals and nations.

> We run, not because we think it is doing us good, but because we enjoy it and cannot help ourselves. It also does us good because it helps us do other things better. It gives

a man the chance to bring out power that might otherwise remain locked away inside himself. The urge to struggle lies latent in everyone. The more restricted our society and work become, the more necessary it will be to find some outlet for this craving for freedom. No one can say, You must not run faster than this, or jump higher than that.

Bibliography

This book rests on the work of hundreds of journalists, sports personalities, social commentators, and scholars. I am deeply indebted to these men and women who have provided me with ideas, theories, data, anecdotes, and perspective. During the past half century the academic community has come to accept sports history as a legitimate area of scholarly inquiry. Since the 1960s scholars have produced a substantial number of significant monographs and articles. Nonetheless, gaps in the scholarly literature are large, especially for the period covered by this book. Consequently, this study has relied primarily on published primary sources, books, and articles by journalists as well as the memoirs and biographical works written by sports figures (frequently with the assistance of a journalist).

Although I have drawn heavily on academic and popular books, this book is based primarily on published primary materials available in newspapers and magazines. Foremost in this regard is one of the best written and edited mass publications in the United States—*Sports Illustrated*. Ever since its first issue appeared in 1954, *Sports Illustrated* has provided an intelligent and perceptive commentary on American sports. The quality of the writing and the depth of analysis that has been a hallmark of this distinguished periodical is unfortunately found only occasionally in daily sports pages and other sports publications. *Sports Illustrated* has been indispensable to me in the preparation of this book. Throughout I have also relied heavily on newspapers—in particular the *New York Times*—and the major news and opinion journals *Newsweek*, *U.S. News and World Report*, and *Time*. Additionally, I have benefited from articles that have appeared in *Life, Saturday Evening Post, Colliers, Look, New Republic, Fortune, The New Yorker, Today's Health, Harpers, New Yorker Magazine*, and *Mademoiselle*. Several important academic journals were consulted, including *Journal of Sport History, Journal of Sport and Social History, Quest, Arete: The Journal of Sport Literature, Journal of Sport and Social Issues, Journal of Sport Behavior*, and *International Review of Sports Sociology*.

Every serious student of sports in modern America must consult Randy Roberts and James Olson, *Winning Is the Only Thing: Sports in America Since 1945* (1989). Their book is especially strong on the issues of international sports, economics, and racism. The best general history of American sports is Benjamin Rader, *American Sports: From the Age of Folk Games to the Age of Televised Sports* (2nd ed., 1990).

Rader provides a meaningful overview of sports in America from co-
lonial times to the present. I have benefited from the insights of the
distinguished social historian Allen Guttmann in his *A Whole New Ball
Game: An Interpretation of American Sports* (1988), as well as his
earlier work, *From Ritual to Record: The Nature of Modern Sport*
(1978). Works of a general nature abound; among those I have found
most useful are Robert Boyle, *Sport: Mirror of American Life* (1963);
James A. Michener, *Sports in America* (1976); Neil Isaacs, *Jock Culture, U.S.A.* (1978); and Richard Lipsky's *How We Play the Game:
Why Sports Dominate American Life* (1981). Jay Coakley, *Sport in
Society: Issues and Controversies* (1982) is very useful, as is Daniel
Landers, ed., *Social Problems in Athletics: Essays in the Sociology of
Sport* (1976).

The enormous body of literature devoted to intercollegiate athletics gives testimony to the importance of this enterprise in modern
America. Its treatment in the media is massive. As is true with other
major themes developed in this book, a systematic reading of *Sports
Illustrated* over its forty years of existence provides a useful frame of
reference for understanding the shifting fortunes of intercollegiate athletics in modern American society. Arthur A. Fleisher III, Brian L.
Goff, and Robert D. Tollison raise fundamental issues in *The National
Collegiate Athletic Association: A Study in Cartel Behavior* (1992).
This book serves as a useful antidote to Jack Falla, *NCAA: The Voice
of College Sports* (1981). Also useful are Donald Chu, Jeffrey Segrave,
and Beverly Becker, eds., *Sports and Higher Education* (1985); James
Frey, *The Governance of Collegiate Athletics* (1982); John D. McCallum
and Charles Pearson, *College Football U.S.A., 1869–1971* (1972); Charles
Rosen, *Scandals of '51: How Gamblers Almost Killed College Basket-
ball* (1978); David Wolf, *Foul! The Connie Hawkins Story* (1971); Rick
Telander, *The 100 Yard Lie* (1989); Joseph Durso, *The Sports Factory:
An Investigation into College Sports* (1975); Alexander Wolff and Armen
Keteyian, *Raw Recruits: The High Stakes Game Colleges Play to Get
Their Basketball Stars—and What It Costs to Win* (1990); John Rooney,
The Recruiting Game: Toward a New System of Intercollegiate Sport
(1987); Charles Thompson and Allan Sonnenschien, *Down and Dirty:
The Life and Crimes of Oklahoma Football* (1990); David Whitford, *A
Payroll to Meet: A Story of Greed, Corruption, and Football at SMU*
(1989); and Murray Sperber, *College Sports, Inc.: The Athletic Depart-
ment vs. the University* (1990). Sperber writes with the authority of a
faculty member at a Big Ten Conference institution who has had the

benefit of witnessing firsthand the operations of a big time program. I have benefited from his insights.

The issue of racism has understandably attracted the attention of journalists and scholars who have produced an impressive array of articles and books on a wide range of specific topics. Jack Olsen's *The Black Athlete: A Shameful Story* (1968) grew out of his illuminating five-part series in *Sports Illustrated* and is reflective of those difficult years; unfortunately, there is no comparable work for later years. For the views of Harry Edwards consult his *The Revolt of the Black Athlete* (1969) and *Sociology of Sport* (1973). Because of its symbolic importance, baseball has attracted considerable attention. Paramount among these books is Jules Tygiel's model monograph, *Baseball's Great Experiment: Jackie Robinson and His Legacy* (1983). Also useful are Harvey Frommer, *Rickey and Robinson: The Men Who Broke Baseball's Color Barrier* (1984); Murray Polner, *Branch Rickey: A Biography* (1982); Arthur Mann, *Branch Rickey: American in Action* (1957); Roger Kahn, *The Boys of Summer* (1971); Art Rust, Jr., *Get That Nigger off the Field; A Sparkling Informal History of the Black Man in Baseball* (1976); Hank Aaron, with Lonnie Wheeler, *I Had a Hammer* (1991); Charles Einstein, *Willie's Time: A Memoir of Another America* (1980) details the career of Willie Mays; Jackie Robinson, *I Never Had It Made* (1972); and Joseph T. Moore, *Pride Against Prejudice: The Biography of Larry Doby* (1988).

Boxing and the question of race has received extensive attention. For starters, see Jeffrey T. Sammons, *Beyond the Ring: The Role of Boxing in American Society* (1988). For Joe Louis, see Barney Nagler, *Brown Bomber: The Pilgrimage of Joe Louis* (1972) and Gerald Aston, *"And a Credit to His Race": The Hard Life and Times of Joseph Louis Barrow, a.k.a. Joe Louis* (1974). For Muhammad Ali see Thomas Hauser, *Muhammad Ali: His Life and Times* (1991); Jack Olsen, *Black Is Best: The Riddle of Cassius Clay* (1967); Norman Mailer, *The Fight* (1975); John Cottrell, *Muhammad Ali: Who Once Was Cassius Clay* (1967); Jose Torres, . . . *Sting Like a Bee: The Muhammad Ali Story* (1971); and Wilfred Sheed, *Muhammad Ali.* For other sports, see Arthur Ashe, *A Hard Road to Glory* (1988). William Baker, *Jesse Owens: An American Life* (1986) is a solid study of an important pre–World War II hero who greatly impacted the postwar years. Althea Gibson, *I Always Wanted to Be Somebody* (1958); Bill Russell and Taylor Branch, *Second Wind: The Memoirs of an Opinionated Man* (1970); Lee Tevino with Sam Blair, *They Call Me Super Mex* (1982) and *The Snake in the*

Sandtrap (1985) provide occasional insights into racism on the tour; Wilt Chamberlain, *A View from Above* (1991) offers a broad spectrum of interesting opinions.

The matter of economics and labor has attracted the attention of many capable scholars and journalists. A good place to start is Paul D. Staudohar and James A. Mangan, eds., *The Business of Professional Sports* (1991). Charles Alexander, *Our Game: An American Baseball History* (1991) provides a solid history of baseball, including important sections on economic forces. See also Gerald W. Scully, *The Business of Major League Baseball* (1989). Lee Lowenfish and Tony Lupien, *The Imperfect Diamond: The Story of Baseball's Reserve System and the Men Who Fought to Change It* (1980) is important. *Baseball and Billions* (1992) by economist Andrew Zimbalist is essential. For labor relations, see especially Paul D. Staudohar, *The Sports Industry and Collective Bargaining* (1986). Also see Robert C. Berry, William B. Gould IV, and Paul D. Staudohar, *Labor Relations in Professional Sports* (1986). Neil J. Sullivan, *The Dodgers Move West* (1987) is excellent. For the best study of the minor leagues, consult Neil J. Sullivan, *The Minors: The Struggles and the Triumph of Baseball's Poor Relation from 1876 to the Present* (1990). Bowie Kuhn's story is explained in *Hardball* (1987), but see Marvin Miller's more revealing *A Whole Different Ballgame* (1991). Useful for an appreciation of economic change is David Halberstam's poignant *Summer of '49* (1989). David Harris, *The League and the Decline of the NFL* (1988) is a hypercritical analysis of professional football's economic history during the three decades of Pete Roselle's commissionership. John Feinstein, one of the nation's best sports journalists, describes the big money involved in professional tennis of the late 1980s in his *Hard Courts* (1991). Terry Pluto chronicles the nine-year fight of the American Basketball Association to survive in *Loose Balls: The Short, Wild Life of the American Basketball Association* (1990). Lewis Cole, *A Loose Game: The Sport and Business of Basketball* (1978), is also useful.

There are many informative studies of the television industry and sports. Best of the bunch is Benjamin Rader, *In Its Own Image: How Television Has Transformed Sports* (1984). *Super Spectator and the Electric Lilliputians* (1971) by William O. Johnson provides useful information and analysis, as does Ron Powers, *Supertube: The Rise of Television Sports* (1984). I also benefited from the insights provided by David A. Klatell and Norman Marcus, *Sports for Sale: Television, Money and the Fans* (1988). Howard Cosell's several books are, if nothing else, interesting: see Howard Cosell, *Cosell* (1973); *Like It Is* (1975); *I Never Played the Game* (1979): and *What's Wrong with Sports* (1991); the latter book provides compelling, if oversimplified, observations on the economic structure of professional sports. See also Don Kowett, *The Rich Who Own Sports* (1977).

The subject of women in sports largely remains to be explored by scholars, although recent books are encouraging. See Allen Guttmann, *Women's Sports: A History* (1991) for a perspective from the ancient civilizations to the present. For the story of one of the world's greatest woman athletes and the dismal sports environment in which she had to compete, see Babe Didrikson Zaharias, *This Life I've Led* (1955), and William Oscar Johnson and Nancy P. Williamson, *"Whatta-Gal": The Babe Didrikson Story* (1977). Billie Jean King, with Frank Deford, *Billie Jean* (1982) presents an illuminating perspective on the changes in women's professional tennis. A recent book by Mariah Burton Nelson, *Are We Winning Yet? How Women Are Changing Sports and Sports Are Changing Women* (1991) provides modern perspectives on the role of women in sports. Pamela Postema presents her unique story in *You've Got to Have Balls to Make It in This League* (1992). See also two books by Adrianne Blue, *Faster, Higher, Farther: Women's Triumphs and Disasters at the Olympics* (1988), and *Grace Under Pressure: The Emergence of Women in Sport* (1987). Bonnie L. Parkhouse and Jackie Lapin present the major arguments on behalf of equal opportunity in sports and present a strategy to achieve their goals in *Women Who Win: Exercising Your Rights in Sports* (1980).

The major literature on youth sports is found in popular magazines and in sports sociology texts. However, see Joseph Kett, *Rites of Passage: Adolescence in America, 1790 to the Present* (1979); Emily Greenspan, *Little Winners: Inside the World of the Child Sports Star* (1983); and H. G. Bissinger, *Friday Night Lights: A Town, a Team and a Dream* (1990). My account of Bobby Plump is derived partially from Phillip M. Hoose, *Hoosiers: The Fabulous Basketball Life of Indiana* (1986) and largely from the February and March 1954 issues of the *Indianapolis Star*. For a balanced consideration of the pros and cons of youth baseball, see Lewis Yablonsky and Jonathan Brower, *The Little League Game* (1979); they ultimately come down on the side of Little League but explore negative viewpoints with sensitivity. Bill Geist, *Little League Confidential* (1992) provides a humorous, but insightful, look into Little League from the point of a coach. I benefited from reviewing a copy of the 1991 *Media Guide* of Washington High School of Massillon, Ohio.

The relationship of sports and American culture is explored by Christopher Lasch, *The Culture of Narcissism: American Life in an Age of Diminishing Expectations* (1979). Neil D. Isaacs, *Jock Culture U.S.A.* (1978) is a thoughtful plea for values in American sports culture. Kenneth Cooper's *Aerobics* (1968) provides a strong medical rationale on behalf of the benefits of exercise, one that greatly influenced me when I read it in 1970. Jim Fixx's *The Complete Book of Running* (1977) became the Bible for a generation of runners. For drug issues see Bob Goldman, *Death in the Locker Room: Steroids and Sports* (1984); Steve Courson, *False Glory: Steelers and Steroids* (1991); and Arnold Mandell, *The Nightmare Season* (1976). There is no substantive book-length study of sports gambling, but Garry Smith, "The 'To Do' Over What to Do About Sports Gambling: Sanitizing a Tainted Activity," in William R. Eadington and Judy A. Cornelius, *Gambling and Public Policy* (1991) provides a good overview. For the view of gambling from the perspective of one of the most successful professional gamblers, see Lem Banker, with Frederick C. Klein, *Sports Betting* (1986). Also interesting is Sonny Reizner and Martin Mendelsohn, *Sports Betting with Sonny Reizner* (1983). See also Richard Sasuly, *Bookies and Bettors* (1982). The March 10, 1986, issue of *Sports Illustrated* considers at length the question of "Gambling: America's National Pastime?" Pete Rose and Roger Kahn deny all in *Pete Rose: My Story* (1989), but see Michael Y. Sokolove, *Hustle: The Myth, Life, and Lies of Pete Rose* (1990) for a much more believable story. Dan Moldea, *Interference: How Organized Crime Influences Professional Football* (1987) is disturbing if less than totally convincing.

Index